LIVES OF HOPE

LIVES OF HOPE

WOMEN'S AND MEN'S PATHS TO SUCCESS AND FULFILLMENT

New and Expanded Edition

Douglas H. Heath

with the Assistance of

Harriet E. Heath

Conrow Publication House

Lives of Hope
Women's and Men's Paths to Success and Fulfillment
by Douglas H. Heath with the Assistance of Harriet E. Heath

Copyright © 1994 by Douglas H. Heath

Copyright under International, Pan American, and Universal Copyright Conventions. All rights reserved. No part of this book may be reproduced in any form—except for brief quotations (not to exceed 1,000 words) in a review or professional work—without permission in writing from the publisher.

Published by Conrow Publishing House
223 Buck Lane, Haverford, PA 19041-1106

Printed in the United States of America
by Thomson-Shore, Inc., Dexter, Michigan

Cover: John Davis Gummere
Book Design: Eva Fernandez Beehler

Library of Congress Catalog Card Number: 94-71918

ISBN 0-9641727-0-4 (paper)

For
Billie, Andy, Marty,
Harry, Jane, Chen, and Jim
and the
Ninety-Eight Other Men and Women
Whose Lives I Gratefully and
Affectionately Describe

Contents

Preface ix

Part One
Understanding Maturity and Success

1. Growing Up to Succeed: Billie Leighton's "Miracle" 3
2. Billie Leighton: Taking Charge of Herself 17
3. Key Paths to Maturity 33

Part Two
Succeeding in Personal Relationships

4. Andy and Marty Miller: A Couple Seeking the Same Path 59
5. Sources of Andy's and Marty's Success 76
6. Marty and Andy: Soul Mates Finding Their Own Paths 93
7. Eleven Insights into Becoming an Adult 108
8. Becoming a Successful Marital Partner 113
9. Finding Sexual Fulfillment 128
10. Harry Barnett: Called to Being a Good Father 140
11. The Character of Fulfilled and Competent Parents 150
12. Succeeding as a Friend 166
13. Ten Prescriptions for Building Strong Families and Relationships 173

Part Three

Succeeding at Work

14.	Jane Allen: Succeeding as an Entrepreneur	183
15.	Chen Lee: Making Work a Calling	202
16.	Nine Steps to Succeed Vocational ly	221

Part Four

Enhancing Other-Centeredness and Well-Being

17.	Being a Model Contributing Citizen	229
18.	Jim Pryor: Creating His Own Religious and Ethical Path to Wholeness	235
19.	A Toast to Good Health and Happiness	252
20.	Male and Female Paths to Physical Health	260
21.	Ten Facts About Other-Centeredness and Well-Being	266

Part Five

Becoming More Mature in Today's World

22.	Men's and Women's Paths to Fulfillment: Same or Different?	271
23.	A Perspective on Hope	288
	Notes	297
	Book Order Instructions	298

Preface

We live in dark times: adolescent homicides, rape and other forms of violence are increasing; political cynicism is rampant; drugs are proliferating; fragmented families prevail; uncertain futures loom over the horizon. Former sources of meaning and purpose—the deep springs of hope—no longer inspire and guide many of us. So we drift and despair. This book features seven remarkable men and women, most of whom have encountered—some are still meeting—dark times in their own lives: parental abandonment and tyranny, crippling childhood handicaps, divorces, alcoholism, life-threatening car accidents, murder, rebellious children, progressive paralyses, homophobia, federal imprisonment, and community ostracism, among others. Surely this is enough grist from only seven people to fill the *National Enquirer's* mill of unbelievable woes and calamities.

Yet none of the seven drifted and despaired. In spite of their dark times—in some cases, because of them—they succeeded in creating meaningful and purposeful lives. Most are devoted family members. Most have been called to heal and serve others. Some are fighting for feminist and sexually liberating visions. Most have fulfilled or are fulfilling their dreams. Some are succeeding far more than they ever expected. Some are nationally—even world—renowned for their discoveries and achievements. Some are millionaires. All have transcended their earlier hurts to become more mature, emotionally healthier, and happier. All are persons of integrity and courage.

So I write about men and women of hope. I seek to understand the strengths necessary to triumph over dark times, to succeed in our varied adult roles, and to live fulfilling lives. I also write to provoke you to reflect not just about how to live more fully yourself but also about how we must change our values, schools, and communities if our children and grandchildren are to grow into their full potential and so live lives of hope also.

What I have learned about how to succeed with integrity has grown out of forty years of following exemplars of successful, self-actualized, and mentally healthy persons as they have lived their lives. In the 1950s, I undertook an in-depth study of young men, first when they were seventeen and again when they were twenty-one who varied in how successfully they were living their lives. In 1965, *Explorations of Maturity* described a model of growing up healthily that emerged from this study. It demonstrated that as we mature, our minds and character become more present to our awareness, other-centered, well integrated, stable, and autonomous. In 1968, *Growing Up in College* reported that this model predicted how other students actually matured from their freshman to senior years. In 1971, *Humanizing Schools* drew out the implications of this research for practicing educators. And then in 1977, *Maturity and Competence: A Transcultural View* showed that the model, based predominantly on the lives of American Protestant and Jewish young men, also described Sicilian and northern Italian Catholic and Turkish Anatolian and western Muslim men.

During the early seventies, I restudied the original participants to discover how and why they were succeeding in their twenties and early thirties. I secured extensive information about them from their closest friends, colleagues, and wives, most of whom I also interviewed about their relationships with their husbands. The model of maturing not only described how they had grown since they were twenty-one but also predicted who would succeed twelve years later. References for the technical articles written between 1976 and 1983 describing these results are included in *Fulfilling Lives: Paths to Maturity and Success.*[1]

In the early 1980s, I returned to restudy the men for the fourth time as well as their wives who also participated as fully as their husbands.

Fulfilling Lives, published in 1991, described the women and men when in their early and mid-forties and showed that they mature similarly.

In 1993, I restudied the seven people this book features when most were in their mid-fifties. I have known the men for thirty-five and many of the women for twenty years.

In 1994, *Schools of Hope: Developing Mind and Character in Today's Youth* described the type of school likely to produce successful and mature adults. It drew on my understanding of such people and on consultations with and studies of hundreds of schools and colleges here and abroad.

Why write about happily married people, good lovers, competent parents, community leaders, and vocationally successful men and women when hundreds of others have already written about some of these topics? So far, no one has identified the core strengths necessary to succeed in all of our principal adult roles, examined how success in one role affects success in others, and explored the meaning of success and well-being in as much depth with both partners. Most have examined *only* marital happiness, or *only* parenting, or *only* vocational success, frequently *only* of men or *only* of women. We have a psychology of each role but not a psychology of persons and of couples who succeed in many roles.

Because the study comprehensively studied the character of successful middle-aged men and women, we can now answer questions that we could not before. What are the core strengths that enable us to triumph over our dark times? Do vocationally successful men and women make good marital partners, parents, and lovers? Does sexual fulfillment mean the same thing for men and women? Is a religious faith necessary for one's well-being? Are virtuous people more likely to succeed and be healthy and happy? Are those feminists correct who assert that healthy persons are androgynous? From what kinds of homes do successful men and women come?

Overview of the Contents

To answer these and other provocative questions about adults who create successful and happy lives for themselves and others, the book is organized into five parts. The first briefly describes the study by introducing you to Billie Leighton, who illustrates the strengths of maturity and androgyny—the two most important personal contributors to adult success and well-being. The second describes the personality of individuals who succeed in creating intimate marital, sexual, parental, and friendship relationships. Though one of the two most successful couples in 1982, Andy and Marty Miller's subsequent trials reveal some of the deeply human complications that trouble many contemporary marriages. Harry Barnett illustrates the traits of men called to be loving fathers. The third part identifies the strengths of successful entrepreneurs like Jane Allen and of those called to and fulfilled by their vocations like Chen Lee. The fourth describes those who extend themselves beyond their immediate familial and vocational roles to serve their communities and devote themselves to religious and ethical ideals, like Jim Pryor; it also discusses the character of healthy and happy people. The last part asks if men's and women's paths to fulfillment are the same or different. It concludes with some reflections about growing up successfully and healthily in these troubling and changing times.

One person's successful life may tell us the strengths that contribute to his or her success; it only suggests but cannot tell us with confidence the core strengths necessary for others to succeed as marital partners, lovers, or entrepreneurs. After describing the person who most succeeded in his or her role, I return to the larger group for clues about what commonly shared strengths distinguish the most from the least successful men and women.

Young adults, parents, and teachers who had heard me speak about the study or read drafts of *Fulfilling Lives* urged me to write for them and omit the technical detail and documentation that professionals demand. I have done so. Other detailed information omitted in this book about the study, together with supporting or clarifying notes and extensive references, can be found in *Fulfilling Lives* and related publications. Only a few of the references I have found most helpful are included in this updated version. While reorganizing, condensing, and simplifying *Fulfilling Lives*, this book, *Lives of Hope*, tells the men's and women's stories as they continued to mature into their fifties. It also introduces Chen Lee to illustrate the character of people whose vocation is a calling. Finally, it expands the stories of others to identify strengths other than those *Fulfilling Lives* discovered are essential to succeed and be happy and healthy.

Readers disagree about what they want from a study about personal, sometimes painfully troubling, ideas and results. Most want

PREFACE   xiii

me to speak directly to them—informally, colloquially, and concretely—which I do. Some have asked me to write more about the lives of the study's 105 men and women, which I also do in this revised updated version. Others more interested in the larger group's results want more abstract summaries, which I also give throughout the book. They may wish to skim these summaries first, before delving into the chapters of greatest interest. Others want me to explore the study's implications for contemporary issues, such as the future of marriage, American families, sexual fulfillment, and ethical values, which I do as well.

Acknowledgments

I dedicate the book with affection and gratitude to the men and women who so openly shared their most personal feelings and experiences with me. I am especially indebted to the principal figures in the book for letting me use their lives to illustrate what men and women are like who succeed and why they accomplish what they do. It is a measure of their maturity that they do not object to my using their names, which I would like to do in order to celebrate their exceptional achievements and lives—as well as their courage. But it is my desire, not theirs, to alter potentially identifying circumstances so that they cannot be recognized. Where such alterations now no longer seem necessary, I have reverted to their original circumstances. I am also grateful to Roger Blake, a perceptive thirty-two-year-old former student when I wrote *Fulfilling Lives*, who critiqued the study's findings from his generation's perspective about growing up to succeed. All of my informants have given me permission to publish what I have written about them.

Fulfilling Lives acknowledged my gratitude to the numerous persons who critiqued that book. I want to thank Michael Murray, Barbara Morrison, Cindy Boughner, and David Mallery again for their thoughtful and wise suggestions about how to make this book accessible to a wider range of readers than *Fulfilling Lives* reached. I am most grateful to Emily Kingham for her years of faithful help with the research. My wife not only kept our family going for the years I spent traveling to all parts of the world to locate the men and women to study but also contributed professionally to the book. As an expert on child development and parenting, she created the study's key measure assessing parental satisfaction; she also critiqued my interpretations of the women's results. I, certainly not she or anyone else, am responsible for any biases and misinterpretations in the book.

The book's last page describes how to order discounted individual or bulk copies of *Fulfilling Lives* and *Schools of Hope*, as well as additional copies of *Lives of Hope*.

Haverford, Pennsylvania　　　　　　　　　　　　　　Douglas H. Heath
June 1994

Part One

Understanding Maturity and Success

Chapter 1

Growing Up to Succeed:
Billie Leighton's "Miracle"

Are you growing in the ways that lead to success? To succeed at what? To fulfill your dreams? Three men and a Ford Escort's bumper sticker tell us how uncertain many of us are today about what we want and what paths to take to succeed and live hopeful fulfilling lives.

What Does Success Mean to Us?

By his mid-twenties, Tom had become a successful group manager monitoring the quality of computer chips in a Silicon Valley factory. When he last saw me, his first words were, "Doug, I want to grow up, but I'm stuck. I don't like my job but I don't know what I want to do; I've struck out with every girl I've ever met; my sex life is dead; all I have every night is TV and pot. I can't give up either. I'd have nothing left."

About the same time, I received a letter from Roger Blake, a thirty-two-year-old former Peace Corps volunteer in Ecuador who had become a popular high school teacher of American history. He wrote:

> I always seem to need an "out," a vision of change, a new destination. That's the restlessness I feel. Why do I feel so vaguely dissatisfied with my job that could inspire and stretch me for years to come? And Beth! Why do I wonder if I can find someone *better* when we have such

a passion for each other and have shared so much? Why do I imagine other places to live when the mountains of Colorado are such a source of joy? When I have a fine apartment and a loving group of friends? Restlessness haunts me. . . .

It all comes down, I guess, to what I value. Maybe I don't know what I value, really. Maybe I haven't been honest with myself all these years. Here I am, thirty-two, and I don't know what I really want. . . . I've got to prioritize my life. . . . Do I want a relationship I can fully commit myself to? Beth wants children; I don't. I'm not into being a father—married or not . . . but I would like to work with Quito's street kids.

It's time for me to grow up, but how?

Adam, a beloved and hugely successful forty-two-year-old minister in my study whom I had known for twenty-five years, matter-of-factly and with no self-pity told me, "At last I feel I've finally begun to grow up. I learned last year that I have AIDS. I finally found the courage to tell each of my parishioners how divided I've felt ministering to them. Most have been understanding. I finally feel I'm now living with integrity. I really feel at peace now. I don't fear what I feel coming." In the time he had left, he worked hard to secure community support for other AIDS patients. He died several years later with great dignity and serenity.

Escorts are also confused about what they want. The bumper sticker of one I followed read, "When I grow up, I want to be a Cadillac." Almost a pathological identity confusion, isn't it?

Tom, Roger, and Adam visibly succeeded in the eyes of others—but not in their own. Tom doesn't know what he wants. Roger restlessly feels unfulfilled but also does not know why. Adam was a divided soul for years. The Escort wants to be something it can't possibly be. It needs a mechanic's therapy to learn it could possibly grow up to be one of Ford's Jaguars.

Why such uncertainty and confusion about who we are and what we want? Our freedom. Freedom often complicates—seldom simplifies—our lives. Parents and society no longer so clearly prescribe what we should want and be. We now can choose between many more options: who to marry; what jobs to seek; who to have sex with; how many children we want.

It is much easier to grow up to succeed—though perhaps not to feel fulfilled in the long run—when we have less freedom to choose. When twenty-three-years-old, my Nepalese trekking guide told me that it was time for him to marry. No, he didn't want to marry until he could support a wife, but his younger brother couldn't marry until he did. No, he wasn't looking for a wife; in his country, mothers arranged the marriages of their children. Yes, he would see whoever she chose for him, but only briefly before the marriage. Maybe in time they would love each other—even become good friends. No, he couldn't divorce her if he didn't like her.

Tom and Roger, however, must work much more self-consciously than a Nepalese guide to create their goals and the mind and character to achieve them. Success isn't just a matter of luck, family privilege, or society's program. It has become more a matter of our character and the way we use it. We have to learn, for example, how to be persons of integrity.

Growing up also means deciding which option or goal is more and which is less important, such as not wanting to have one's own children but wanting to work with Quito's street kids instead. It means accepting that we cannot be everything we would like to be, a Cadillac instead of a Jaguar. William James, one of America's most influential philosophers, told us this a hundred years ago when he wrote psychology's first textbook.

> I am often confronted by the necessity of standing by one of my empirical selves and relinquishing the rest. Not that I would not, if I could, be both handsome and fat and well dressed, and a great athlete, and make a million a year, be a wit, a *bon-vivant*, and a lady-killer, as well as a philosopher, a philanthropist, statesman, warrior, and African explorer, as well as a "tone-poet" and saint. But the thing is simply impossible. The millionaire's work would run counter to the saint's; the *bon-vivant* and the philanthropist would trip each other up; the philosopher and the lady-killer could not well keep house in the same tenement of clay.[1]

Harriet, my wife, questions James's idea that we have to have a number one self or one identity. "Why couldn't James be simultaneously fat, a wealthy philosopher, and a lady-killer?" She argues that James's belief that we must have a number one self is a male view of growing up. Men have always had one identity—their vocations; women have had at least two—wives and mothers—until recently. Superwoman now wants three: a successful career as well. Not even Superman could manage two successfully; he lost his superhuman power when he chose to marry Lois Lane.

What does success mean to you? Clarifying our priorities about what we want is the first step in achieving them. Why not rank the following twelve goals that most people would like to achieve? Then you can compare your personal meanings to those of college-educated adults who have similarly ranked their values. Rank your most important goal or value a 1, the next priority goal a 2, and so on. To discover just how clearly ordered your priorities are, try not to give tied ranks.

High income	____
Leadership and power	____
Having a close friend of the same gender	____
Fulfilling sexual relations	____
Being a contributing citizen to the community or nation	____
Competence in a satisfying vocation	____
Competent and satisfied parenting	____
Religious-ethical ideals	____
Happy marital relationship	____
Physical health	____
Psychological maturity; good mental health	____
Self-fulfillment; happiness	____

To compare your priorities to those of several thousand college-educated thirty- to fifty-year-olds, just reverse the order of the priorities listed.

Self-fulfillment and happiness are invariably selected by most as their highest priority; they next rank psychological maturity and good mental health. Most rank high income and leadership and power to be their least important values.

Men and women differ in a few of their priorities. Men value a fulfilling sexual relationship and high income more than women do. Women rank a close friendship with someone of the same gender and contributing to their community more highly than men do. Later we'll discover the why of these differences and some of their consequences.

Why We Know So Little About Well-Functioning Adults

Once we are clear about what is most and least important to us, we can then ask what paths we should follow and what strengths we need to achieve our hopes.

Ultimately, we have only one way of ever learning much about men and women who turn out to succeed as partners, parents, or contributing citizens. We must empathically and nonjudgmentally go with them over the years as they create their individual paths to success and happiness. However, uncertainties and formidable barriers make such thirty- to forty-year trips difficult not just to initiate but to sustain. And the practical problems are daunting. Studies that continue for decades are expensive; funding agencies shy from supporting them. They are also time consuming. They don't lend themselves to rapid and frequent publications; some publications, like this book, emerge only after years of work. More important, securing the cooperation of just one partner, let alone two, as well as of close friends and colleagues, tries one's patience. Incomplete information about some types of success bedevils such studies and increases the unreliability of some findings. The physical stress of constant weekend travel and even being way for weeks at a time over a period of several years can cause severe health problems.

For me, the emotional stress of becoming so involved in the inner dramas of others is the most compelling reason why our knowledge about successful adults is so thin. A few of my many adventures illustrate why going "out into the world" to study individuals so intimately for long periods of time can be emotionally perilous.

My visit to see Marc Taylor and his wife, Roberta, illustrates the logistical problems of such research. I had taught Thursday afternoon and just made my flight, which arrived late in the evening in Bogata, Columbia. Marc met me at the airport wearing a shoulder holster and gun. I apprehensively asked why.

"We're driving into the jungle. Bandits have been reported in the area."

I shrank. Great. Just what I need. Will I get home in time for my seminar Monday evening? (I had promised myself I would never let the research get in the way of my commitment to my students. It never did.) And then I said to myself, "If we're attacked, I'll whip out my Rorschach inkblots, flash them at the bandits, and promise to tell them their fortune, which would include a happy future if they let us go unscathed."

Only later on the return flight did I remember that my long forgotten Italian would have been no substitute for Spanish. I returned emotionally exhausted, but I was prepared for class Monday night.

Another tale explains why we know so little about the most personal lives of effective adults. It is emotionally risky to enter as deeply as I did into the inner secrets of families. And I found no family that was secret-free. Since I (and the Internal Revenue Service) paid for my own research expenses for the middle-aged studies, I tried to see several people who lived in the area during the same visit. On one of several trips to the Chicago area I saw Barb and Bob Henry and John and Mary O'Neil. When I first saw Barb, whom I hadn't met before, I felt that she was subdued and preoccupied. She smiled dutifully, almost plaintively. I sensed some inner dark cloud that I had little inkling of from the hours of test and questionnaire material she had earlier returned. After about twenty minutes of our first interview, I began to feel sad.

When I asked what she was most proud of in her life, she answered, "Nothing. I've had a lousy marriage; I love my kids but I sometimes wish I didn't have them."

A few minutes later, she broke in to ask, "Everything I tell you is just between us, isn't it? Bob won't know?"

"Yes. I feel strongly about that."

At the end of the interview, she tearfully said, "I've had enough. I'm thinking of ending it all."

I couldn't sleep that night. What should I do? There was no question what was most important: Barb, not the study. I decided to ask her if she really wanted to continue. The next morning, without my asking, she drew me aside to say she wanted to go on. "I just needed to feel understood." But we worked on the pain later. (No one in the study has committed suicide, though one child of the participants has.)

Late the next day I arrived at the O'Neils. John's first comment was,

> I'm awfully sorry. I hope we haven't messed up the study. We didn't have time to let you know. Martin [their fourteen-year-old son] ran away from home last Tuesday, stole a car, and cracked it up. He refused to tell the police his name. We've been going crazy. Mary's had a rough time. We just found him. He's okay now but he doesn't want to meet you.

How could I help John and Mary? I could be there for as long as they needed me, and for several years after, whenever they needed support.

The Men and Women I Am Accompanying

With only a few exceptions, the men and women went to college. Many, including the women since their marriages, have gone on to graduate and professional schools. They, again including the women, are physicians, scholars, ministers, journalists, teachers, research scientists, poets, singers, lawyers, managers, entrepreneurs, and owners and presidents of businesses. No women are mathematicians, engineers, or physicists, though more than a few had the temperament and talent to succeed in these fields. In their early forties, about two-thirds of the women worked outside the home. In their fifties, almost all did.

The sixty-five men that I studied in their mid-forties were more homogeneous as a group than their partners. All are white. Most came primarily from middle- and upper-middle-income families; all attended the same small liberal arts college (Haverford), though not all graduated. They were selected from five successive classes. Some were chosen randomly and others nominated by judges for their interpersonal, extracurricular, and community success or failure. I had extensive information about them when they were about seventeen, twenty-one, thirty-two, and forty-five. I have since secured additional information about the four men, now in their mid- to late-fifties, whom this book features.

The forty women are the partners of the men. They vary more than the men in their ethnic, national origin, and social class backgrounds. They attended diverse colleges. They ranged in age from twenty-six to fifty-two, though they averaged thirty-nine when I last visited and studied the entire group. I had known two-thirds of them when the men were in their early thirties. At that time, they had completed extensive questionnaires about their partners and provided more limited information about themselves. I have revisited the three principal women of the book now that they also are in their late forties and early fifties.

All but five of the men had married. Five percent had divorced by their early thirties, 30 percent by their mid-forties, and 40 percent by their mid-fifties. Four have divorced twice. Adam and one other, the most brilliant of the group, died of AIDS since I had studied them in their forties. All but one couple have children; they now range in age from nineteen months to thirty-six years.

What I Know About the Men and Women

I have thousands of bits of information about each person—more about the men than the women since I have known them since they were in college. I know of no other study that has gone into such depth in all of the principal areas of both men's and women's lives or obtained such extensive information about their success and well-being from their partners, friends, and colleagues.

Because I included many different ways of assessing how successfully the women and men achieved each of the twelve goals you rated, I was able to check the results of one measure against the results of several others. For example, I measured marital success by each participant's ratings, each partner's ratings about the other, and their closest friends' ratings. Each also completed a comprehensive marital scale that described what researchers had previously identified as characteristics of happy marriages. In addition, each answered interview questions about the relationship, as well as created an imaginative story to a picture of a middle-aged man and woman embracing. This allowed them to reveal less conscious feelings and attitudes about such relationships. Finally, I lived with most of the couples for several days and observed how they got along with each other.

Mental health and psychological maturity were similarly assessed in as many different ways as possible: psychology's most widely used paper-and-pencil tests and imaginative measures of mental health; self-, partner- and close-friend ratings of psychological health; interview questions about coping ability; transculturally validated measures of maturity; and behavioral tests of different aspects of maturity, among others.

Casting such a wide net increases the odds that I actually am identifying who is more or less successful in their various roles. I took special steps to prevent my biases—both those I know about and those I don't—from influencing whom I chose to tell you about. I have relied *only* on the study's objective measures and the judgments of the participants' partners, friends, and colleagues about their success and well-being.

Learning About Successful Men and Women: Billie Leighton

It's now time to tell you how I learned about why men and women succeed. I introduce you to Billie Leighton, the study's most successful woman, and describe how we worked together to understand the strengths that enabled her to work her own miracle of growing up.

If any of the study's women merit the label of "Superwoman," Billie Leighton does. She is the most all-round successful and fulfilled of the forty women. She had created one of the happier marriages, become a successful physician, and scored among the top three in leadership, ethical character, and maturity. She rated herself to be very happy and fulfilled; her three peers also rated her that way. When I first identified her as the study's most successful and fulfilled woman, she fell down only in her satisfaction as a mother. She scored "average" on a measure of parental fulfillment, possibly because she, childless herself, was a part-time mother of two stepdaughters, instead of a full-time mother of her own children. So she is not quite the ideal Superwoman.

How did I go about understanding Billie? What did I learn? Chapter Two will describe how and why she had grown during the ten years since I had first met her and the lessons she teaches us about the strengths of those who achieve what they've worked a lifetime for.

As I describe her, you might enjoy looking for clues in her story that explain why she succeeded so eminently. Then you can compare your strengths to those Billie and I came up with and to those the larger study identified to be central to both men's and women's overall success.

Billie was the second wife of Allan Leighton, a successful corporate lawyer, who had participated in the study since he was seventeen. I knew a great deal about her from the six to seven hours of questionnaires and tests that she had completed. Billie had been married to Allan three years when I first met her on a Friday evening in April 1983. She appeared younger than her forty-one years. Though she was five feet nine inches tall, she seemed more petite, due to her carefully trimmed auburn hair, willowy movements, and simple, almost plain dress. She was not a frilly woman; she seemed to be very much a piece of her Boston townhouse, which was understatedly decorated with modern Danish furniture. Her aura, not her appearance or that of the house, captured my memories that spring day: calm, composed, "down-to-business," efficient, purposeful.

As with every person in the study, within the first hour I gave Billie the Rorschach inkblot test, one of psychology's most revealing personality tests. I asked her to tell me everything she saw in each of its ten cards. To make sense of a vague inkblot or a summer's cumulus cloud, we must find images in our minds that fit the blot or cloud. Such images, like those of dreams, are openings to our inner lives. They can reveal our unfulfilled urges and fears, the intensity of our energies, the cast of our mind that organizes our images, and our ways of coping with stress.

I next gave Billie other tests as well as the first of two several-hour interviews, which I taped and typed, that focused on her past history of accomplishments and worries, ways of coping with them, and present feelings about her work, marriage, family, and friends. In the interview's first few minutes, she said, "A lot of people who know my family story believe that it was very unlikely that I'd grow out of it. As a child, I truly believed I never would become old enough to be a parent, probably because of my fear of not surviving. . . . When my mother was murdered by her fourth husband, my first husband said, 'Given your relationship with your mother, you're better off that she's dead.'" So Billie introduced me to her family story. No self-pity. No dramatics. No blame. No excuses. Acceptance. Matter-of-fact. This was the way it was. A "What do I do about it?" attitude.

Billie's family life had been abysmal. It had few of the *loving, democratic,* and *firm* values that mark the homes that I have found contribute most to later adult success and happiness. She declared that her beautiful mother's artistic talents had led her into an erratic bohemian way of life. When Billie was five, her mother had divorced her husband because he physically abused her. She subsequently remarried three times; each new husband reminded Billie of her own father. He had also remarried but shortly afterward divorced his second wife to marry another. Billie was shuffled back and forth between her mother, father, and maternal grandparents during these marital games of musical chairs. On the previsit questionnaire, she rated her parental home as tense and conflictive; her parents had argued frequently about her and money. She never had the feeling that they had enjoyed being her parents.

As Billie said (later confirmed by her tests), she still felt deeply ambivalent about her mother and other women who took on the role of a "mother" to her. She saw her mother as having been a socially outgoing, effervescent, energetic woman who enjoyed exploring new ideas. She had encouraged Billie's independence and willingness to take risks which made living exciting. But Billie also recalled that her mother had been sexually maladjusted, physically unhealthy, and so mentally unstable that she was hospitalized twice for depression. Too self-absorbed and self-centered, her mother seldom made herself accessible when Billie really needed her. Though she emphasized that Billie should do well in school, she never, for example, helped her with her homework. To the item, "I felt rejected by my mother," Billie checked "Quite true." However, she felt gently ignored, really casually abandoned, rather than hostilely rejected. Her mother wasn't an authoritarian or severe disciplinarian. Billie didn't feel particularly close or temperamentally similar to her mother; she only moderately respected her as a model of the woman she should become. But she still was not emotionally free of needing her. To an incomplete sentence that began, "When she thought of her mother, she . . .," Billie poignantly replied, "wanted more."

Billie talked much more about her father than her mother in the first interview, perhaps because he was no longer an *unresolved* painful "presence" in her life. She felt that he had really loved her when she was a child, which contributed to her trusting men, even though he had later run out on her. "When I was a little kid, he loved me; he paid attention to me and provided for my physical needs through my teenage years. He stimulated me intellectually. When I was a little girl, he would read passages to me out of an encyclopedia, which gave me a sense of learning. That was important to me. When older, we'd sit at the dinner table and talk about theories of evolution."

However, like both stepmothers, who she felt didn't like her, her father became more authoritarian, severely disciplining and regulating her social life in her teenage years. He enforced "ridiculous rules, like I could go out only one night a week, and restricted me in other ways not at all in line with my peers." Her father was more loyal to his wives than to her, which he later admitted after his second divorce. He never sided with her when she desperately needed his support. On Billie's seventeenth birthday, he told her that she was now "emancipated"; it was time for her to be on her own. Billie returned to her grandparents, who remained her "real" parents.

Without rancor, Billie said she had never been important to her father. To a questionnaire item, "I felt rejected by my father," she checked, "Quite true." Not actively concerned about her or her welfare, he, like her mother, never made himself accessible when she needed him. Billie felt that he did not understand her, perhaps because they were so dissimilar temperamentally. Nevertheless, he felt more warmly toward her than her mother had; so she felt closer to and loved him more than she had her mother. Though she still visits him occasionally, he has never visited or telephoned her. He has emotionally passed out of her life.

Despite her unsettled home life, Billie enjoyed school, where she did so well that she became overly sensitive about appearing to be too smart and competent. Believing "that the only pathway to love and approval was through perfect performance," she participated in every challenging academic and extracurricular activity she could. She made the state's debating team, became a leader in her state's athletic association, and won awards for scholarship as well as leadership. Excelling in school and extracurricular activities and assuming household responsibilities in her father's house left little time to develop other interests. Although sharing interests typical of girls her age, she felt that she was different—a feeling that persisted into her forties. She had some close friendships with other girls and boys but was not sexually active until she married in her mid-twenties.

Needing the security of her grandparents, she remained home with them while attending what she called a "mediocre" state-run college with "very mediocre teachers," rather than going the several hundred miles to the university, which would have been more appropriate for her talents.

Growing up in a stable and conservative Catholic neighborhood with an eventually thrice-divorced mother and with a twice-divorced father had made her feel that she was "from the wrong side of the tracks." So after graduating from college, she married Frank Peters, who came from the "good side." She felt a special duty to prove her own credentials to him, so she supported him during his graduate work for the five years they stayed together. But the marriage became rockier and rockier.

When her mother was murdered by her fourth husband in an ugly drunken brawl, Billie inherited a small insurance policy that (unknown to her at the time) eventually became her life raft to a much happier and more productive adult life. Doubtful about her future, increasingly unhappy with a marriage that wasn't meeting her needs, feeling stuck, and unable to grieve her mother's death, she used the insurance for short-term counseling from a local community clinic. At one point, her counselor asked her, "What is it you really want?" For forty-five minutes, Billie talked about what her grandmother and husband wanted of her. So he repeated the question, "What do *you* want?"

> I burst into tears, for no one had ever asked before what I wanted. When he then said, "I hear you saying you are in a terrible marriage and really want to get out," a light bulb flashed. He was giving me permission to ask something for myself. It took me another year and half to get out. My husband didn't pass his grad school prelims. I bought him a car and got him an apartment so I could leave him as free of guilt as possible. I left and felt free for the first time in my life.

Deciding to go to medical school, she paid her own tuition and living costs by working odd hours at any job she could find. (A "miracle," her advisor later told her.) She got her medical degree, became associated with Yale's medical school, and shortly afterward met and married Allan. She left her tenure-track position to be with him in Boston and help raise his two daughters. So began my intensely concentrated visits—first, the Rorschach and some other tests, then the first of two taped-recorded interviews.

Next morning, Billie and I got right to work to complete several other questionnaires and the second taped interview about how and why she had changed in the past ten to twelve years. She rated how influential fifty possible causes of her maturing had been (personality of spouse, type of occupation, and so on); and then explained their effects. She next answered other questions about how the changing roles of women and men had affected her. I then reviewed with her a report about her tests results that I had completed the night before. That afternoon I began to work with Allan, who had considerately taken their daughter on an outing near the harbor.

As others had done, both thanked me for the "gift" of my visit, perhaps because I genuinely tried to listen and understand without making judgments even about what they might have felt were awful, perverse, or wicked wishes and deeds. It was a measure of Billie's maturity to trust me—almost a stranger—and to agree to share her life so publicly with you, the reader.

We are now ready to understand the key reasons why Billie has succeeded as well as she has. The next chapter describes our hunches ten years ago, describes how she has grown since, and then reexamines the reasons for her success.

Chapter 2

Billie Leighton:
Taking Charge of Herself

If you enjoy figuring out Agatha Christie's mysteries and working with Jessica Fletcher to solve her weekly murders in CBS's *Murder She Wrote*, then become a psychological detective and join Billie and me as we look for hunches about why she succeeded. Her life story seems to defy the lessons that our current Dr. Spocks and psychologists have taught us about the families that help us to mature. How could Billie, given such a disruptive family, rejecting parents, mediocre schooling, and a failed marriage, pull herself up by her bootstraps to become the study's most competent, mature, and fulfilled woman? What strengths enabled her to resist and free herself of the potentially damaging effects of her early life?

Most of my hunches are based on the tests I gave Billie. You may feel they are arbitrary, even dogmatic, pronouncements. But Billie agreed with and amplified them with other examples from her life.

The summary of her tests identified the core strengths that contributed to her success. "She has an unusually rich number of intellectual and personality potentials to use for adapting. Her most salient specific strength can only be described as an androgynous judiciousness. What is most striking is her accessibility in a balanced way to stereotypical feminine and masculine strengths. She is one of the more psychologically healthy, emotionally stable, and mature persons of the entire group." Billie's success and fulfillment were due to at least three prominent strengths: her cast of mind, her androgynous character, and her maturity.

Cast of Mind

I could not tell how much her genes, constitution, family climate, parents, schooling, and other events contributed to how she turned out. Surely she must have inherited some impressive intellectual and energetic genes that enabled her to withstand and overcome the corrosive effects of her early family life. What is important is how she developed and made use of her potential intellectual strengths.

What strengths of mind contributed to her ability to cope? She herself identified her principal ones, which were independently confirmed by the tests.

"Ever since I can remember as a child, I have been both very introspective and very socially outgoing. I have an analytical side to me. When I had a bad relationship with someone, I'd think about it, work it through in my mind until I understood it and why it happened. It helped me to change my behavior. I did a lot of analytical work when younger; I kept a log, not exactly a diary, in which I wrote about what was troubling me and how to change myself."

Billie coped with her disruptive family life by consciously developing what she called a "problem-solving" approach to living. The Rorschach showed she could note details and put them together in clear, realistic, and practical ways—hence her judiciousness. Her mind was more practical than fanciful. I wrote, "She has beautiful control as well as resiliency, but her inner clarity seems to preclude turmoil and disorder as well as the strange and bizarre" (qualities that tend to mark the minds of creative persons).

She spoke of the intellectual strengths that contributed to her adult success this way: "I was always very good at remembering things and making relationships between things. Now I am much better able to do the next step of analysis . . . the grander relationships. One skill I have is being able to see a patient, analyze seemingly separate and discrete symptoms, pull them together in a whole, and then bring out the various approaches to treat the problem."

Years of practice trying to figure out each of her four fathers and three mothers and how to get along with them must have strengthened her reflective problem-solving skills, such as planning "proactive" steps, as she called it, to resolve family strains and anticipating their consequences.

Androgynous Character

High intelligence, introspective and reflective control, analytical ability, and practical problem-solving skills aren't enough to account for her success, however. We must look to her character. Billie shared the typical strengths of both women and men to an unusual degree. Her androgyny consistently emerged in three different ways. She populated the vague Rorschach inkblots with well-defined wolves, bears, giants, and alligators—all typically aggressive images that males tend to give. But she also saw princesses, bunny rabbits, sea cows, and a baby's head—images that females typically see more frequently in the blots.

She was temperamentally similar to persons successful and happy in *both* typically feminine and masculine occupations, as measured by a widely used vocational interest scale. Unlike others in the study, she resembled successful persons in most fields of endeavor: in the expressive arts, probably reflecting her mother's bohemian inclinations; in mathematics and science, reflecting her father's scholarly temperament; in entrepreneurial activities like business, politics, and law; and even in adventurous, risk-taking vocations like the military.

I had analyzed Billie's tests before I examined how she, Allan, her closest female friend, and a colleague had rated her on 100 personality traits. Twenty of the traits indexed typical masculine strengths like assertiveness and self-sufficiency; twenty measured typical feminine ones like compassion and sensitivity to others. Such strengths are not exclusive to one's gender; everyone shares both masculine and feminine characteristics to some degree. Allan, her friend, and a colleague rated her to be not only the most masculine of the study's women but also its third most feminine woman. Adding these two high scores together made her the most androgynous woman. That three diverse measures—an inkblot test, psychology's most reputable vocational interest scale, and judgments of the three persons who knew her most intimately—identified her to be androgynous, rather than only feminine or masculine, suggests that her androgyny was probably close to the core of her identity. Billie did not dispute these objectively based hunches. She told me, "My colleagues tell me that I don't think like a woman. I think like a man. They mean it as a compliment, not realizing it is insulting. I've also been very aware that my name is androgynous.

That must've influenced me in some ways when growing up."

In her formative years, she probably developed both masculine and feminine strengths without clearly identifying with either a fixed female or male gender role. So she is open to and accepts the potentials of both. What is intriguing from a developmental point of view is that this amalgam did not result in a diffuse sense of self or identity, lack of a strong will, or paralyzing emotional conflicts. Instead, she learned how to reflect judiciously, analyze, and integrate such potentially contradictory strengths in healthy and mature ways. In some ways, her basic identity is organized around her own image of herself as a problem solver who can cope, not around her femaleness or maleness. Her androgynous character provided her with rich and diverse gifts on which to draw to succeed in her familial and vocational roles.

Psychological Maturity

That her psychological maturity was so formative didn't surprise me. My earlier research had shown over and over that more mature people continue to grow more rapidly and healthily than immature ones; they also cope with adversity more effectively throughout their lives. Maturity is a foundation for further maturing. Billie's maturity enabled her to use her intellect in the way that she did to succeed. (The next chapter summarizes what my research and Billie tell us about the strengths of maturing persons.) When asked what she was most proud of in her life, Billie instantly replied, "I feel that I've now come to terms with what I am and am functioning as a healthy adult for the first time in my life. I am ambitious, set high goals for myself, and work hard to get there. But I don't walk over other people. I really have a strong need to be loved and have loving friendships. Because of that, I have sought out mother and father figures in my friends and colleagues."

So why did Billie turn out so successfully, overcoming seemingly devastating odds? We don't know with certainty, for her early childhood experiences and other causes remain obscure. But native talent and temperament contributed to her special coping skills. Probably, in a perverse way, her parents, by not being emotionally compelling and respected models, didn't confirm her in either a rigidly feminine or masculine role. Familial insecurity was the goad to learn how to survive. School was where she succeeded and discovered her own competitive worth. Supportive grandparents provided her the safe harbor to which to retreat and from which to sail forth.

Billie had learned to survive and flourish on the basis of her *own* maturity and determination to produce that "miracle" of putting herself through medical school. By the time she remarried, she had developed the good judgment to marry a man who, sensitive to her needs, supported her professional career by making adjustments in his own life.

Ten Years Later

I revisited Billie for a three-hour interview late one afternoon in December, 1993. Earlier, she had completed and returned several tests and questionnaires.

Since my last visit, Billie and Allan had made several career-related moves and now lived in an affluent rural community near the Adirondacks. Their rambling 200-year-old, historic white clapboard home was as tastefully decorated and immaculately ordered as their Boston apartment had been. To my eyes, Billie had not changed except for a few strands of gray hair; she claimed, however, that she was now ten pounds heavier as a result of an early menopause. Though having worked all day at her hospital, she was just as alert, lively, even vivacious, and comfortable to be with as I remembered her having been ten years earlier. After a simple but elegantly served dinner that had tasty traces of her month's cooking lessons while she and Allan had vacationed in Italy, we settled into our interview. It focused on questions that were updated versions of those I had asked ten years earlier.

Three themes criss-crossed during the evening and illuminated the strengths that contributed to her earlier success as well as her adaptability to the three crises she has faced since. The themes were the death of her grandmother, the intensification of her nurturing needs, and her expanding career success and its conflict with Allan's.

Death of Billie's Grandmother

Shortly after my 1983 visit, Billie's grandmother unexpectedly died of a heart attack. "I was absolutely shocked. Totally. I was prepared for my grandfather to die. He was dying from Alzheimer's. I thought of her as still young. I really grieved. It also brought up unresolved issues and feelings about my mother's death." As Billie described her grandmother, I realized how incomplete my understanding had been of how she had survived her chaotic upbringing and rejecting parents. Her grandparents had not just been a "safe harbor." Billie's grandmother had been the mother she never had had who loved and affirmed her in a way that enabled her to grow healthily. She had opened up the world to Billie and given her hope for her future.

> She adored me and let me know it. She took responsibility for me. She clothed me when my parents were irresponsible or left me alone. She enriched my life. She gave me piano lessons. She encouraged me to take ballet. She assumed I would read all of the time and never limited what I read. She encouraged me to read adult books; she'd give me a book she was reading. She talked about her work as an attorney, which she loved. She assumed I'd go to college and assumed I would be an attorney. She would let me know how proud of me she was. She was very affectionate; she loved to hug and kiss me. She would literally bite me on my cheek and say she wished she could eat me up. I knew what she meant. I just knew I was important in her life. As an adult, I asked her for advice, which she would give, but she never interfered in my life. When I first bought my house in New Haven and needed help, she shared in the expenses. When it came time to sell, she expected she would get her share back, just as she expected the change back if I went to the grocery store. She was always very clean about those things.

What better model of the loving, democratic parent who respects her child's individuality but who holds her child to firm expectations of how to behave?

Intensification of Nurturing Needs

Shortly after her grandmother's death, Allan and Billie decided to have a child. But she was devastated to discover she could not become pregnant. In the sterile words of her physician, she was an early "outlier in the statistical distribution of the age of menopausal onset." "It was really hard for me. I was angry at Allan because I partially blamed him for not wanting a child, but then I realized I too had stalled making the decision, though why I'm not sure."

Though she felt she had accepted her childlessness, her need to be a "nurturer" had become even stronger than I had noted ten years earlier; it was an insistent theme throughout the interview. She now ranked being "a supportive and fun parent/grandparent" as her most important wish to fulfill before she died.

Erik Erikson, an influential psychologist, claims that middle-aged persons must find ways to fulfill their needs to care and be responsible for others—the stage of generativity—if they are to continue to grow healthily. How did Billie adapt to her intensifying nurturing need in ways that might contribute to her further growth and well-being? Since the death of her grandparents, she has self-consciously recreated an extended family for herself to nurture. Her first words in the interview set the nurturing theme of the remaining hours. Describing her feelings about her stepdaughters (now adults), she said "They have been wonderful for me. I had anticipated what being a mother to children would be like, but I didn't imagine how much I would enjoy being a mother to adults. I really like it. And I like them as people.... I love Allan's children. That is one of the biggest gifts he gave me."

To my question, "In what ways have you been a good parent?" Billie replied without hesitation, "I've been very direct and honest. I've loved them a lot and they know that and I tell them that. I have tried to be there when they needed me. I have tried to improve their relationship with their dad. I tell them often and sincerely how much I care about them and what they have meant to my life. I really wanted them to know that they mattered to me and what good people they are."

The birth of her stepgranddaughter provided her with "baby experiences, which are really wonderful. I find babies to be endlessly entertaining.... My grandchild is just a delight. She's cute, smart, and I bonded to her very quickly. She gave me smiles when three days old."

Later, she mused, "I've gotten to be a grandparent and I have become interested in a family in a different way. Rather than seeking out parental substitutes for myself, I now seek opportunities to do parenting."

Billie's nurturing impulses are overflowing her immediate family's channel and rippling into others' lives. She now volunteers one evening a week to work in a pediatric ward because, in her words, "I love being with the kids so much." She has also resumed frequent contact with her stepsiblings. Both she and her stepsister agree that Billie has taken on more of a maternal than a sisterly role. "I feel responsible for her. I have a life insurance policy in her name and am taking responsibility for sending her daughter to college."

Her caring for others has also spilled over into her relationships at work. As the director of a medical program in her hospital, she is responsible for teaching and encouraging the growth of residents as well as for generating the funds necessary to sustain some of the staff. She is so worried that she might not be able to support her staff because of her hospital's current financial plight that she sometimes can't sleep at night.

The rippling effects of her nurturing desires (combined with her professional and leadership skills) are now spreading beyond her community to state and national activities. She voluntarily works to obtain food donations for a local battered woman's shelter. Because of her empathy for and desire to help families who have parents with Alzheimer's, she voluntarily works on a state Alzheimer's board as well as on other statewide health-related boards.

Career Conflict with Allan's

Before I describe how Billie worked to resolve her third crisis—about Allan's and her career problems—let's pause to do an exercise. In a moment, I'll give two of her responses, but first, why not try to answer these questions yourself? Without hesitating, write down or say out loud the first five words or brief phrases that come to mind about each of the following periods of life, whether you have reached them or not. Don't worry if what springs to mind is not related logically to each period.

- Mid- and late forties
- Early thirties
- Late teens and early twenties
- Mid-fifties

Like the others interviewed, Billie did not spontaneously cite unhappy, depressive, or anxious words or phrases. She also did not describe herself on the questionnaires or interviews as discouraged, pessimistic, or paralyzed during her middle years.

About the mid- and late forties, Billie impulsively said "interesting, active, transitional, more fun than I thought they would be, settling and settled."

About the mid-fifties, she commented, "more focus on family, very active, healthy, considering retiring, and grandparenting."

All of Billie's crises, as troubling and painful as they were at the time, drew on her coping skills and the optimistic attitude implied in her view of the forties and fifties. This approach spurred new growth. Billie's and Allan's career conflict was no exception. Her move from Yale to an administrative position in one of Harvard's teaching hospitals opened other opportunities. Her leadership skills blossomed. She is looked to as someone who can motivate others to work collaboratively as well as resolve a group's interpersonal conflicts. Editing books and preparing chapters for others and being skilled in securing research grants have also led to increasing professional recognition, the development of a network of professional friends, and more demands on her leadership skills. Recently, she was selected to chair a long-range planning committee for a national organization responsible for veterans' health and nominated for a major governmental position in one of the national health agencies.

Meanwhile, Allan's career blossomed publicly as he moved up his company's administrative ladder, but increasing discontent drove him to quietly search for another position. One day, with little warning, he told Billie he had been offered a more desirable position in another state that would require her to leave Harvard. She was furious, disappointed, and sad. Furious because "he was not altogether honest with me . . . not upfront, and we were not doing it together." Disappointed because "I was feeling torn for there was no position for me. . . . It was really depressing and a little insulting to have to make 'cold calls,' as salespeople say," to seek out and then to discover there were no openings in nearby hospitals. Sad because she knew it was the right decision for Allan, though not for her. It brought him recognition and was an exceptional opportunity to be a director of an important division. However, just as she had given up Yale's tenure track for her marriage, now she faced giving up her Harvard position for her husband's fulfillment.

How did they cope with this hardest and most troubling period of their eight-year-old marriage? Relying on what she called her "usual approach," she systematically thought through all of their options. They decided to purchase an apartment in Cambridge for her and their current house for Allan. They lived apart for two years, though it was not an angry separation. They talked every day by phone and then took turns visiting each other on weekends. "Though little bubbles of anger ... [occurred] over the inconvenience, I was no longer deeply angry." Billie eventually became director of a program in a neighboring hospital and moved to be with Allan, who was flourishing in his new position. However, she misses Harvard's intellectual stimulation.

Their resolution to never again act as two separate people but only as a couple so strengthened their marriage that when asked, "What is your greatest accomplishment or happiest experience of which you are most proud since our last visit?" she replied,

> I am very proud of making a stable, happy marriage given my background. I didn't know if I had the capacity.... We continue to work at making a good relationship. Both of us work on the natural ups and downs. As soon as we see a down we both work at making it go up. We are much better at expressing when we are not feeling close, what is upsetting us, and sharing concerns. The first time you have a valley all you can imagine is that the valley will last forever. Now we recognize that is normal but that we have some control to keep it from reaching the nadir and that we can bring it up faster. Also, [we have] the confidence of a history together; we trust that we can really get it to be better.

Why Billie Continued Her Growth into Her Fifties

Billie moves into her fifties an even stronger and more fulfilled woman than when she entered her forties. She is creating her own paths to fulfill her more insistent nurturing needs, fashion a sturdier relationship with Allan, expand her vocational success, and use her impressive leadership strengths to serve an ever-widening community. Her mind's strengths—judiciousness, reflectiveness, analytical ability, and organizational problem-solving skills among others—have served her well. Her androgynous character enabled growth in both typical feminine nurturing and masculine achieving and leadership activities. Billie's sound health and maturity buffered her against the potential defeating and paralyzing effects her major crises could have provoked. Her maturity empowered her to wrest greater fulfillment from her crises.

Life-Affirming Vitality

Relying solely on the test information I had about Billie a decade ago, I underestimated other core strengths that have since emerged more prominently. One is her life-affirming vitality, whose sources may be both constitutional and psychological. Perhaps because she feels as if she is fifteen years younger than her fifty-one years, she says she is on life's "expanding and growing," not contracting or downhill, trajectory. In the past decade, she has become even more optimistic and hopeful about her future. Living is an opportunity for new learnings and growths, even when approaching death itself. "I don't want to be dead... but I also view being terminally ill as a period of potentially tremendous personal growth." No other person in the study viewed the crisis of dying this way. Her vitality overflows into her recreational skiing and hiking activities; she has energy for new interests and is eager to use and improve her skills, such as cooking for her 150-person Christmas parties. She has also become more assertive, forceful, and decisive as her leadership skills have been called on.

Interpersonal Strengths

The psychological tests also did not adequately assess her other major strength: her interpersonal needs and skills. Billie is very clear about their importance to her. "I am an intuitive 'people person'; people are my species." When I asked, "From what do you draw your staying power?" she said emphatically, "My relationships with other people. That is what is important to me. That is what gives me the most energy and hope and enthusiasm."

Though judged a decade ago to be the study's second most androgynous person, now (as then) she identifies her masculine rather than feminine interpersonal character to be more prominent. However, the abrasive potential of her increased forcefulness, aggressiveness, and decisiveness is moderated and mellowed by her growth in sympathy for and sensitivity to others' needs. She is learning how to use her androgynous inclinations and strengths to be the effective leader that she is emerging as.

But, as I learned belatedly, she did not do all this alone. Opportunities that can draw out our latent strengths are essential to our success and well-being. Though I gave her chapter in *Fulfilling Lives* the subtitle *Succeeding on Her Own,* I failed to understand how much her grandmother had contributed to her strong sense of self and drive to grow.

Billie's life suggests how crucial the death of a mother can be to a woman's healthy growth and subsequent fulfillment. Far more than the study's men, its middle-aged women were still deeply enmeshed in and distressed by unresolved feelings, especially anger, toward their parents, almost exclusively their mothers. Not until Billie's grandmother—her emotionally good mother—died could she finally let her biologically bad mother go, as she had let her father go more than a decade earlier. Mourning her grandmother's death may have freed her of her intense need for a mother—any kind of mother—to take care of her. Might she no longer have needed her bad mother against whom to drain off her resentment? Her forty years of hurt no longer nagged at her confidence about what kind of mother she could be. Now emotionally free to have her own child, she discovered it was too late, prompting her to explore other ways to fulfill her persistent nurturing needs.

Billie adapted to the crisis of her grandmother's death and her inability to have children in a very human way. She became the kind of mother to her step-daughters, and subsequently to her granddaughter and stepsister, that her grandmother had been to her. Did you notice that she used similar words to describe her own parenting and the way she had been parented? She had not described her parenting that way ten years earlier. A healthy way to mourn loved ones is to make their strengths—interests, values, even skills—our own. So our departed loved ones can persist in our character as our strengths. They have become part of us.

Allan's Character

I also don't want to repeat the same error I made about Billie's grandmother by ignoring Allan's contribution to Billie's success and fulfillment. He is the most important and central person in her life.

Recall her reply to my question about what she was proudest of: "I am very proud of making a stable, happy marriage given my background. I didn't know if I had the capacity." However, two people are necessary to create an enduring loving relationship. What was Allan like that made such an achievement possible for a woman like Billie?

> Allan is endlessly interesting. I like him better now than when I married him. He is very loving and makes that absolutely obvious. He cares about me and . . . [values] my needs as important. He has given me a lot of self-confidence from his positive feedback about my work and cooking. . . . He is proud of me and he makes me feel that way. My successes are not threatening to him. And he is . . . always interested and interesting to be around. We have fun together; we have four theater subscriptions; when we go to plays we analyze, argue, and talk about them. We often listen to the same recorded book or read the same one. In bed Saturday night we do the *New York Times* crossword puzzle together. He does the Roman numerals and sports and I the popular culture items. . . . And then we share similar interests about our administrative problems at work. We spend a lot of time talking with each other about our work.

Though not nearly as androgynous or as interpersonally skilled and needy as Billie, Allan ranked third among the study's men in his maturity. Maturity gave him other strengths with which to learn, with Billie's prodding, how to create the mutual relationship of which she was so proud. "I love to cuddle, be affectionate, and snuggle—something he has learned to enjoy."

What Billie's Life Tells Us About Becoming a Successful and Fulfilled Person

When some hear Billie's and Allan's stories or those of others, they ask, "Aren't they so unique, so different from the rest of us, that there's little their lives can teach us?"

Yes. I cannot assert with great conviction that some findings—say about the contribution of Billie's androgyny to her vocational fulfillment—describe successful blue-collar steelworkers or migrant Hispanic farm workers.

Possibly. The remarkable changes in women's roles in recent decades may limit some findings, such as those about the character of happily married career women, to those of Billie's generation.

And no. Billie and Allan are human beings who had to learn to cope with universal life challenges, such as marriage, children, vocational conflicts, and aging. For centuries, people have sought to understand human nature and how to live fulfilling lives by observing how others have lived theirs. Euripedes and Shakespeare told us about ourselves by using fictional characters such as Medea and Hamlet. Freud told us about ourselves by describing only a few unhealthy patients and himself. Abraham Maslow, the first psychologist to write about self-actualized persons, selected people like Abraham Lincoln, Eleanor Roosevelt, and unabashedly himself—so I am told—as exemplars. But as insightful as the great playwrights and the Freuds and Maslows among us are, they don't tell us what the critical, the shared, the core character traits are that contribute to most people's success and fulfillment. Are Billie's androgyny and maturity the really important keys to success and fulfillment for the rest of us, or are they only her unique ones?

The only way to discover if Billie's keys open others' doors to success is to go beyond the playwrights'—even Freud's and Maslow's—literary approach to studying the character of other successful and fulfilled people. If I did not, I would have no reliable clue about which strengths are unique to a Billie and which are shared by most who succeed. As I will do for each individual that the tests and judges identified to tell you about, I will return over and over to the larger group to search out which strengths most consistently appear in the lives of successful and fulfilled people generally.

The larger group of men and women identified from their own experience the core strengths necessary to succeed as citizens, marital and sexual partners, parents, friends, and workers. Since Billie is the study's most all-round successful woman, see if you can recognize these strengths from my description of her. Eleven core strengths are necessary to succeed in all of these roles. The most important are *caring*, *honesty* and *integrity*, and a *sense of humor*. Every major adult role involves other people; our success, like Billie's, depends on the quality of our relationships with them. When we care, we affirm to others that they count, are important, are valued, or are even loved. We have seen how caring Billie is. When we speak honestly and act out of our hearts with integrity, we create trust. Billie said of herself, "I get teased about having an overdeveloped conscience. I don't cheat." And when we bring the perspective of humor to our relationships, we help each other transcend the pain of frustration and anger that inevitably arises in our relations with others.

The next core strengths needed to succeed are *openness* and *lack of defensiveness* about sharing our feelings with and *tolerance* and *acceptance* of others' quirks and failings. With no hesitation, Billie openly shared her feelings and intimate experiences with me, a stranger, and with you.

Other strengths are *dedication* and *commitment* to fulfill our different roles well. Without such commitment, work becomes sloppy, marriages are unstable, good parenting is unreliable, sex is only sex and not intimacy, friendships are untrustworthy, and community contributions are ineffective. Billie excels in her dedication and commitment to her work and to other people.

The men and women then identified the interpersonal strengths of *understanding, respecting*, and *empathizing with others* and rounded out the list with *adaptability* and *self-confidence*—again clearly seen in Billie.

Billie and the others, judged by their partners, closest same-gender friends, and most knowledgeable colleagues to have such strengths in abundance, turned out to be the happiest and most fulfilled persons of the group. They were more happily married, interpersonally intimate, and vocationally successful than those judged to have fewer of the eleven strengths. And they were the most ethical and idealistic—though not necessarily the most religious—of the 105 men and women.

If you want a simplified prescription for how to grow up to succeed, the two most salient general personality strengths to develop would be your androgyny and maturity. As we will learn later from others' lives, androgynous men and women feel fulfilled and make good marital partners, vocational colleagues, close friends, and responsible community members.

Your maturity is the most powerful contributor to your future success and fulfillment. Mature men and women are more likely to be happily married; good parents; sexually fulfilled, compatible with and faithful to their partners; vocationally satisfied; and healthy, happy, fulfilled, and virtuous. No wonder adults select maturity, after happiness and self-fulfillment, to be their most important value. They are right to do so. It is the most important key to success in most areas of life.

Billie's story suggests ideas about maturing, success, and fulfillment that we should keep in mind when we later sort out what is unique to other adults from what is common to those who succeed in their different roles.

- Destructive and unhappy families do not inevitably doom us to stagnation and failure.
- It can take a long, long time of hard personal work to really feel "grown up."
- Too-rigid demands to be a typical male or female can get in the way of developing the rich strengths needed to succeed later in life.
- Psychologically mature adolescents have the skills and values to take charge of and direct their own growing up.
- Mature and androgynous persons can transform the crises of living—whether the death of loved ones, frustration of intense needs, or conflicts with partners—into opportunities for new growth and fulfillment.

Doesn't Billie's image of herself as a problem solver model the character we need to develop to adapt to the uncertainties of the twenty-first century? Her approach to living transcends the traditional role categories that have become increasingly dysfunctional in our society. Her life is really a story about hope. It tells us that we don't have to succumb passively to today's dismally disintegrating families and societal values. It begins to illuminate the critical character strengths necessary to create healthier, more fulfilled lives. We can assert control over our lives and work to change them for the better. This sounds like a sermon, but it expresses what Billie reaffirms for me.

Let's now examine in depth the meaning of Billie's maturity—the principal key to her growing up to succeed and be happy.

Chapter 3

Key Paths to Maturity

Each of us can tell our own special story about how we have grown up. Billie's may feel foreign, even unbelievable, to you. Few, if any, of us have had seven "parents" raise us and witnessed the murder of our mother. However, the major spiritual leaders, philosophers, and psychologists tell us that we tread a common psychological path when we are growing healthily and becoming more whole, authentic, and self-actualized persons. Whether they call it the path to "salvation," "*Sahaja*," "enlightenment," or "maturity," most identify similar signposts along that way. Their view of how humans mature tells us to become more aware, other-centered, harmonious, committed, and self-disciplined. Furthermore, whatever their century or background, people highly value that path. Buddha, Jewish prophets, Christ, Mohammed, liberal educators, philosophers such as John Dewey, psychologists such as Maslow, and the men and women I have canvassed around the world have agreed, though each in his or her own words, that becoming more mature is an important goal. Wise observers of those who have lived their lives well sense, with good reason, that this is *the* key to the good life. Research agrees. Our maturity helps us marry successfully, be good parents, feel fulfilled vocationally, act virtuously, and be happy and healthy, among other successes.

This chapter tells you how mature you are. It identifies the commonly shared strengths of men and women, of young and old, of Catholics, Protestants, Jews, and Muslims, and of Americans, Turks, and Italians who follow the path to maturity. To get in touch with how you have been maturing, why not ask yourself and then answer this question and the others in the next few paragraphs: "How effectively have I fulfilled my responsibilities, say as a parent, lawyer, or citizen?" A history of doing many things well tells us that we are on top of our talents and can make them work for us.

Then ask, "How excited, even passionate, am I about my work, hobbies, community, or world events? Do I have energy left over for initiating new friendships and interests?" A mature person's energy is available for spontaneous adventures and new commitments, not tied up in conflict or exhausted by day-to-day tasks. I once was on a committee to nominate seniors for prestigious international awards. We turned down the college's most distinguished scholar, primarily because he reacted to the question "What have you contributed in the four years you've been here to the life of the college?" with, "I've been so busy with my academic work I've had no time or energy to get involved."

The next question to ask yourself is, "How fully present am I in my relationships with others?" By relationships I don't mean infatuations or sexual affairs. I mean sensitively aware, compassionate, cooperative, sturdy, nondefensive relationships, including those with our own children and parents—probably the most difficult persons with whom to get along maturely.

And finally, ask yourself, "How well do I keep my sense of humor, even in distressing relationships or situations? Do I have enough perspective about a troubling issue to laugh at myself?" A hearty laugh from deep in our gut about ourselves and our current predicaments with our colleagues or partner is not just cathartic and health sustaining but also a sign that we have transcended pride. Mature persons can play spontaneously, too; they don't have to use drugs to anesthetize their consciences or dissolve their self-control. As Jesus implied, they can act like children again.

These visible signs of maturity just don't happen instinctively. They result from taking some paths rather than others while growing up. Before looking at the map of maturity's principal markers, find out if you have been following its path by answering questions like those I asked Billie. For example, ask yourself, "How have I changed in the past ten years since I graduated from school or got that new job or got married? How am I different now?" Or "How has my partner's personality or my divorce or my children changed me?" Then see if you can locate your changes in Table 3.1. Or you might even rate on a five-point scale just how much of each of the map's strengths you have and then ask which strengths have contributed most to your own success. I will use Billie's map to illustrate other signs of maturity. The map of maturing summarizes the common core strengths we need to adapt successfully. The first column in Table 3.1, labeled "The person's strengths," lists the three principal facets of our personalities: strengths of mind, strengths of character, and strengths of self. The next five columns, comprising "Developmental Dimensions of Maturing," identify the underlying organizational principles that guide our growth in each facet. Our personalities mature in five predictable, interrelated ways. As we grow, we become increasingly more able to put our experience into some kind of language; we also become more other-centered, integrated, stable, and autonomous, as the map shows, in the way we use our minds, express our character, and use our self's potentials.

The map's last column, "Visible Signs of Maturing," lists the main visible signs of the maturity you questioned yourself about. I now describe each of the five developmental principles that organize the growth of our minds, characters, and selves. Keep the whole person in view. Remember what St. Paul told us in I Corinthians 12:12, 17:

> For as the body is one, and hath many members, and all the members of that one body, being many, are one body.... If the whole body *were* an eye, where *were* the hearing?.... If the whole *were* hearing, where *were* the smelling?"

He is right. We grow healthily as persons, not just as minds or in personal relationships. Growth in one facet on one dimension affects growth in other facets on other dimensions. So we are not just eyes or ears, bits and pieces—we are adapting, whole persons. As Maslow reminded us, we are like indivisible, multifaceted crystals. We sparkle differently depending on which facets the light strikes, but each facet is an integral part of the whole crystal. I describe each dimension and the strengths of mind, character (including our interpersonal skills and values), and self that its maturing produces. I will be somewhat arbitrary as I tell you about each in isolation from the other, but I have no other option: I have to focus first on one facet and then on another to describe each sign of our maturity clearly.

Table 3.1 Model of Maturing: Strengths That Contribute to Success

The Person's Strengths	Developmental Dimensions of Maturing						Visible Signs of Maturity
	Symbolization	Other-Centeredness	Integration	Stabilization	Autonomy		
of Mind	Aware of how own mind works	Empathically grasps others' views	Thinks relationally and sees the whole picture	Functions well and resiliently under stress	Educates self and can create novel solutions for varied situations		Increased mastery, competence, and power
of Character	Sensitively aware of and reflective about relationships and values honesty	Cares for and values others' welfare with compassion	Creates mutually cooperative relationships and consistently lives values with integrity	Relationships endure and values persist with commitment	Self-reliantly forms selective relationships and stands up for considered principles with courage		Increased ability to create intimate and loving relationships and freed energy for new interests and enthusiasms
of Self	Accurately understands self	Accepts self as fully human and understands how others see self	Self is so together that it is able to act naturally and spontaneously	Has strong sense of self and is confident about wants and needs	Affirms own worth and directs and controls own growth		Heightened capability for self transcendence, objectivity, and sense of humor

Becoming A More Reflectively Aware Person (Symbolization)

In this section, I'll address several key questions.

Are You Becoming More Aware of How Your Mind Works?

Maturing people become more reflective. Billie did. She reflected on how she went about solving problems. In her own words, she described how our minds mature on all of their dimensions—the leading edge of her maturing during her forties: "I've become increasingly reflective (Symbolization) and analytical in my work as well as in my personal relations. I've learned how to approach a problem in a very ordered way. . . . I know now how to analyze and clarify a problem, collect information from others (Other-Centered), find a way to reconcile the different viewpoints (Integration), and then try testing them out to see which one really works (Stabilization). I do that in my personal relations as well as in my work with patients" (Autonomy). She has made the process so much her own that she can autonomously apply it to most areas of living.

The ability to use symbols to reflect about our experience is our most important adaptive power and distinguishes us from other animals. We can put into words, figures, art, music, and gestures the simplest to the most complicated ideas. We can mentally represent what we feel and believe or what our senses see, hear, and touch and then think back in time about it. We derive extraordinary power when we can precisely describe to another how to drive from Denver to Miami, recall where we were last Christmas, imagine, anticipate, and plan for the birth of our child, or monitor our ongoing arguments or plans. To be able to represent and then manipulate reality in our minds before we act in the world is a remarkable strength. Mature persons like Billie, who have perfected their awareness of how they can use their mind's coping skills, can therefore get along more successfully.

Are You Becoming More Aware of and Reflective About Your Relationships?

Mature persons, like Billie, are more aware of their relations with others. Her maturity gave her the ability to reflect about and figure out why she was having difficulties with her stepmothers and stepfathers. Not knowing how to understand others and reflect on our relationships undermines succeeding in these relationships at home and work. Remember Roger Blake, the high school teacher, who wrote, "Restlessness haunts me"? After he wrote that, his relationship with Beth became increasingly tumultuous and painful. Mystified by what he called her "guerrilla campaign" to make him more sensitive and responsive to her needs, he asked me what she meant by the following excerpt from one of her letters:

> You are easy to love on the one hand and yet difficult to love on the other. Easy because you ask for nothing and yet accept whatever you are given at a shallow level. I give and give to you and it all seems to go down a black hole. Difficult because your soul, your very being, seems enclosed so very deeply, hidden by layers and layers that even to catch a glimpse of a flicker of its flame is rare. In times of stress you seem to sink even further into yourself. . . . I so desire you to be fully alive, to feel the pain and the joy but most of all to be there 100% and not only just a flicker.

Roger dismissed what I felt was a devastatingly accurate description of him and their relationship by pushing it down his "black hole." Puzzled about what she really wanted from him and hurt by her persistent attacks, he decided several months later to leave her. He had not yet learned what Billie had taught herself for years to do: to reflect about his relationships with others and why they were so disruptively painful.

Are You Becoming More Aware of Your Values and So a More Honest Person?

Another maturing change that contributes to our success is our increasing awareness of our values. "Values" are what initiate and steer everything we do: our goals, preferences, motives, biases, and prejudices. Growing up means becoming more aware of what is more and less important to us and why. To be aware of what we want and don't want and why we believe and act or do not believe and do not act as we do vastly increases our ability to get what we want. Not until Billie's counselor prodded her to reflect about what *she* really wanted out of her marriage did she feel "free for the first time" to plan her future to fit her own needs.

Freud taught us how powerfully our behavior can be influenced by wishes and needs we are unaware of. Pushing our desires or impulses deep into our inner "black hole" can so drain our vitality that we become just a "flicker" of what we could be. Like Roger, we don't understand why we are restless, indecisive, and act in ways that aggravate others.

Roger had begun to get glimmers that he didn't know what he wanted. "Maybe I don't know what I value, really. Maybe I haven't been honest with myself all these years. Here I am, thirty-two, and I don't know what I really want."

In the mysterious way that our unconscious self communicates to us, Roger and I got clues about his future growth and why he acted as he did with Beth from three different types of drawings he had been experimenting with. The first were meticulously precise, overcontrolled, literal black-and-white pen sketches devoid of all life. The next were explosive, barely controlled riots of color that gave the impression of disruptive passion that hadn't yet been channeled well. The last paintings beautifully brought together the disciplined control of the black-and-white pen sketches with the vivid yellows, oranges, browns, and blacks of his watercolors. The artwork heralded his growing intellectual and emotional integration.

But it was the theme of passages that struck me in the three watercolors that made up the third group. The first showed in perspective a black mine shaft tunnel with a blocked door at the end. The second was of the same door, closer up, but now partially opened with light shining around it. The last was even closer up, with brilliant yellowish orange light streaming through the completely opened door and gloriously illuminating the tunnel's rich brown and black beams and walls. Intuiting that these passages might reveal something about his restless indecisiveness, I asked Roger to make up a story about his pictures. He said that an old man dresssed in black wearing a tall hat was standing in the doorway and a thirteen-year-old boy holding a burst balloon stood next to him. Suddenly, several playful dogs bounded out of the door. The boy began to play with them but the dogs began to snap and growl at each other so viciously that he became scared, cringed, and backed through the open door, which he managed to shut.

I asked, "What are the first words that come to mind when I say 'dogs'?"

"Passion. Degenerate," he instantly replied, in that order.

Then I said, "Old man."

"Superego." Roger impulsively added, "Dogs are id"—Freud's words for conscience and animalistic impulses.

What might such rich and suggestive images mean? Could Roger's accepting, "easy-to-love" mask be shielding him from aggressive, sadistic male impulses that scare him and that his conscience keeps from bounding out of him because such intense passion is "degenerate"? To understand why he closes the door to them, I should have asked what happened in his relationship with his father when he was thirteen. Whatever his drawings may mean, they beautifully portray how what is unconscious begins to sneak into awareness, though still in disguised form. As we become more mature, our inner doors open up and our darker passions as well as repressed goodness become accessible for more conscious and constructive use.

Accurate understanding of our motives enables us to be more intellectually honest with ourselves. Roger was psychologically right when he wrote, "Maybe I haven't been honest with myself all these years." He had much growing up ahead of him to better understand his own motives and apprehensions.

How Accurately Do You Understand Yourself?

A classic sign of growing up is increasing *self*-insight or *self*-understanding, not just of our relationships and values but also of our personality and how we have become what we are. Accurately understanding our strengths and weaknesses contributes immeasurably to how well we succeed. Men and women who accurately understand themselves succeed in their principal adult roles.

The roots of our maturing self-awareness reach far down into our earliest years. We learned in first grade, for example, why we were put in the bunny rabbit but not the teddy bear reading group. I learned in third grade that I might become a teacher when Mrs. Simpson asked only me to read to the rest of the class when she had other things to do. When in adolescence our reflective ability begins to approach that of adults, we turn inward to make sense of our changing selves. One self-conscious, introspective teenager told me, "Well, any sort of criticism, even if somebody curses me out and calls me a dogmatic bastard, which happened recently, I think about. You see, I try and see why am I really a dogmatic bastard."

Billie's years of laborious effort to understand herself and her relationships may account in part for the singular inner clarity that I noted in her reactions to the inkblots. She knew herself so well that the tests I had given her told her nothing that she had not already discovered about herself. With a minimum amount of training in understanding symbols, she could have interpreted her own images. (Roger probably couldn't.)

Becoming a More Other-Centered Person

Like the previous section, this section also addresses several different questions about the maturity of your mind, character, and self.

Are You Becoming More Able to Empathically Grasp Others' Views?

The course of healthy growth moves from self- to other-centeredness. Intellectually a child sees the world only from his or her point of view. As five-year-old Jimmy was departing after our son's birthday party, his mother told him, "Tell Mr. and Mrs. Heath good-bye and thank them for the ice cream and cake." Jimmy turned to ask us, "Where are you going?" An adolescent acknowledges others' viewpoints but still believes his is *the* right one. A mature adult knows that others have their own views about an issue, each of which may contain elements of the truth. The mature mind thinks more relativistically. Our judgment and objectivity improve as we grow beyond thinking in terms of only either-or and black-or-white positions. We learn from discussions and arguments how to analyze and don't accept simplistic opposites, like "You're either for or against me" or "You're a self-righteous religious bigot or a wimpy, fuzzy-headed liberal."

Some women told me that their husbands and children prodded and encouraged this growth of their minds.

> My husband is a lot more direct, concise, penetrating, down-to-earth. So I look to him for answering the question of how do I see what I see. . . . [I] like to check out reality with him. . . . I have taken in his way of looking at the world, so it also affects my way of looking at the world. He is rather analytical. This has been foreign to me. He has showed me how to break down a problem into stages without becoming confused and how to work to a logical conclusion.

Another woman said of her thirteen-year-old son:

> He is more of a challenge than I really need. I really need to know what the hell I am talking about to communicate with an adolescent. . . I have to learn how an adolescent would think, put myself in his shoes when we disagree. He can drive me nuts. [She laughs.] Not really. He's an interesting little person. Take his snakes. I'd never ever look at a snake or rodent and now I realize that they can be very interesting things. He brings them home. Just as long as they are not contagious, I don't care now.

A sign of becoming more other-centered is not just an increasing ability to think like another but also to feel what another feels. Beth may have been complaining that Roger wasn't entering into *her* world, understanding *her* needs, feeling what *she* was feeling. If Roger had empathically understood her viewpoint, he might have talked for Beth this way: "I'm now thirty-four, have been your faithful lover on and off now for more than twelve years, may never have another, and face a 'maritally' empty and childless future as time runs out for me to fulfill my dreams. You keep coming back to my bed, but I still don't know your real 'intentions' or if you'll ever commit yourself to me or anyone else."

Are You Becoming More Caring About Another's Welfare?

It takes a lot of maturity to value and then develop more other-centered *relationships* in which we genuinely care for others who differ from us. Billie and her peers believed that she was a caring person. She valued being a nurturer most highly (so much so that she couldn't leave her first husband until she had bought him a car and an apartment).

Empathy, sympathy, and caring are typically feminine interpersonal skills. The men did not stand out as mature in their empathy, possibly because American males are not expected or taught to develop such other-centered skills. Being a parent contributed to the empathic growth of about 25 percent of them, however. They had to learn such skills "on the job," so to speak, as one father said about his three-year-old son. "He taught me. . . that being a little tiny guy, while I'm a great big guy. . . that a tiny guy has feelings, thoughts, and reasons for doing things, too. And because he is tiny and little and inexperienced does not mean that he is stupid or insensitive. Brought a greater sense of empathy and sympathy for him."

How Much More Compassionate Have Your Values Become?

Learning how to take someone else's point of view, to analyze a problem from different perspectives, also affects our values. When we truly understand others' viewpoints, we can emotionally appreciate their values and interests, and we more readily tolerate views that disagree with our own. We begin to value giving to others, even though we have no personal relationship with them and may have to sacrifice some of our own interests and desires. Mature Haverford alumni, for example, give more to their college's annual fund campaign and to charity than immature alumni.

We develop more humane values when our role prods us to learn how to care. Compassion becomes a cardinal value. A new father eloquently described how his child had begun to affect his values this way. "The feeling that you have toward a helpless baby and later a growing child of enormous protectiveness and affection and love and wanting to shield and ensure happiness for her can't help but make you feel a little better and more home conscious—and less pleasure oriented, too."

Are You Becoming a More Self-Accepting, Humane Person Who Understands How Others See You?

Mature persons also have more other-centered images of themselves. They become more self-accepting over time. They have shed their adolescent idea that they are so unique no other person can understand them. By accepting more of their own humanness, they rejoin the human race and become less self-righteous. By seeing everyone in themselves regardless of their gender, ethnic background, or nationality, they gain access to a wider range of adaptive potentials. By accepting her masculine strengths, Billie developed the assertive will to compete successfully in a male world.

Our ideas of ourselves become more other-centered as a result of our relationships with others. Becoming parents and grandparents like Billie nurtures our empathic skills and alters our values and priorities. Becoming a parent can change our attitudes about ourselves. Another father captured how his view of himself had changed in this beautifully insightful comment: "I'm certainly different now in that I approach selflessness with my child more than I do at any other time. ... I'm also now more concerned for people other than myself. You become oblivious to yourself... your attention becomes focused on the children and you are concerned with their development and really for the first time in your life, your self really drops out of your own thinking." My daughter, reflecting on how Benjamin, her first child, had changed her, also said, "He's made me much less selfish and self-centered. He comes first now."

As we mature, we not only develop more other-centered self-concepts but also understand more accurately how others view us. This empathic understanding of others' opinions about us powerfully predicts our maturity and success in our marital roles as we and our partners evaluate our maturity and success.

Becoming a More Together Person (Integration)

When he was a freshman, Roger told me, "I feel like a thousand bits and pieces going in a thousand different directions." I recall at the time that I felt he was painfully trapped in an inner maelstrom, but it was a good kind of turbulence. He was in a state of high educability and potential growth, as when we are in love: vulnerable, hypersensitive, flooded by poetry, coursed by strong emotions, confused, awed, and asking, "What is happening to me?"

Such times of personal chaos are potentially precious gifts that can promise new integrations and so new growth. It is agonizing to feel we are only bits and pieces of contradictory values and habits that undercut each other and trip us up from being as decisive and successful as we feel we could be. But it is also exhilarating, for example, to be so possessed by love for another that we become unrealistic, preoccupied, inefficient—even so irrational that Freud likened falling in love to becoming insane.

We are built to make sense of our pains and exhilarations, to order and make more consistent our views of ourselves, to create coherent meanings about our world. When religions talk about becoming more inwardly harmonious, as most do, they acknowledge that a healthy growing person becomes more consistently integrated. Biographers also know this truth. They search for the core themes that make sense of and give consistent meaning to the people they are bringing to life. I similarly tried to make sense of Billie and will try also for the other principal actors and actresses in the book by identifying the keynotes of their success.

As we mature, our values, temperaments, interests, and personalities increasingly come together to help us achieve our goals; parts of ourselves don't work against and undermine other parts. I remember watching my youngest teach herself to play the piano when she was seven. I heard a particularly discordant note, saw her slap her left hand, and then heard her indignantly exclaim, "Stop doing that." Her two hands had yet to work well together and with her brain.

Do You Think More Relationally and See the Whole Picture Better Now?

I'll go back to the mind's earliest signs of integration. Newborn infants take no more than a few days to convert their first clumsy efforts to suck at the breast into an efficient, seemingly reflexive effort. They quickly learn how to bring their thumb effortlessly to their mouth to suck when their mother is not present, and eventually they watch their thumb as they wave it back and forth. Wiggily Benjamin, two and a half months old at the time, taught me again how early such integrations occur. While I was baby-sitting him, he reached for the first time to some colorful keys hanging on a string over his head and pulled them to his mouth to suck. He had never done that before. I witnessed the birth of a new, more complex visual-motor skill that combined looking, grasping, pulling, locating one's mouth, and sucking.

Out of such beginnings and much subsequent practice will later come more complex adult physical and mental skills. When he was twenty months old, Benjamin was fascinated by trucks with hitches that pulled trailers. He loved to attach his toy trailer to his truck. When visiting me, he saw my trailer parked under the trees and my Escort on the other side of the driveway. Guess what he mentally put together? Right. He pulled me over to the car, pointed to the hitch and looked at the trailer. The mind's miraculous ability to generalize and put things together blossomed right in front of me.

Such early visual-motor coordinations provide the templates of how we get ourselves more and more together. Piaget, psychology's most careful observer of children's developing minds, showed us how an adult's mental skills evolve out of such early experiences. These experiences are the roots of our ability to combine ideas, take them apart, and recombine them to make different patterns or hypotheses. We actively seek more information and learn new skills to increase our perspective and create new ideas (or even books like this).

The mature person's mind is relational and contextual. A business manager selected his community's choral group as one of fifty possible influential causes of his mind's maturing. Then he explained how it had enriched him: "I just got a broader- and broader-based frame of reference. While you learn the music strictly speaking, you also get a commentary about interpretation and comparative analyses of the piece's similarity to other pieces we have done, which is very satisfying and stimulating. My musical background just has a richer context to it."

Billie has already told us how skillfully she could put ideas together to form insights about her patients' illnesses as well as her own interpersonal relationships.

How Much Better Can You Create Mutually Cooperative Relationships Now?

Mature persons create open, cooperative, harmonious relationships with others. At ease with themselves, they are nondefensively open with others. Like Billie, they feel comfortable sharing their feelings about even the most personal of topics, such as their dreams and failures, with trusted others—including me. They trust themselves to be themselves; they don't try to seem what they aren't in their relationships.

Their cooperativeness makes possible a deep mutuality or "*we*ness." Such times of "communion" occur in many different situations: five basketball players effortlessly playing as one unified team; the couples gracefully and flawlessly dancing in the Olympic ice skating contest; the shared mutuality I felt with eight rebellious Jesuit priests in the early seventies illegally taking communion while circling their makeshift altar under the eaves of their monastery; or the corporate pride of a Vietnam combat platoon that never left a wounded buddy behind. Episodes of mutuality may be transitory or longer lasting. They are enhanced when the participants have the maturity to overcome their own imperious needs and become attuned to and adapt to those of the group. Billie's maturity enabled her to draw on her collaborative skills, which contributed to her success as a leader. Not unexpectedly, mature men and women create more enduring and happy marital and sexual relationships.

Are You Living Your Values More Consistently Now with Integrity?

Growing up means making one's values and acts more consistent with each other. So we act with greater integrity. We also develop priorities; we figure out what is most important to us. Consider Dave Corcoran, a seemingly successful corporation lawyer who had been deeply divided for years between what he thought he should be and what he wanted to be. He wrote me on his thirty-eighth birthday to say that he had just abandoned his lucrative seventy-hour-a-week practice to "have a bash!!!" He had *adjusted* well to his career's expectations: He was highly skilled and competent, thorough, reliable, responsible, respected by his clients and colleagues (even by his paralegal aides), and wealthy. But Dave had not *adapted* as well to his career. He had become more and more restless and dissatisfied. For years, he had gotten out of bed each morning feeling that life was passing him by.

Why? Programmed to be a lawyer since he had been just an idea in his lawyer father's head, he had adjusted too well during his high school and college years. Dave had worked compulsively in high school to get into Haverford and, while there, diligently pursued a narrow prelaw program. In law school, he kept his nose in his books and made the law review. Too obsessed vocationally, he had never explored his other potentials and interests—even his own adolescence. He had too many wild oats left to sow. So one morning, upon awakening, he had his "mid-life crisis." He impetuously decided that the day had arrived to have his long-delayed "bash!!!" and satisfy his increasingly clamorous need for adventure.

Self-fulfillment temporarily triumphed over adjustment. It took Dave several years of self-indulgently reliving his teenage years and trying different jobs before he discovered how to balance his needs with those of a career and family—that is, becoming more well adapted. Learning that he had a flair for administrative leadership, he secured a position in a large, bureaucratic insurance company that gave him more time to be with his family and to indulge his newfound passion for flycasting. He had become better integrated after his "crisis."

I don't know how you will react to Dave Corcoran's story. Do you envy, disapprove of, condemn him, or judge him to be a sick, self-seeking neurotic because he abandoned his lucrative law practice? But he felt that he wasn't together and was stuck. He had the strength to give up a way of life that he knew did not fit what he could be—though at the age of thirty-eight, he had to endure the anxiety of not knowing how he might come out of his own self-induced chaos.

The integration of values was a principal form of growth that the men and women experienced in their fifties. Like Billie, they no longer felt torn and divided between several inconsistent and conflicting values, beliefs, and desires. They acted with greater integrity.

Are Your Ideas of Yourself So Together Now That You Act Naturally and Spontaneously?

Finally, a growing person develops an increasingly coherent and consistent self-image. What mature persons think they are is what they predict others think they are; mature persons don't play roles and put on masks to appear what they aren't. Adjectives like *genuine*, *natural*, and *spontaneous* describe them.

Billie thought of herself as one piece. She gave herself the highest score possible in her early forties as well as fifties when rating how accurately statements like the following described her: "I seldom feel I am a divided, inconsistent, and contradictory person. I am reasonably sure of what I am and what my direction is." "I actually am what I believe other people think me to be."

I have often wondered if Norma Jean Baker committed suicide because she had always been a deeply divided person. She had apparently never found a way to bring together her private self-image as Norma Jean Baker and her public one as Marilyn Monroe. She reputedly didn't feel she could be herself wherever she was.

Literature is full of examples of divided souls, like the hero of Dostoyevsky's *Crime and Punishment*. Wouldn't you say that Reverend Dimmesdale in the *Scarlet Letter* is the best example in American fiction? Hawthorne brilliantly described how the Reverend's divided soul produced his psychosomatic symptoms. Remember that the Puritan divine got Hester pregnant. She refused to name him as the father, was imprisoned in the stockade for adultery, emerged wearing on her breast the brilliant scarlet A that she had embroidered, and was banished to an isolated house on the outskirts of the community. He, on the other hand—the most respected member of the Puritan community—did not confess his sin. Never betraying the Reverend, Hester grew in inner strength and saintliness throughout the book, while the divine's guilt slowly split his righteous public self and his sinful private one. His suffering, witnessed by incapacitating physical symptoms and paralyzing despair, powerfully depicts the consequences of a divided self.

Becoming a More Stable and Autonomous Person

I discuss how we become more stable and autonomous together, not because they cannot be theoretically distinguished, but because I have had a lot of trouble untangling them when testing for them.

Does Your Mind Function Well Under Stress, Educate Itself, and Create Novel Ways of Solving Problems?

Benjamin's rapid growth in his early months illustrates how our two last organizing principles, stabilization and autonomy, guide maturing. To enable him to survive outside the womb, his neurologically wired sucking reflex had to be strengthened immediately. However, he could not initially nurse successfully at his mother's breast, so she wore a breast shield. The next day at home, he didn't work hard enough at first to fill himself up. After a lot of wailing and maternal frustration, his skills of rooting and sucking became graceful and efficient. Later, after stabilizing the skill of looking at his thumb, grasping it with his other hand, and bringing it to his mouth to suck, he instructed his grandfather how to reach for keys dangling in front of him and bring them to his mouth to suck.

One night, months later, after Benjamin had stabilized many other complex skills, he was squirming in his chair at the dinner table when his mother hastily ran to a pot boiling over on the stove. Curious Benjamin seized the opportunity to pull the tablecloth to his mouth to chew. Plates crashed to the floor. Frightened, Benjamin fell apart; he then giggled. Piaget would say that he had learned to use skills originally acquired to satisfy his hunger needs to create crashing effects. His grasping, pulling, and chewing skills had become freed, more mobile, and autonomous of the original needs whose satisfaction had led to their stabilization. He now could explore his world by looking at, grasping, sucking, chewing, banging, and dropping any toy he found in his crib. He could freely use his skills any time, any place with any other skill, and with any object he wished to explore, know, or destroy or to which he was attracted.

Mature persons have more stable and autonomous intellectual skills available for adapting than immature persons. Their skills have become an integral part of their personality. In a new situation or crunch, they don't fall apart; their skills and knowledge are readily available. Billie could be certain that she had a stable marriage because she and Allan had taught themselves how to bring their relationship back up out of its dark valleys before becoming overwhelmed or immobilized by frustration and anger.

Stable and autonomous skills enable us to resist or quickly recover from the disorganization that stress can cause. Surgery, probably more than most professions, demands that feelings and apprehensions be kept from interfering with one's mental efficiency under stressful conditions. The study's one heart surgeon claimed that operating every day had forced me to become very good at what I do. I am much better now in my judgment and technique. I've learned from my mistakes and am now very efficient. Surgery is a decision business; you are constantly making decisions. How should I make this incision? How deeply should I cut? Should I take this cancer out in this elderly person? I make such decisions much more easily now. I could always make decisions easily but now I am not afraid to deal with the unexpected; I don't get flustered, even when a patient is close to dying on the table, as happened this afternoon when inserting a pacemaker.

"What happened?" I asked.

"He died," he replied, almost too calmly. I felt more troubled than he did.

As our intellectual skills become more stable and autonomous, so that we no longer have to pay attention to their use, energy becomes available for other purposes. What we do becomes automatic, like reading or typing. We take such skills with us wherever we go. We don't have to use energy to be aware of them; we use them with minimal attention. Habits free our energies for other activities.

Are Your Relationships Becoming More Enduring, But Can You Tolerate Aloneness If Necessary?

Mature persons develop more stable and loyal relationships than immature ones. Like Billie, mature men and women create more sexually compatible and faithful marriages. I don't know if this result will hold in the future, given changing values about extramarital relationships, but the model suggests that immature more than mature persons seek out and run from one "friend" or lover to another.

Other signs of immature autonomous relationships are excessive "neediness" (incessant demands that others approve of and love us) or falling apart when alone or not being circled by admirers. To get along with aloneness is a great test of our interpersonal maturity, *provided* we can still love another.

Are You Increasingly Able to Commit Yourself to Values You Defend with Courage?

Growing up also means deepening our interests and values, which we pursue more persistently even though we may not fulfill them for years. We make our values so completely our own that we accept full responsibility for their consequences. Billie tested her maturity by putting herself through medical school. She had what our society used to value—an old-fashioned calling that supported her heroic determination. To be steadfastly committed and persist in the face of criticism and adversity is a hallmark of a mature person.

Developing doggedness, commitment, and the courage to stand up for what they believe in is one of the more salient types of growths people experience in their forties and fifties.

Are You Developing a Stronger Sense of Self-Confidence, Self-Worth, and Control of Your Own Growth?

Finally, growing up means feeling a sense of continuity and being in charge of one's self. Erikson's idea of "identity" refers to just such a strong sense of self. Our self yesterday is what it is today and what it will be tomorrow. Billie learned what she could and could not do, accepted and liked herself, and felt confident in her ability to succeed. Middle-aged women like Billie who have a strong sense of themselves are mature, succeed in their principal roles, devote themselves to their communities, and have been predictably happy and fulfilled since their teenage years.

Stability is not rigidity in mature persons; they are open to new ideas about themselves. Their mature autonomy enables them to separate true from false ideas about themselves. Mature persons can act independently of the opinions that others have about them. They can affirm their own worth even in the face of their in-laws', lovers', and friends' doubts and criticisms.

Seeking to understand the sources of Albert Einstein's genius from his collected papers, a reviewer pointed to both his strong sense of self and his autonomy:

> Albert had an early, strong sense of autonomy as expressed by his leaving home [early] . . . [and] refusing to let his

> mother dictate [his] personal relations. [His] sense of self-worth had much to do with a supportive home environment. His mother was immensely proud of Albert's early intellectual achievements.... What Einstein had was the special balance of intense early nurture and autonomy that gave him a self-esteem that would carry him through the years when he was homeless, degreeless, and jobless. He was consequently never hopeless or loveless.[1]

This insightful comment illustrates the balance between other-centeredness, stability, and autonomy that we need to mature.

Such are the signposts of growing up. The model central to this book brings together and makes explicit the wisdom of writers, prophets, philosophers, and psychologists as well as the results of years of research about what maturing means. This model provides a comprehensive but manageable map to guide efforts to understand healthy growth. It has led to many interesting discoveries. For example, I know now that our ideas about ourselves—especially their accuracy, other-centeredness, integration, and stability—more powerfully predict our effectiveness than other facets of our maturity. And that our maturity as a teenager predicts our maturity when thirty-two, which in turn predicts our maturity when we are in our forties, and most likely when we are fifty-five as well. Billie's history shows us that also. As a teenager, she had been more mature, stable, and autonomous than 90 percent, 80 percent, and 98 percent respectively of the other women when they were adolescents. Her adolescent maturity gave her the strengths to continue growing healthily into her early forties, when she ranked third among the women in maturity.

I have also learned that we are equipped psychically with what I call an *equilibrating principle* that protects us from breaking apart when emotionally "stretched" too far. We can be emotionally pummeled, hurt, and squashed just so much before we resist, rebel, and compensate, sometimes in extreme, seemingly unacceptable and self-destructive ways. Sometimes like a rubber band stretched too far out of shape, we either break or resist further stretching by shooting off in unpredictable directions.

Dave Corcoran's abrupt decision to abandon his corporate law practice told me just how far he had been stretched out of shape for years. Billie's consuming professional development in her thirties and early forties may, at a less conscious level, have intensified her maternal nurturing needs in her late forties and driven her to recreate her extended family. Her maturity aided her in coping healthily with her crises rather than being thrown into a paralyzing mid-life crisis.

Whether we deliberately disrupt our existing way of living, as Dave Corcoran decided to do, or are upset by others, as Roger was by Beth, the equilibrating principle is the steward of our psychic health. It doesn't always intervene as dramatically in our lives as it did in Dave's. More often than not, it speaks softly—so quietly we may not hear it clearly. After an intense lecture schedule one spring, I retired to our Maine coastal retreat, taking my computers, boxes of research, and numerous books, some of which I had carried back and forth unread for three summers. After the first few days doggedly writing, what predictably happened? My thoughts wandered to the dying trees outside my window that the family of porcupines nesting under our cabin during the winter had stripped of bark. The trees needed to be cut up into firewood. I dreamt of laying up a stone fireplace for our guest cabin. I also yearned to survey a road I wanted to put in. Instead, I forced myself to write *Fulfilling Lives.* My system rebelled. Its equilibrating principle noisily warned me that I needed to live in my body all year round, not just in my head during most of the winter and spring.

Excess in fundamentally healthy human systems naturally provokes warnings that we must change how we live our lives. If only we had listened more sensitively to what we could be hearing, we might not have been so prone to that heart attack, ulcer, or depression. I listened that June. So I worked ten hours a day cutting the trees down and surveying another portion of the road. I just wish I could have exorcised the guilt I felt about how slowly my writing was going. And each year my body tells me a little sooner that it is getting too much of this physical trauma. I should run my life differently during the winter to avoid being so strenuously stretched out of shape by June.

Ways Growing Up Gets Off-Track

How does growing up go wrong psychically and impair us? I'll mention a few examples. If you have also felt stretched out of shape at

Key Paths to Maturity   55

times, you might want to figure out why you have sometimes been knocked off-track on each of maturity's five dimensions.

Inadequate or excessive *awareness* limits our ability to adapt. Unreflective people take a long time to learn from their mistakes. Roger needed to become more adept at reading the signs his unconscious mind broadcast so loudly while he produced his drawings. If he does not become more psychologically minded, he may repetitively get lost in the same emotional black tunnels with his next lover.

Awareness can also be forced or excessive when it comes to maturing on other dimensions. We become obsessively introspective, or hyper aware of our motives, or self-conscious about our relationships or ourselves. We become paralyzed and can't act. A student sought my advice. He had stewed for weeks about dropping out of college, then had begun to fret about his stewing. He went over and over every monumental and infinitesimal reason why he should and shouldn't drop out. He began to pace so frantically around my office that I thought he was working himself into an anxiety attack. His central issue was not whether to drop out or not; it was his inability to decide—about anything.

The second way we grow—becoming more *other-centered*—can also be under- or overdeveloped and so limit our ability to achieve what we want. American males are traditionally undersocialized and females oversocialized in other-centeredness. I know many more egocentric males than I do females and many more accommodating females than males. Roger paid a steep price for his lack of empathy and sensitivity to Beth's needs. I don't need to belabor how excessive other-centeredness can distort healthy growth. Billie told us of its dangers. Remember how she felt compelled to set up her first husband in his own apartment and even buy him a car before she could divorce him? Caught in the grip of her need to nurture and please, she could not initially develop a well integrated, strong sense of herself and become healthily autonomous.

We can also be inadequately or overly *integrated.* While Reverend Dimmesdale's psychosomatic descent, due to his divided soul, was dramatic, the effects of poor integration on how we succeed are typically more subtle: unpredictability, inefficiency, emotional sloppiness, or the restlessness of a Roger. Paradoxically, we can be too well integrated, relative to growth on other dimensions. Though compulsively efficient automatons or machines in our work, we may lack spontaneity, earthiness, and warmth in our marital or love relationships. Drugs and alcohol deceptively make such persons feel less uptight, more loose, free, "together." Maturely integrated persons do not need such crutches to play spontaneously and childishly. They can will their own temporary "disintegration," for they can confidently recover their integration by their own willpower. Not surprisingly, those who experience transcendent mystical experiences are indeed more mature. They can allow their controls to dissolve, surrender, even disintegrate in the presence of the ineffable.

Excessive *stability*, again relative to growth on the other dimensions, is rigidity and thwarts further integration and new growth. Eventually, rigidity brings boredom, stasis, and deadness, predisposing us to throw over the traces, injudiciously seek new experiences, and act out of character. The media delight in titillating us with tales of impeccably righteous TV evangelists, like Jim Bakker, or closeted homosexuals, like Roy Cohen (the aide of Senator McCarthy), who suddenly are wallowing in sin. Such unexpected acts are telltale signs that the sexual puritan and drug "prohibitionist" are not what they had tried to be. They had failed to integrate healthily what they had labeled "morally wrong" into their values and personalities.

Overexaggerated *autonomy* leads to self-centered self-sufficiency. It brakes further growth, especially in other-centeredness. If such people escape becoming loveless hermits, their love selfishly takes more than it selflessly gives. The Achilles heel of the typical masculine male is his overdeveloped self-sufficiency and of the typical feminine female her underdeveloped autonomy. Can you think of examples from your life of autonomy gone off-track?

We are now prepared to better understand Andy and Marty Miller. When writing *Fulfilling Lives*, I was delighted that their tests and peers identified them to be one of the study's two most successful couples. I felt that they were at the edge of an advancing cultural change in our familial relationships and so would illuminate the path ahead for others. Since then, Marty's and Andy's collective equilibrating principle intervened to shatter their fulfillment as a couple and severely test their individual maturity.

Part Two

Succeeding in Personal Relationships

Chapter 4

Andy and Marty Miller:
A Couple Seeking the Same Path

In their middle years, the Millers represented the values you ranked in the first chapter. Neither Andy, a biological researcher, nor Marty, a feminist lawyer, was the study's most fulfilled and competent parent or happily married, sexually fulfilled, vocationally satisfied, or happiest person. This chapter examines how they had grown to become the most all-round successful and fulfilled *couple* as of 1983 when I visited them. The following two chapters describe their growth since then and probe to discover their strengths that accounted for their success.

Two warnings, though. Don't expect that a successful *couple* doesn't stumble along the way—even very badly, as Andy and Marty did. They illustrate the pain of deteriorating modern marriages and how a couple tries to recreate a happier and more fulfilling one.

Also, don't expect to meet two ordinary, typical, run-of-the-mill, Main Street Americans, whoever they might be. However, when we go more deeply into the dilemmas the Millers faced trying to adapt to the changing role of women to create a viable two-career family, I think you will see many of the issues that millions of other couples are currently struggling with, each in their own unique ways. I can't emphasize enough, therefore, that Marty and Andy are every modern woman and man, despite how exaggerated and dramatic their lives may be. They stumbled trying to reshape centuries of emotional conditioning of what femaleness and maleness have meant and how women and men should get along with each other. Just as Billie prefigured how many modern women may be growing in the future, so the Millers prefigure the route many couples may find themselves taking, if they want to remain a *couple.*

As you read their stories, why not ask yourself these questions: "How has my maleness or femaleness affected how well I get along with my partner, children, and friends?" "What do Andy's and Marty's strengths tell me about the ones I need in order to create and sustain a healthy family life in these times?" "How would I have met the kinds of trials that Andy and Marty faced?"

I arrived in Atlanta one Friday afternoon in October 1983 to interview Andy Miller, then forty-six, and his second wife Marty, then forty-two. I saw Andy hovering along the crowd's edges, almost shyly; I knew he was trying to protect his shortened right leg, which had been partially paralyzed as a result of a crippling car accident when he was sixteen. Because he could feel few sensations in it, he never knew what he might be stepping on. He had to be constantly alert about where he put his cane to keep from tripping, losing his balance, and severely wrenching himself.

Limping beside me as we walked to his Buick, he seemed tired and in pain, though he did not mention either. (He never complained about his disability during any of my visits.) "Andy, you seem more thin and tired than I remember."

"Yeah. My muscles are weaker now. We're doing some tests to find out why I have so little stamina. I need to sleep now in the afternoon. And my headaches interfere with my concentration. They're the same symptoms I had when I was knocked out in that accident."

He later pluckily insisted on persisting with the six to eight hours of tests and interviews, despite frequently asking me to repeat the questions and occasionally grimacing and hiding his eyes as if he were in pain.

Marty was waiting for me when we reached their home, which was deceptively small on the outside, spacious but simply furnished on the inside. The living room opened onto a swimming pool which Andy used daily. I had never met Marty before; Andy had married her after my last visit. Compared to Andy's almost fragile ganglines that made me feel his tentativeness, Marty's five-foot-ten-inch frame, broad shoulders, flowing black hair, dancing eyes, earthy expressive voice, and exuberance instantly gave me a feeling of rootedness, solidity, feminine power—even mystery. She immediately hugged me, saying, "I feel like I've known you for years." I felt similarly—and was already very much at home.

So began my intensely concentrated visit, first with Andy and then Marty, following exactly the same procedure that I had used with Billie and Allan Leighton. What routes had each taken before they began traveling together for the ten years before my visit?

Andy Miller

Andy was the fourth and youngest of a long line of Maine Millers. His father, a small-town and not too successful Methodist minister, "never made enough money but always made me feel there was enough for the important things, like sending me to camp or allowing me to go to any school I wanted to." Andy felt that when he was an adolescent his father had been emotionally detached and uninvolved in the family and its conflicts. Though taciturn and not emotionally warm or expressive, he was not hostile and rejecting. To the phrase, "My father . . ." Andy wrote, "is a marvelous, lovable man but ill at ease with his feelings," and to "Remembering his father, . . ." he wrote, "he felt some sadness but deep affection and love." From his "impractical but high-minded" father, more interested in ideas and causes than in earning money, Andy got his social liberalism and interest in writing. "He really fulfills the old joke about a mother who takes care of the house and a father who takes care of the rest of the world. He has given me a strong streak of idealism."

His mother, feeling neglected by her own mother (who had been married to an alcoholic husband and so had had to work), stayed home to always be available to her children. After Andy left home, she opened her house to any stray hurt child who needed a temporary home. She was an active, energetic, and socially outgoing person, too attuned, according to Andy, to her social status among the neighbors. To the phrase, "My mother and I . . ." he wrote, "are good friends," and to "When he thought of his mother, he . . ." remembered a strong, loving woman whom he admired." Ten years later, Andy answered my question about how he might feel when she died: "I thought a lot about that. Be sorrowful and go through a period of grieving. I feel basically we have had a good relationship that has grown through the years; I feel close to and loved by her and she by me."

In recalling both parents, Andy said, "I felt loved and appreciated and got lots of strokes. My mother hugged me; my father never did. He really cared though; I know he cared. It wasn't until I took the initiative when I was thirty-five to embrace him that we ever touched each other. They didn't always understand me, but they stood by me through thick and thin. They've provided me a safe place to go back to."

Andy had been all-boy as an adolescent. He had enthusiastically participated in team sports and extracurricular activities, was elected president of his class, had close male friends, had begun to be drawn to girls, felt at home in social situations, and generally had the interests typical of boys of his age.

Then, when he was sixteen one of his gang careened off a curve on a rainy night and caused a car accident. The accident almost killed Andy, permanently changing his life though not his basic psychic healthiness. Thirty years later, I interpreted his test results to suggest:

> It's as if his mind and self-awareness come constantly between his impulses and the external world, so diluting passionate spontaneity but also restricting aggressive energy for coping . . . I feel this constant self-awareness and monitoring may be limiting the full integration of his potential in action. . . . The amount of energy tied up in awareness of and sensitivity to his body must take energy away from other activities. However, his basic concept of his bodily self seems to be quite healthy. I don't detect any morbid, self-rejecting, or negative feelings about his body that could undermine his self-esteem.

Andy broke in at this point to say, "I am always aware of my body."

With prodigious determination, he recovered enough from the accident's maiming effects to teach himself to walk again before entering college two years later. His high school counselor recommended him to Haverford, saying he was "serious-minded and hardworking with a high sense of responsibility." Haverford's admissions director recognized that such strengths would compensate for Andy's undistinguished verbal and quantitative aptitude test scores and his 40 percent score on the English achievement test.

True to his character, Andy threw himself into numerous extracurricular activities. Musically talented, he became president of the college's orchestra and played the piano with a jazz band as well as with a semiprofessional orchestra. Typical of his felt sense of responsibility and capacity to work hard, he also assumed the demanding editorship of the student literary magazine.

Believing that he was not as intellectually gifted as others, Andy worked hard to achieve his solid B academic record. Anticipating a medical career, he majored in biology. However, he discovered from work in the arts and English that he was a scientific humanist at heart and so decided, after a good but not stellar academic career, to get a Ph.D. in mammalian physiology. His senior advisor said Andy had been a "fundamentally serious and responsible worker, well-balanced, most likable, superior person all-round" and rated his determination, intelligence, and originality to be good but his emotional stability and personality to be excellent. At Harvard, his evolving research interests eventually drew him into applied biohumanistic problems, such as developing therapeutic exercises for various sexual disorders. He feels good about his work; he ranked fifth among the sixty-five men ten years ago in his satisfaction with his vocation. His earned income placed him in the top fifth of the men at that time.

Andy's relations with women have been less successful. In graduate school he fell in love with a woman who, after several months, precipitously left him to marry a classmate. Two years after getting his Ph.D., Andy married, only to become increasingly unhappy. Four years later, unable to bear his wife's interminable "hostile sarcasm" any longer, he persuaded his reluctant wife to see a marriage counselor with him. "In just a few sessions, the counselor convinced her of what I had known for a long time. We were incompatible. I felt good about it. It was a healthy step. Even though divorce had a negative stigma for me, I felt good that I had asserted myself and taken charge." Two years later, he met Marty while working for the peace movement during the Vietnam War years.

Martha (Marty) Wood

Marty's route to her marriage with Andy had been filled with a different, less visible kind of hurt. It was so festering that she was still trying to heal it by psychotherapy when I saw her when she was forty-three and by more counseling through her early fifties. She had grown up in a rigidly conventional and culturally unstimulating Catholic home dominated by an unstable mother in constant conflict with an alcoholic husband. Marty, the eldest of five children, had had her parents to herself until she was five, when her first sibling was born. Her mother expected her to be her "assistant, not a daughter," and take care not only of the four rapidly appearing kids but also of her. She said of her parents, "At a time when I needed them, they were experiencing so much pain that they needed me to parent them. I've been resentful and angry all my life. I learned that men were incompetent and women were out of control. When my father wasn't drunk, he'd play with us, just as I now play with my kids. But mother . . ."

To the phrase "When she thought of her mother, she . . ." Marty impulsively wrote, "cried." She replied similarly to a similar phrase about her father, whom she described as "a frightened man." She felt that her mother and father had not enjoyed being parents; they had never respected, loved, or shared their ideas and feelings with each other. A lingering special hurt for Marty was that neither parent valued her mind nor encouraged her to use it in school. In her mid-teens, they sent her to a Catholic girls' boarding school, where she blossomed. Like Billie and Andy, she participated in organized team sports and extracurricular activities, remained an active member of her church groups, and was looked to by the other girls for leadership. Isolated from boys and naive about sex, she became emotionally attached in eleventh grade

> to a very cruel female teacher. She was a lot older and used my infatuation for her own purposes, I now realize. She then withdrew from me, shut herself away from me. I was crushed. I didn't know why. I blamed myself and felt terribly guilty and didn't tell anyone for a whole year. I thought I was going crazy. I couldn't sleep at night. I couldn't work. I went to a counselor, who told me that there was nothing wrong and to use the experience as something to learn about my own intense needs to be close to other women. It sparked a wonderful change in my life. I started to collect very close women friends and learned what real friendship is all about.

She entered a convent to become a nun, but later left to go to law school. Law did not turn out to be her vocation, though. She got swept up into the women's movement, joined the National Organization for Women, aided in creating one of the country's more radical feminist groups that rejected males and their domination, and used her legal talents to further the cause of feminism. Her "calling" has remained to this day that of a feminist. When asked what her bedrock faith, her strongest conviction and commitment, the ultimate source of her energy and hope, was, she instantly said:

> Fighting oppression of any kind. That just expresses itself in everything I do. I want to create a community of women. I want my girls to become strong women. Women who are physically strong can defend themselves. Big women who can walk with a strong stance; who have strong minds; who can take stands; who have strong spirits, strong emotions; who see their emotions as signs of strength, not weakness. Anger and sadness and joy and silliness. Everything.

How vocationally successful had Marty been? Very. She preferred female clients. She had gained a reputation in her metropolitan area for legal and, increasingly, marital and sexual counseling. She was an expert in cases of sexual abuse, harassment, rape, and other forms of oppression that women are especially vulnerable to. She also had published popular articles on women's issues and achieved considerable influence through her public lectures, workshops, and organizational political activities. Her outspoken advocacy of feminist issues had propelled her into such prominence among women's groups that she had become a guru, even a priestess, for some women. Very satisfied with most aspects of her work, she ranked fourth among the women in her vocational fulfillment, fifth in her colleague's assessment of it, and among the top four women in earned income.

But it is her growth as Andy's marital and sexual partner and her children's parent that is most instructive about women's and men's changing relationships. After living together for two years, Marty and Andy married ten years prior to my first visit. Their early marital years were happy and fulfilling, with one exception: Marty had trouble conceiving. Shortly after they decided to adopt, she became pregnant and had no difficulty with her next pregnancy. During the next several years, Andy was productive and happy but Marty became increasingly troubled and dissatisfied with her life, the children, and Andy.

> I felt trapped and that had a lot to do with Andy's disability. I survived the early years of our marriage because I was living out the typically feminine mode of thinking. I was a good person. I would take care of him. I was a sacrificing kind of person. A martyr. I really started to resent him tremendously. I thought he fell into that. We both just drifted into agreeing that I would be the one to take care of him. So I felt I had three kids again.
>
> I know now that his disability does not make him a powerless person. But I used to see him as the person who was having just one fresh crisis after another . . . like being newly handicapped every day. I'd work all day with women suffering as women and then come home to two screaming kids and a disabled husband who didn't, really couldn't, help much around the house. He couldn't easily lift the babies or change their diapers. Caused me to think more and more I was the victim of patriarchy. I didn't want to be just a wife and mother, a traditional homemaker at that time of my life. But everything was pushing me that way emotionally.

Andy did not dispute Marty's description of their troubles. He was thirty-six when Jeannie was born and didn't have the stamina, or ability, to be physically involved with her and their next child. He just didn't feel "bonded" to them. Besides Marty breast-fed the children and ambivalently resented Andy's efforts to help as intrusions.

> She was becoming more hostile and angry that I wasn't more involved. She saw it as part of a more general behavior pattern of mine, which she interpreted to mean I wasn't emotionally committed, that I didn't care, that she should do all of the work. Since she was the primary nurturer, she was the primary parent. All of the feelings she felt during her own childhood were coming back to haunt her. Here she was living with a man who also wasn't available or supportive.

> At the same time she was being aggressive about her nurturing role. She didn't make it easy for me to be involved. She would jump in and take over too quickly. She felt that only she could solve the problem, only she could be the nurturer, only she could provide the right amount of support and understanding and care and that automatically excluded anyone else from being involved.

Marty agreed. The shadow of her own mother and her own childhood nurturing memories shrouded all that she did as a mother.

> I immediately felt out of control. When they were babies and crying a lot, I couldn't stand their continuous demands. I couldn't stand that I couldn't relieve their every cry. I would wake up in the middle of the night to their crying, which I couldn't stop. I'd start crying, go into the kitchen to pound the cabinets, run out of the house, fight with Andy—blaming him for my being out of control. No matter what he did, it wasn't good enough. Poor guy. He didn't know what hit him. He withdrew more and more and that made it worse. If only he had gotten angry I would have felt better.
>
> My main problem was that I was identifying with my mother, who couldn't drive a car, had no college education, had five kids and an alcoholic husband. I started acting out all of her behavior; I felt totally responsible for them and totally inadequate.

All the while, Marty found increasing support from her feminist friends and the ideology of the movement. Despite his sensitivity, Andy acted more typically male, an attitude that Marty had begun not to value. She felt that he expected her to mother him and didn't value women as women in their own right. Though "he doesn't make comments like most men when driving along the street about a beautiful woman's tits, his first comment is about how attractive she is." She became increasingly sensitive to the subtle ways men have historically controlled women. For example, she resentfully saw him playing old and familiar tapes, such as "Yes, I'll help around the house," but fading behind the newspaper when he came home from work and the kids needed to be tended to, or dozing off when the table needed to be cleared.

Andy became more aware of a darker current troubling Marty that his own maleness had been unconsciously aggravating, more aware that what he called his "male strengths" had their own pathology. He knew that he was not carrying equal weight in running the house and providing Marty with the emotional support she needed.

"How were you typically male in your thirties?" I asked Andy in an interview focused on the effects of our society's changing gender roles. He replied:

> I was very work-oriented, task oriented. Very conscious of my role as principal provider. Aware that I was a person responsible for providing the main income and would be when we had a family and my wife had to stay home and raise the kids. I was very competitive athletically, and was always aware of the professional accomplishments of my colleagues. I was concerned about matching and surpassing those. I also wasn't aware of, in fact, didn't value, emotional kinds of behavior. I saw emotions as weak, womanly. I have to be dominant, in control, an expert at work before my peers.

He felt like a "victim" of his upbringing and cultural training as a male because he wasn't as demonstrative and effusive as Marty needed him to be. She saw him as "relatively aloof, cold, and uncaring," a view that he didn't fully share about himself. "She's been tough to live with. With her emotional crises, I've been a patient and understanding, sensitive person and willing to listen and take a lot of her verbal abuse . . . . She kept saying, "If only you were more caring . . . ," implying it was all my fault.

Not surprisingly, the doubts, strains, and accusations found their way into the bedroom. For Marty, sex eventually became the most available playing field on which to strike out at what she felt was patriarchal domination.

> I didn't enjoy sex at all, and I worried about this and thought about it a lot. I just grinned and bore it. After we got married, I never really enjoyed sex the whole time. I had always loved my sexual fantasies, enjoyed sexual play and its novelty. I enjoyed talking about sex but didn't enjoy

> intercourse. As I started to resent Andy for other things, I started to avoid sex even more. I hated its messiness, his thrusting, his dominating male violence. I felt no woman should enjoy that kind of violence. And that was part of what was happening when I tried to connect with women.

As Andy picked up the story,

> Marty had become increasingly involved in the feminist movement and more doubtful about her own feminine identity. One night she came home to tell me that she had "fallen in love" with a woman, had never been in love like this since high school, and wanted to remain living in the house but spend more time with her than with me. I said, "Absolutely not," and told her to get out. It was a difficult time, because she didn't want to leave. But she did and we separated. We got a housekeeper and agreed we would co-parent the children, each taking them half of each week. We were really headed for a divorce.

Marty's reaction to those bitter moments was, "We were ugly and cruel to each other. He cut himself off from me. I know now he was very hurt because of what I was doing. He was very rejecting. We both got angry and screamed at each other and said things that were exaggerated. "You don't really care about me." "You're selfish."

How did they deal with their pain? Marty turned to other women for the tenderness, intimacy, and support she felt she hadn't gotten from Andy. He was left, in his words, "bereft and lonely without the emotional and physical support Marty had provided." In the space of two years, his ratings of his energy, mood, productivity, and fulfillment plummeted on a 10-point scale from a 9 after the birth of his second daughter to 1. Marty's ratings eroded more slowly from a high of 9 shortly after her marriage to 0 when Andy told her to get out.

As I heard their stories, I felt I was reliving a Greek tragedy. They were like fated lesser deities being controlled by more powerful Olympian gods; they were neither fully responsible for nor had much control over the moves they were being forced to make. Just as humans have sensed for centuries that Oedipus, King Lear, and Faust are larger-than-life representations of themselves, so I felt that weekend that the

Millers were magnified projections of so many torn contemporary couples that I knew.

Their Three Paths

How did their tragedy unfold? What route did each now take? How did they find a way to travel together again? What do their lives tell us about how modern couples are resolving centuries-old patterns that are now no longer adaptive?

Marty's Route

Marty said, "When I separated from Andy, I deliberately threw all of my values to the four winds and decided that I wasn't going to value anything. Probably didn't throw all of them away. I sure acted like I did. I had a real, 'I don't care attitude' about what people thought I should do. I was testing my values."

Marty recaptured her happier convent days by plunging fully into her feminist community of close friends. She said of them,

> I had a fantasy that what I needed was to be with women all of the time, to be happy in women's bars. I would be happiest meeting radical feminists discussing our oppression. But I found I wasn't. I don't know if this has to do with such feminists. They were very angry. I didn't enjoy that continuous state of anger. Also, it was very incestuous. Everyone knew everyone else's business and personal lives. It also affected my legal practice. I had a lot of clients who knew too much about my personal life and it became increasingly difficult to maintain my professional distance.

So Marty began to turn away from her more radical friends to become closer to other feminists, particularly one married, very reflective woman who helped her ground her feminism on a less angry but much firmer spiritual foundation. Her new network of friends created religious rituals with each other to bond themselves together more communally.

She also turned back to men to satisfy her sexual needs, though she later regretted that she had not really learned how to become friends with them. Marty learned from these experiences that "I didn't absolutely need my husband and that I could make friendships and relationships work with other men also." She made up, so she said, for her delayed adolescence, when she never had any close emotional or sexual relations with males in school or college.

Andy's and her earlier experiences at Esalen—a popular California human growth center of the sixties and seventies—as well as their encounters with other similar groups created a common bond, to which they returned during the two years of their separation. They attended a workshop together where Marty was surprised to learn that her husband "was not the only sensitive man in the world," a revelation that some men had the courage to examine their own feminine side and the meaning of their sexuality. She slowly became less hostile to men.

Her primary route back to Andy, however, was psychotherapy. She began to understand how her childhood and adolescent experiences had affected her marital and sexual relations. With Andy and then separately, Marty began to explore with her therapist the meaning of her relationships and feelings about the traditional roles of wife and mother, roles that she came to realize she really loved. "I learned that I try to make people dependent on me and then I get angry at them and reject them. I also learned that I use sexual seductiveness when I want nurturing. I really do love my husband and like to feel safe in a family system."

About a year after their separation, Andy told her that he wanted a divorce, which "totally devastated" her. When asked why, she said that she had always viewed the separation as a temporary period during which each would learn how to grow up and become healthier. She fell apart, couldn't go to the office, and "felt really knocked off center for several months."

To better understand Marty's less expressible feelings about Andy and their relationship, I gave her a picture of a woman holding onto a man who is intently looking toward the viewer. There is a partially clad woman in the background. I asked Marty to tell as imaginative a story as she could about what these people were feeling and thinking. She said animatedly,

> This is a story of a relationship. It has a pretty typical beginning. A woman is feeling like she needs the man very badly. And he looks like a very harsh kind of person. Not

in touch with any kind of gentleness or sensitivity. There is a picture on the wall that shows he views women as sexual objects. And in his attempt to use this particular woman that he loves, he is discovering some pain in himself and that he would like to relate to her in a more sensitive and caring way. And he doesn't know how. And he's pulling away. He won't talk to her about his feelings; he doesn't know how. She is trying to understand him, trying to make contact with him in more mutually satisfying ways. I think he's going to leave. He has been touched by her in some way, but he can't put it all together. He is going to spend some years struggling with that, and she's going to need to let him go. But she'll be all right.

Andy's Route

As his relationship with Marty "deteriorated," Andy sought counseling from a therapist who specialized in working with men "in crisis." Andy joined the therapist's ongoing men's group that met twice a week. Each man had the telephone number of the others, whom he could call at any time. With this support, Andy bounced back to begin dating again. He realized that he was a "marketable single male" whom women still found attractive, despite his partially useless leg.

Andy initially found the responsibility of taking care of the children to be unexpectedly arduous. But he also discovered that he could be a good parent, particularly when he could get along with them on a more verbal level. He got in touch with his feelings about how he wanted to raise the kids, and he felt relieved to not have to discuss or argue with Marty about how caring and firm he should be in setting limits for them.

But he emotionally held on to his relation with Marty, not only cooperating with her in taking care of the children, but also seeing the therapist with her and hoping that they could work out a different relationship. By focusing on Andy's half of the responsibility for their rupture, the therapist refused to allow Andy to blame Marty for the breakup. What did Andy learn about how he got along with women?

> I had become overly involved in Marty's life, as she had in mine. We lost our boundaries and became too fused and

wrapped up in each other. I wasn't in touch with my strengths. I wasn't strong enough about my own territory, about my own role. I didn't stand up to her. I guess I tried to be sensitive and aware and flexible. She was testing me and interpreted my flexibility as weakness. The more she would test, the more I looked weak. Then she could despise me for that. It was during a period of maximum feminist rhetoric. She found it very easy to lump me with all other men as a chauvinistic pig and insensitive bastard. You know, all of that. I worked on becoming more self-contained, independent until I emotionally felt totally separated and ready for the divorce. I took the initiative to get it started. She kept resisting, dragging her feet and it wasn't until she was ready to get a legal divorce six to eight months later that she also began to feel free of me. We both felt so free of each other that we were able to say, "Hey, let's talk about starting over." I felt much better about myself. More self-reliant, independent, able to survive without Marty.

Andy's and Marty's Route

As Marty's imaginative story suggested, not until each, paradoxically, had become maturely more autonomous and free of the other could they return to walk the same path together, which they had been doing for six years until my visit in 1983. How successful were they as marital partners, lovers, and parents?

I asked Marty how good a wife she felt she was. She thought she was "quite good" but not "very good" and explained why.

> Very good seems to be too good. If I were too good a wife, I would have too much invested in staying a good wife. To be quite a good wife is as good as I want to be because that means I'm taking care of my needs as well . . . I tried for a very long time being a very good wife. Somehow that means to me staying home more and taking care of all of the needs of the family. But as a quite good wife I can be successful in my work and feel good about myself and have some of that rub off on the family relationships.

Defining "marital success" is obviously going to be more complicated in the future for those studying happily married women. Although Marty scored in the top 25 percent of the women on a conventional marital happiness scale that described all of the principal characteristics of happy marriages, she felt extremely happy in her marriage. When rating how well Marty fulfilled the six most important attributes he had learned that a marriage required in order to be happy and fulfilling, Andy gave her the highest ratings on five of the six, including trust, shared values, common interests, ability to grow, and ability to be her own person.

Though still feeling that he was not as emotionally demonstrative as Marty would like, Andy rated himself to be a very good husband, mentioning that he had continued to co-parent the children, thus showing his commitment to an equal division of family responsibilities. He, as Marty also, felt that he was happily married. Marty saw both of them as equally sharing four of her six attributes of a successful marriage—for example, good communication skills, shared values, love, and mutual respect—but she felt that she was less independent than he and that he was less nurturing in the relationship than she was. These days, however, what more stringent measure can there be of a man's success as a marital partner than to have his spouse say of him, as Marty said of Andy,

> He's a really sensitive and loving and strong person. And because he's stuck with me through all of this, I feel wonderful. I feel I have such a supportive and loving partner and that frees me up also to make friends, to interact with other people without having to make that so intense. It's hard to put into words. I feel so safe with Andy and so completely accepted by him. He's been so open to change and to growth. He's taken so many risks with me that I feel that I have not just a safe place but a very real and honest relationship. I now have more energy to be friends with other people, because I have a strong and caring partner.

Sexually, Marty rather dubiously enjoyed marital sex now, varying in her ratings about how she felt. She rated Andy to be high on the strengths that she believed described a good lover: respect, self-confidence, playfulness, willingness to experiment, and giving. Andy enjoyed sex with Marty and felt she was a considerate and good lover: comfortable with sex, open in talking about her sexual feelings, and willing to give and be playful sexually, which he valued highly.

Finally, both rated themselves and each other to be very competent parents. In terms of satisfaction and fulfillment in the parental role, Marty ranked in the top 25 percent of the mothers and Andy in the top 10 percent of the fathers. Both saw Andy as generally more "parental" than Marty, primarily because both agreed that Andy was firmer and more consistent in the way he reared the children. Marty pinpointed the differences when she said, "The kids will tell you that I'm a softy. I'm not consistent and don't set limits as strongly. He's much more patient. He can teach them. If they don't learn fast enough for me, I get angry. I'm much more physical and do much more hugging and kissing [I also observed this; Marty would wrestle with both children on the floor, which Andy obviously couldn't do] . . . Andy is very intensely engaged with them now."

Numbers and percentages can't possibly express the messages of the heart, of just what another really means to us. To Andy, Marty

> was a warm, caring, loving, giving person. She's a good mother, a good companion. She's been very supportive of me in my work, especially in terms of my emotional growth. She's helped me by sharing her own insights into feminism and what that has meant in getting in touch with some of my latent powers. She has the remarkable ability to face unpleasant things, to try to deal with emotional problems right now, not put them away and pretend that they're not there. We have an openness and ability to communicate that is really very remarkable. We can talk to each other about almost anything. That's what Marty has done for us.

And how happy were Andy and Marty? Very. Each felt happy and felt the other was, and their closest friends agreed. And how fulfilled and satisfied were they with their lives? Andy, Marty, and his closest friend all agreed: He and seven others in the study were the most fulfilled of the sixty-five men. Marty's restless dissatisfaction with herself, however, kept her in the top 25 percent of the women.

Before traveling further along Andy's and Marty's path, I pause to reflect why they had succeeded as well as they had by their mid-forties.

Chapter 5

Sources of Andy's and Marty's Success

As with Billie, I knew nothing about how Andy's and Marty's genes, hormones, and constitution contributed to their success. Nor had I known or observed them as children in their formative years. I know about them and their parents only through their adult eyes. Despite these limitations, the hours of tests and interviews generated some insights as to why Andy and Marty had succeeded as well as they had by their mid-forties.

Andy: Growing into a Mature Androgyny

Five factors nourished Andy's success:
1. Loving, basically respectful parents who had firm expectations of him and who remained available when he needed them
2. An androgynous inclination both intellectually and emotionally
3. Adolescent and adult psychological maturity
4. Marty's provocations which taught him how to continue to grow by way of his femininity
5. Much pain and an optimistic attitude that he could triumph over it himself

Loving Parents

The first key to understanding Andy's growth was his feeling that he had grown up in an emotionally safe and loving home, to which he could comfortably retreat when he felt miserable and emotionally wrenched during his separations and other crises. His parents had always been available when he needed them. Actively concerned about his growth, they encouraged him to achieve in school and sports and become independent at an early age. While holding him to firm expectations, they had not severely disciplined him or given him the feeling that he wasn't accepted or loved. They were basically respectful.

I said that they "basically," not "fully," respected him, because of a central theme of Andy's psychological tests that I must explain. His relationships with women were too mixed up with his relationship with his mother. He had changed from his early thirties to his late forties in his attitudes toward them. My report about that change stated:

> He still doesn't feel as connected and secure with women, who seem to be unpredictable to him. In contrast, however, to his early thirties, he has matured considerably, now seeing women more as adults, not just as mothers. He depends upon them much less now for nurturance as well as being less submissive in trying to please them. He is now more certain of his own sexual identity in such relations and has established a firmer sense of his own self in his relationships. The foundation for this movement is a growing confidence about his own sexuality.

I had not known that a focal issue in Andy's counseling had been his relationship with his mother. He explained it to me this way. He felt that she loved him but only "conditionally"; he had to earn her love by doing well, particularly in school. Although both parents expected great things of him, his mother had higher hopes and assiduously worked with him to attain them, such as helping him with his homework.

Two effects of her conditional love lingered into his middle age. We agreed that to get her love, he had learned to value and work hard for professional success. Her less healthy effect intensified his emotional dependence on women. He feared that they might not love him and so would abandon him. He needed to become part of them, in his own words, to "fuse myself with them," to continue getting their love. When a relationship started to go sour, he protected himself from any confirmation that he was not loved by initiating separations. His attitude was, "If I separate first, then she hasn't separated from me, so she still loves me." Not until he first left Marty did he learn to let go of his need for her approval and so become his own independent man. His tests showed how much he had grown as a result of his therapy and Marty's provocations from his late thirties into his fifties.

Andy felt more temperamentally similar to his father. He respected him for his ethical idealism to which he traced his own humanistic values about applying basic research to human concerns. But he apparently also learned from his father that he should be an emotionally reticent, inexpressive, and stoical male, traits that later got in the way of succeeding as a husband and parent. Although Andy believed that he had broken out of his emotional straitjacket with Marty's help, he continued to understate how he felt about his pain and underlying low spirits—which I only gleaned from his asides and other fragments of interviews and questionnaires.

Androgynous Inclinations

Andy explicitly singled out his androgyny as the second and most important key to his success. I had not anticipated that the more successful men and women, selected solely by objective signs of their success, would be so androgynous. By his mid-forties, Andy had learned how to moderate his adolescent overdeveloped maleness. He had brought what he called his hidden "feminine parts" into awareness so that he could more consciously use their strengths. He was one of the two men described by three peers as equally balanced in their masculine and feminine strengths—a stricter way to define androgyny. Compared with the other men, he was more masculine than about a third and more feminine than 90 percent of them.

Raised as a typical male, Andy had learned to achieve, compete, and control— if not suppress—his emotions. He had participated in the usual adolescent male activities. Rigorous schooling had encouraged what he called his "male-dominated left-brain" strengths: analytical, objective, scientific modes of thinking. Andy was familiar with the discoveries that the left and right hemispheres of the brain contribute to different abilities and rates of growth. The left brain mediates more typical masculine modes of thinking like analysis and linear logic; the right brain encourages more typical feminine modes like empathy, intuition, esthetic values, and contextual thinking.

Possibly the car accident when he was sixteen—which closed off growth in typically vigorous and competitive male activities—opened up the path to more introspective and typically feminine interpersonal growth. He was not surprised by what his tests showed. His "feminine mind," which he defined for me as its "subjective emotive aspects," was truer to his given native talent than was his conscious analytical and conceptual mind. He had devoted most of his life to developing this more masculine way of thinking to be able to compete like a male. Clues to his undeveloped feminine mind's potential were his adolescent interest in literature, the discovery of an ability to learn and enjoy languages, and his movement away from "straight" biological research to its humanistic application in the area of sexuality.

The reasons for Andy's vocational creativity and recognition are instructive, for they show just how one-sided his education had been and why traditional school credentials do not predict adult success well. Schools value and measure stereotypical masculine talents, such as analytical, logical-deductive, and critical thinking, more than they do stereotypical feminine ones, such as empathic, intuitive, and contextual thinking. Identifying analytical and conceptual thinking with intelligence, Andy has thought for years that he was less intellectually capable than his colleagues.

> I don't see myself as phenomenally gifted in intelligence or IQ. Yes, I'm bright and articulate and introspective. I like to write. I grew up in a left-brain environment. Most of my education and training also emphasized and focused on left-brain qualities. My intellectual abilities are primarily left-brain ones, and throughout my life I have compared myself with other academic colleagues primarily in terms of them. I don't feel that I'm in the 99 percent of left-brain performers and as a result have discounted my abilities. I have become more aware that I have right-brain emotional skills, which may be stronger than my left brain ones. These are valuable and important, and it is the synthesis of the two halves that is most important. I feel I have an exceptional ability to synthesize the two halves.

Andy's synthesis of his femaleness and maleness, the yin and yang, became the pathway to increased creativity, as others studying creative persons have also noted. His emerging vocational recognition paralleled his growing openness to and integration of his more feminine parts into his more masculine mode of research. Prodded by Marty, reinforced by his Esalen and other similar group workshops, and furthered by his therapy, Andy said, "I became more comfortable with my own feelings, and that made me more comfortable with issues in my professional life. I became more willing to look at my work from other perspectives. I became more open, accepting different approaches to problem-solving, more tolerant of ideas I would have considered to be kooky, far out, nonscientific when younger."

Psychological Maturity

The third key to Andy's success was his maturity, both as an adolescent and as an adult. When he was a teenager, he ranked seventh among the sixty-five men in maturity. His years of arduous growth had led to a healthily balanced androgynous personality.

Mature for his age in his relationships, self-aware and self-confident, determined and purposeful, Andy had the personal resources to learn to live with the shattering injury to his right leg. They enabled him to cope at the vulnerable age of sixteen, an age when the implications of such an injury for athletic skill and physical image can be traumatic. Andy did not resort to self-pity or neurotic withdrawal; instead, he took himself in hand and taught himself how to walk again, just as he is teaching himself in his fifties how to get along with his spreading quadriplegic disabilities.

I wondered how his shortened, almost useless leg had affected his image of himself as a "regular guy." It could have turned him away from the rough and tumble of male competitive prowess, heightening his sensitivity to his body and therefore to his feelings and others'— particularly women's—reactions to his disability. When I asked Andy directly about his accident's effects on his view of himself and his future, he replied, "There is no reason why I can't live a very full rich life in the domains of my life—the intellectual, emotional, and spiritual. I just have to live within a smaller perimeter." Andy never let his disability excuse his failures and contract his perimeter; instead, it prodded him to work even harder to succeed vocationally. However, marital and parental success demand more than determination and hard work or even interpersonal skills. His disability limited his familial perimeter in ways that provoked Marty's resistance to take care of him. Imagine so needing to protect one's useless leg that one fears picking up a three-month-old daughter or even changing an infant's diapers.

Andy was the study's most mature middle-aged man, which gave him the strengths necessary to learn from both his separations how to adapt to being a part-time father. Since maturity stimulates further maturing, it was not surprising that just as he grew as a result of adapting to his disability, he matured as a result of adapting to his separations. His first separation from Marty

> had a profound impact on how I got along with my kids . . . in understanding the dynamics of child-rearing, the stages that children go through, and in being able to appreciate and experience how they felt and how to respond to them appropriately . . . . The separation was a wrenching traumatic event and through getting insight into what led up to it and my contribution to it, I developed a better understanding of how I had been dealing with women. I became more comfortable as a husband and a more effective one too, when she came back to me two years later. It made me much more aware of what other couples might be experiencing, more empathic, and at the same time perhaps more inclined to encourage them to seek counseling, be more persistent in their efforts to salvage their relationship.

Andy's maturity enabled him to adapt resiliently to one of the most hurtful events of his life. He rapidly learned from his men's group and counseling how to be more aware of and put into words his feelings about Marty and their relationship. As a result, he became even more interpersonally sensitive and effective in his other relationships.

When studied in his forties, Andy was a superb example of one of the study's principal findings: Men's success in their vocations, marriages, and relationships tend to go together because each draws on the same underlying strengths that describe maturity. Both Andy's vocational achievement and his relations with Marty and the children improved as he became aware of "the many dimensions of . . . [his]

own sexuality." Paradoxically, but quite understandable psychologically, as he accepted and expressed his more emotional, affectionate, and nurturing self, he became, according to Marty, more self-reliant, more independent, and more in control of his own life. And, according to Andy himself, he became more creative in his research; he stood at the threshold of singular vocational recognition and honor.

Marty's Provocations

The fourth key to understanding why Andy succeeded was Marty's confrontational feminism. Andy could not escape her challenge to his maleness; fortunately, he had the maturity to endure the suffering necessary to alter years of living as a typical male, the courage to risk refashioning his sense of self, and the flexibility to persist in changing how he got along with Marty and the children.

Andy's Pain and Optimism

The last key to Andy's success in his forties was the unremitting pain of his injury, which he was forced to adapt to constantly. Andy does not give up because he has hope. His hope is similar to the hope that helped Billie work for her success; in both cases, hope is an offshoot of maturity. Andy is an optimistic person who highly values continued growth and feels he can control how he matures. He believes that living means growing and that growing takes effort; it doesn't just happen. I asked him these questions: "Where is your potential growing edge? Where could you be developing more?" He answered with a mixture of hopefulness and realism:

> I am just aware that nothing is static. You don't achieve one level of excellence and move on to the next. You constantly relearn and repolish and repractice skills that made you productive at a previous level. I am really aware that my past glories and triumphs either become memories or if I want to retain those skills and qualities that led to the triumph, I must work, constantly work. Like my marriage. Just getting back together was not enough. We have to keep working. The same is true in being a father.

> I think I have lived life very fully. It has been a very rich life, full of a lot of pain and worry and setbacks, but what I haven't done very well is to integrate the pain and the triumph. I sort of see that as my next task.

I also asked him, "What role does faith play in your life?"

> I believe that humans are basically good and that collectively we are slowly and painfully learning from our mistakes. The majority of people in the world are interested in bettering life for their children and want to see life on the planet continue. I believe that we are evolving toward a higher state of raised consciousness, an awareness that we are a large family flying together among the stars.

Though Andy's story is as special as Billie's, I sense that his has much to teach us men about our maleness. Andy shows us how we may need to alter its historic meanings if we are to become more whole and healthy in the future. We also may need to follow his lead if we are to succeed in our relationships with emerging modern women, such as Marty, who want to be empowered in their own right to live fulfilled lives. What does Marty's story tell us about why she succeeded as she did?

Marty: Growing into Her Vision

When I first met Marty, I felt her to be special, different, even charismatically so, as her friends said of her. When I met her, she was in psychotherapy. She was self-absorbed in exploring her "unordinariness," as she described it, as well as her feelings about her parents, particularly her mother. Since I had no measures of her pre-therapy self, I could not determine how her therapy affected her judgment and views of herself and her parents. Therapists focus more on parents' and clients' weaknesses than on their strengths, more on what went wrong when they were younger than on what went right. Marty's complicated personality and history, combined with her therapy's effects, may have obscured psychologists' more conventional ways of understanding her evolving strengths.

Five keys—configured in a more complex pattern than Andy's—helped Marty and me understand her success:

1. Caring but unstable, powerless, and inept parents who propelled her to get in touch with her own resources in her early growing-up years
2. A sensitive, supportive husband, very similar in values and interests, responsive to the egalitarian, companionate heterosexual relationship that she wanted—and didn't want
3. A perhaps biologically-given erotic intensity that opened her to sources of feminine insight and power that enabled her to articulate for other women their historic strengths and goodness
4. An androgynous predisposition whose nurturing femininity and independent masculinity were simultaneously set when younger
5. An involvement with the feminist movement, which provided her the social forms and support to explore an egalitarian vision whose time had come

Inept Parents

The first key—Marty's caring but inept parents—contradicts what psychologists have known and what the study's results of its 105 men and women also showed: Generally speaking, successful adults come from favorable home environments. Since exceptions that violate our expectations frequently produce new insights, we must closely examine Marty's unfavorable home environment. (Only two other women reported as unfavorable a family during their childhood and teens.) Just how unfavorable was her family in Marty's eyes? Very. She reported few strengths in her parents and in her early relationships with them. Marty believed that both parents had poor mental health. She regretted more what her parents did *not* do than what they did do. Like Andy, she never felt that either parent had rejected her. She did feel let down that they had not loved her more or encouraged her athletic, outdoor, and especially intellectual activities. (A signal event in her growth occurred when her parents went to one of her therapy sessions. She asked them to hug and love her like a little girl again—and they did so.)

Her alcoholic, physically unhealthy father and incompetent and helpless mother did not give her models of a man and woman to respect and emulate. Like Billie, she felt closer, though ambivalently, to her father than to her mother. She depended on him emotionally but stubbornly rebelled against him. (Only one other woman reported disagreeing more with her father about vocational, political, and social values.) Therapy, of course, seeks to resurrect our parents so that we can learn how to get along with them more maturely or relinquish them as continuing influences in our lives. Marty had not yet emotionally freed herself of her parents. She ranked sixth among the forty women in feeling her mother to be a strong, vivid, and internal presence *still influencing her life.*

We do not know the strengths Marty absorbed from her parents the first five years before her sister arrived. She must have become intensely uncertain, most likely jealous, about being displaced by her three sisters and brother. To then be expected by her mother to grow up overnight from being a child to being her "assistant"—even a "mother"—responsible for taking care of her rivals as well as her own parents galled her for years.

Sometimes, however, it is just such parental weaknesses that prod children to develop compensating strengths. Andy's father's taciturnity and emotional restraint caused him later in life to learn to be affectionate and even cry. Marty's out-of-control, powerless mother and weak, incompetent father may also have perversely provided the impetus for her to value and develop control, power, and strength.

Parents may indeed give us more strengths than we may be aware of or wish to accept. Marty's resentments when she was five colored her memories of her parents for years. Not until such feelings began to pass in her early forties did she begin to appreciate their strengths. Unanticipated by Marty, her mother demonstrated a nurturing competence by supervising visitors to patients in a local hospital; her father had summoned the will to free himself from alcohol for seven years. And both parents came to her aid when she called out to them for help, even after Andy had told them why he had kicked her out of their home. So Marty had begun to accept and respect her parents. As her anger abated, she discovered that she, too, was a good person.

Psychologists only recently have begun to understand why some hurt children, like Billie and Marty, draw strength from their parents' weaknesses, while others can't. Parentally hurt but resilient children have usually had at least one trustworthy, loving experience. For infants, this may have been a close bonding relationship with a mother or, particularly for vulnerable girls, an identification with a father.

Older children may have had supportive siblings or adult relatives (like Billie's grandparents), or even helpful neighbors and teachers. Natural "self-righting" or equilibrating strengths can help children like Marty overcome the potential long-term damaging effects of their vulnerability.

Caring teachers and rewarding school experiences can also provide hurt children the nurturing security they need to outgrow their parents' limitations. Unfortunately, Marty's female boarding school provided neither affectional security nor intellectual support. Hungry for affection, unsure of her own feelings and identity, isolated from boys and men, she was drawn into a romantic crush on an older mother figure. Despite her teacher's cruel rejection of her, the experience led her to discover and later value close female friendships. They became her principal path to growing up and provided the interpersonal model for her feminist vision.

Like Billie, Marty discovered her leadership strengths from her athletic and extracurricular activities, which opened up her vocational path to adult success. Although she was very bright, her intellectual strengths did not become a major route until she was older. Neither her parents nor her teachers modeled or encouraged her mind's growth. She didn't discover how much her teachers had let her down until she tried to argue logically with Andy. Like Billie, she felt her teachers had been mediocre, rigidly emphasizing memorization and never challenging her latent intellectual talents. So, again, like Billie, Marty was forced to turn to her own resources. "Getting angry about all that they didn't teach me has sort of freed me up to be bright all on my own."

Andy's Character

Marty agreed that a second key to her success was Andy. He adapted in ways that let her integrate her nurturing maternal needs with her achieving career desires. Psychologists have underestimated the maturing effects a loved partner can have on our growth. The women judged their partners' personality to be the most important of the fifty causes I examined of their growth into their middle years. In their thirties, the men rated their wives as most influential, but when they were middle-aged, their wives came second to their occupation in influence.

Andy's love for her and willingness to stand by her as she explored her bisexuality gave her the emotional space she needed to discover her own sexual and parenting needs.

Others have had unfavorable family lives, incompetent parents, and uninspired teachers but have not succeeded as Marty did. Why? The next two keys—her eroticism and androgyny—found their integration and social support in the last key, her involvement in the feminist movement.

Marty's Eroticism

Not until I had analyzed Marty's inner life as projected onto the Rorschach inkblots did I understand the third key to her success: why she felt different and valued strength and power so highly, and why other women called her their guru, even "priestess," during the heyday of the women's movement.

> She seems to have opened herself to what are typically less conscious and conventional images and sources of energy. A dominant theme in her imagination, almost of obsessional vividness, is her preoccupation with all varieties of erotic activity. She is in touch with sexual energies of all forms: voyeuristic and exhibitionistic needs, heterosexual and homosexual impulses, birth and menstrual fantasies—and can willingly allow their access into awareness without anxiety or defensive efforts to repress or avoid them.
>
> Now these erotic fantasies and needs seem to be vehicles for expressing forces even more primitive, archaic, and fundamentally human, which I have rarely seen expressed in the fantasies of most others. It is almost as if she has direct access to what Carl Jung calls "archetypal" sources of power. [Archetypes for Jung are inherited universal and primitive templates energized by instincts of such power to potentially overwhelm a person's control.] So she has available mythological, religious, universal symbols of great energy on which to draw for insight and staying power. She is probably sufficiently aware of them to fear

being taken over and lived through by transcendent powers. She could well emotionally identify with very primitive myths of the *magna mater,* the universal earth mother, the power of middle earth, mother ocean, the life energy—the sources of feminine mythological insight and power. Such images contain so much energy and power that she may feel she is every woman, rooted in and living out centuries-old myths of feminine mystery.

The quality of Marty's power that I tried to communicate when she was in her forties may seem elusive, even unfathomable, to you. If you are a humanist, you could tell me that the power of a Shakespeare, Hawthorne, or Tennessee Williams comes from their access to such universal symbols of human passion and insight. I sensed a similar power behind the doors of Roger's watercolors, except that for Marty, the door was wide open and she welcomed everything that bounded through it. In its extreme uncontrolled form, such power is seen in the mentally ill person who feels possessed by demons or angels whose intensity is so great that they come alive in hallucinations. In its public, more socially acceptable form, the power is seen in religious and political leaders who are so possessed that they move others to fanatical devotion, even self-sacrifice. It is seen in creative persons who become transfixed by an idea or a vision whose sources are felt to be transcendent. The same power is felt in our daily lives when we are so caught by a feeling, such as falling in love, that we are compulsively driven to act beyond our rational control.

What implications did this way of understanding Marty's familial and vocational success in her mid-forties have for her? Three questions immediately occurred to me. What was the source of such felt power? Did Marty have control over her inner myths, or was she controlled by them? What did feminism mean to her success?

I felt that there was a strong constitutional basis to Marty's energy, dynamism, and earthy eroticism. In psychoanalytic language, she had a strong id. By *erotic* I—like Marty—do not mean simply sexual energy. I am using the term (the way Freud used it) to refer to an energy that clamors, excites, disturbs; an energy that impels us to risk, to be attracted to, to reach out to touch, to connect, to be a part of, to merge with others, a cause, or a transcendent being. We know that infants temperamentally vary greatly in the intensity of their needs, energy levels, alertness, and outgoingness. Such infants, like my energetic grandson Benjamin—who apparently needs only four or five hours of sleep a night—can drive their parents to distraction, as he does his sleepless, weary mother. Yet such vitality can be a priceless strength when appropriately channeled. Marty's erotic vitality was her great strength. It propelled her into the world of others, which became her route to growing up. In her words, she was a "networking" person, seeking to connect with others, creating groups, participating in communal rituals, nurturing other women, and learning from her own therapy to be nurtured by others. Marty's life force was strong. Other women sensed it, were inspired by it, and sought her out as a counselor, not just for legal advice but for affirming support of their identities as women.

Androgynous Predisposition

The fourth key to understanding her success is her androgynous predisposition, probably also constitutionally rooted. Children of such insistent vitality need help to learn how to control and use its associated intrusive, aggressive, self-assertive, frequently dominating energies. Girls in particular can become conflicted about such vitality when they are raised to be properly feminine. Marty and I agreed that the early channeling of her vitality into becoming a "nurturer" when she was five had several enduring unhealthy effects. She became an "adult" before her psychological time. Her feminine nurturing skills of reaching out and connecting with others were unduly strengthened, as were her masculine initiating, assertive, independent, and self-reliant ones. She is aware that the name she prefers—Marty—can also be a man's name. So her erotically strong temperament combined with her early assumption of responsibility for raising other children strengthened her androgyny even more. (In her forties, her peers described her to be the second most androgynous and feminine and fifth most masculine woman of the study. Marty, restlessly conflicted about her self and needs, initially had not fully accepted the strengths her peers had noted; by her mid-fifties, she had.)

What happens to a girl who must nurture others before she has had the opportunity to fulfill her own needs to be cared for and loved?

The need to be child again lingers on for years in adult fantasies, as Marty tells us in the picture she imagined for a blank card.

> There is a park or forest with a clearing in which there is a group of children playing, around whom are parents sitting watching them play. They are obviously ambivalent about whether they would like to play or go and work. The children beckon them to come and play with them. Little by little, the adults move to the center to play with their children. They start to collect ribbons, putting them in each other's hair, and they learn they can go back and forth easily . . . back to their work and back into the circle . . . . They decide to meet there every so often to remember how to play with each other.

The emotional price that Marty paid for the opportunity to develop and stabilize her androgynous strengths too early was high. It complicated her marriage, pushed her into therapy, and initiated her inner restlessness that drove her for years to explore ways to grow more healthily. As she explored society's prescribed marital and parental options, lesbian bars, and indiscriminate sexual liaisons, her equilibrating principle—the guardian of her wholeness—intervened each time to say "no, not the way."

How vulnerable was Marty to being possessed by her archetypal power? Two strong bulwarks fortified her in her forties when her power was most intense: her basically good health and the women's movement (the fifth key). As an adolescent, she was quite mature, particularly in her interpersonal relationships. As a middle-aged woman, she rated herself as more mature than only a fourth of the women, most likely because therapy unsettles clients and accentuates weaknesses rather than strengths. Her tests showed that she was basically emotionally healthy and interpersonally mature, had good judgment and reflective control, and could resiliently recover from being overcome by her power. But in my concluding summary of all of her tests, I suggested that "the only limitation I could foresee, and it might not be a limitation if she wished to move others, might be that in her struggle to reconcile the opposites of maleness and femaleness under the dominance of feminism, she could be vulnerable to imposing arbitrarily a preconceived ideology on her experience—

and perhaps risk being possessed by the idea of being a great earth mother."

Marty emotionally understood my reservations. Unbeknownst to me, she had focused in therapy on how "to understand and be more conscious of my charisma and always remember that I am ordinary," that she was not the powerful great earth mother, the priestess of all. "I'm not extraordinarily good and holy and wonderful. I am not extraordinarily awful either." She succinctly and vividly interpreted the meaning of her own power. "I think much of my trouble has been my struggle with my power. I see myself as a powerful person and I need to make almost everyone else powerless to take care of them and I resent that because who would then take care of me?"

Marty's commitment to feminism was her way to integrate her own androgynous strengths; she used her masculine, forcefully assertive leadership talents to fulfill her feminine nurturing image of the ideal marriage and world. She could thus keep her intense feminism from leading to a single-minded fanaticism, as has occurred throughout history in members of religious cults. This single-mindedness could result in her losing control and so becoming unhealthy.

Marty's Feminist Vision

Just what did feminism, the fifth critical key to understanding her success, mean to Marty? Feminism provided her with the route back to the instinctual strength of her own femininity. She only began to accept it when she overcame her childhood resentment about her premature nurturing role that tenaciously held her in its grip for some thirty years. In her mid-forties, she said of her feminism:

> I have made a commitment to women. I always will be committed to women. I believe that by our nature as women that we are priestesses. Because of our cyclicity, the cycles we experience, the possibility of birth and death every month, we understand the cycles of the universe, the change of the seasons. We have the ability to celebrate life and death and all of their transformations. I celebrate all of the problems that have given women trouble in the past. I love that I can menstruate. I love that I am able to bear and

nurse children. I love that I am empathetic, as long as I am taking care of myself. I love that I can connect with other women and form very supportive groups and experience a spiritual bond with my sisters. I love the history I have as a woman and all of the models I have of women throughout history.

At the end of my first meeting with Marty, she told me of her compelling vision that gathered up all of her talents and energies to which she felt called to devote her life. It was a vision of "total equality in which women are in all positions of authority in business and government, where other married couples are experimenting [with] exchanging roles so ours doesn't look so strange. And where men can form their own brotherhood and not depend on women to help them learn how to connect with each other and us."

I, Andy, and Marty believed at the time I first described their story in *Fulfilling Lives* that they would travel the same path the rest of their lives. From what you now know of their story and of the equilibrating principle, can you guess where their future paths led them? And can you guess why ten years later, they would not have been selected by all of my tests and their peers as the study's most all-round fulfilled *couple*?

Chapter 6

Marty and Andy: Soul Mates Finding Their Own Paths

For several years after my visit in 1983, Marty and Andy felt good about each other and their lives. About Marty, Andy said, "We call each other soul mates. We think in complementary patterns, which is very unusual, very hopeful, and very productive. She was very good at getting me to be more expressive about my feelings," which he had claimed ten years earlier to be the opening to his creative energy.

About Andy, Marty reflected, "I loved Andy so much. We are soul mates. We connected from a very core place. We didn't have to explain [ourselves on] core issues. Our leisure life was very connected. We could play together very well. Our sex life was quite wonderful. . . . We really connected at the core with very strong emotional feelings. We still cry with each other." Intriguingly, both continue to this day to refer to the other as a soul mate.

Both also continued on the same professional path they had been traveling for years. During these busy years, Marty collaborated with Andy on his burgeoning research and writing projects. She also co-authored a feminist book, continued to provide workshops, and organized women's self-help groups. Recently, she has begun to shift her energies from political activism to empowering women by means of private counseling and to creating healing spiritual communities for women.

Andy's years of hard work began to pay off in exceptional achievement and recognition shortly after my visit in 1983. His years of research on male sexual disorders, a pioneering discovery of a new neurological disorder, and the creation of a model treatment center—now replicated in more than sixty locales—have been recognized by numerous national and international awards. He has reported his biomedical research in more than eighty technical articles, authored and edited four books, contributed more than twenty chapters to standard textbooks in his field, keynoted international conferences, given more than seventy conference presentations, and is a reviewer for and/or on the boards of more than ten prestigious journals and organizations. His leadership potential has been recognized by appointments to national commissions in his area of expertise as well as to various university administrative positions. Research continues to be his first love, however, and he continues it to this day in America and abroad with other colleagues. Recently, he has been nominated for a prestigious award honoring productivity and character.

Andy has received numerous unsolicited job offers for years. "Every time I open one door, five others are now available to me." Succeeding, as he exclaimed, "beyond my wildest expectations," Andy finally received an enticing job offer neither he nor Marty could refuse. It appealed to both to return to the Boston area, where Marty could be near her family and they and their daughters could become part of a cultural milieu they valued.

Their move to Boston proved to be bittersweet. It culminated in the destruction of their marriage by the god Bacchus and the poetess Sappho of the Greek island of Lesbos. The tragedy I had previously sensed was gripping them fatefully played itself out to its inexorable ending.

Marty's Path Through Her Crises

Marty's high hopes for recreating her former productive life in Boston collapsed. Physically severing her relationship with her co-author disrupted their collaborative interpersonal style and led to mutual recriminations, feelings of rejection, and torturous efforts to complete the book. She encountered much more difficulty than she anticipated reestablishing her counseling practice in Boston's more staid and closed culture. More discouragingly, Marty "couldn't find . . . [her] tribe"—a congenial feminist group that had always been a source of her strength and vitality. Andy's focused absorption in reestablishing his program in an inhospitable setting only contributed further to their drifting apart, which they didn't discuss. Emotionally bereft and lonely, Marty turned increasingly to alcohol's solace and soon "hit bottom."

Crisis after crisis then cascaded on Marty to make her question if life was still worth living: Deepening alcoholism. The death of her father, with whom she had become reconciled. Increasing strains with Andy, who she felt did not understand and support her. The intensification of her sexuality and coming out to Andy and her daughters as a lesbian. Andy's response—the divorce he initiated, his precipitous remarriage, and the arrival shortly thereafter of another daughter. Andy's second near-fatal car accident and declining mobility. Acute worry about their adolescent daughters, one of whom required a month-long hospitalization for anorexia and depression. The daughter's subsequent promiscuous sexual AIDS-risking activity which may have been a delayed reaction to possible sexual abuse by a relative and to the loss of a drug-dealing lover in a car accident.

Marty's alcoholism, emergent lesbianism, and divorce were her key crises that sorely tested her emotional resilience and ability to create a healthier path to wholeness.

Alcoholism

"Marty, what do you mean by your alcoholism?" Her paraphrased explanation was:

> I had to drink every day by noontime. I stopped eating lunch and took a lot of wine. When I came home, I would be frantic if there was no wine. I drank bourbon as if it were wine. I fell asleep early, only to wake up around three in the morning to take Valium, which I did on a daily basis. I never drank, however, upon awakening. I was irrational a lot of the time. I got angry, yelled, shut myself in my room, and thought the world and the kids were against me.
>
> My grandfather was an alcoholic. I think I was an alcoholic all along. It was a good place to hide from my sexuality. My drinking goes back to the years in Atlanta. I do not remember many aspects of the move to Boston outside of my alcoholic blur. I lost touch with all of my wonderful resources: my strengths, adaptability, courage. Andy continued to be my drinking buddy. He introduced

me to taking Valium after I had been drinking; he was taking a lot of Valium himself. He did not understand me; he was in a state of denial until just recently, when he admitted I may have been alcoholic. I was really angry with him. But I still feel it was my responsibility; I was an adult.

Puzzled why Marty did not feel that Andy understood and supported her, I asked how good a partner had he been since their move.

"Not very good."

"Why?"

Testily, Marty replied "He was a good partner as long as he was the sick one and I was the able one. As soon as I became disabled, he couldn't take over the other role. He resented me for not being the strong guide, the supportive woman."

Confronted by her daughters and another drinking buddy, who told her that she was an alcoholic, Marty attended Alcoholics Anonymous sessions, which she still goes to. Sober for five years, she ranks as her most important goal to fulfill before she dies to "stay sober a day at a time."

Andy agreed that Marty felt he hadn't stood by her during her alcoholic crisis and then indignantly claimed, "That's bull shit. I started to go to Alcoholic Anonymous meetings with her. She wanted me to go to Al-Anon meetings with the fervor that she went to AA meetings. I wasn't feeling the pain that she was feeling. She kept working, kept mothering, and kept being a wife though our sex life had dried up. She was functioning, not having alcoholic bouts."

Lesbianism Out of the Closet

Marty's offhand comment that her alcoholism was a "good place to hide from her sexuality" provoked me to probe what she meant by "her sexuality." I had earlier thought she had fully accepted and integrated it with her calling as a feminist. Despite loving Andy, her soul mate, and despite her deepening devotion to her daughters, Marty's inner restlessness had persisted. "My lesbianism was bubbling under. . . [my drinking] the whole time." Then one day she no longer denied its full expression. She emotionally accepted and "owned . . . [her] authentic self as a lesbian."

Because I have long felt that gayness has a different meaning to males than lesbianism does to females, I asked her to tell me what lesbianism meant to her.

> Being a gay male is based much more on sex. Being a lesbian is more about empowerment as a woman: loving myself as a woman, socializing with women, praying with women, which is why I entered the convent. I love watching women growing and getting stronger. Because I love myself as a woman . . . [I have a] real sense of sameness and of relationality.

"Why call this lesbianism?"

> Because it is shared erotic intimacy. Erotic for me is about mind, body, and spirit, not specifically genital. For me to call myself a lesbian is . . . [to make a] political statement. It is important to name it; naming is empowering. I want to be very clear that it is not just an eighteenth-century passionate friendship. It is a commitment to share my life, my love, my politics, my spirituality with another woman. I give it the name *lesbian* because I want it to stand out, to be known and seen. That is why I have a rainbow sticker and pink triangle on my car. I don't want my lesbianism to so blend that we are hiding it.

"How does being a lesbian differ from being a sister in a convent?"

> Because of the erotic piece, though that piece was there also for a lot of women. . . . I am realizing just how spiritual sex is. Like for me a spiritual experience, a transcendence, . . . a real letting in. . . . A woman's body is like a cave and it's a very sacred space, from where we come, our children come. For me to go in there is for me to go into a very sacred space where I have to light candles and incense and play music.

Finding out that she was a lesbian did not surprise Andy, but it caused the final separation he had seen coming for some time.

Divorce

Preoccupied with transferring his research to Boston and maintaining its momentum but aware of Marty's increasing involvement with lesbians, Andy did not have the energy to open old wounds again. "After having gone through a previous separation and feeling we had repaired a leaky boat I was not anxious to repair the boat that was leaking again. . . . She has this gift for picking out lesbian women. She had friends who came from Atlanta. They were all lesbians crawling out of the woodwork. It had happened before, so I wasn't really threatened by it."

"But Andy, you have known for more than fifteen years that she had lesbian friends and was probably a lesbian. What changed to lead to the death of your marriage this time?"

Marty's therapist in Atlanta had felt her lesbianism was part of a lingering adolescent phase that she was still going through. So Andy replied:

> I was willing to accept that. She loved me and I loved her. I knew she was probably bisexual. We were sexually active again. So I thought she had gotten her homosexuality out of her system . . . . [But that] was only temporary and came back stronger than ever. . . . Our marriage wasn't going to continue if she is an openly declared lesbian. . . . Sexual relations are important to me. I don't want to share her with anybody. Being a lesbian is not just a question of what you do in the sack. It's a whole lifestyle—your friends and social activities. There was absolutely no way I could do it. At this point, I didn't want to invest anything more about making her bi or hetero.

To prepare their daughters for their divorce, all four entered family therapy which helped their relationships, especially Marty's and Andy's. Marty said that "we shared moments of recognizing our closeness. There was a lot of love and affection there."

Andy did not look forward to another separation, living alone, and trying to manage the daily tasks of living given his spreading disability. So it was not long before he began dating Betty, an unmarried woman in her early forties, who was sympathetic to his disability. Andy's and Marty's separation had been "reasonable." They continued to work together to help their daughters, but when Andy told her about Betty, Marty exploded. According to him, "She went into a rage. She was jealous, angry, made obscene phone calls to me. It was awful, just awful.... [She accused me] of ruining her life. Extraordinary." According to her, "We were really tearing each other apart during the divorce. I especially was very angry, but I am now at a different place about that."

Two soul mates can be tightly entwined. Ferocious anger sometimes is the emotional knife necessary to cut the ties—though I doubt Marty's and Andy's ties will ever be fully severed. While listening to them, I felt not only their respect but also their enduring love for each other. Their tragedy is that the gods on Mount Olympus refused to allow them to live out their lives as a couple.

Marty's Path to Wholeness

When I met Marty again for our interview, I immediately sensed a difference. Her greeting was as warm and exuberant as it had been our first meeting. But this time I felt a more gentle, inwardly composed, almost serene, presence—not the forceful, absorbing, almost larger-than-life presence of a decade ago. How had she moved through her stormy crises to draw out their potential for continued maturing?

Fully accepting and affirming her lesbianism to Andy, her daughters, her mother, (and the world by way of her car stickers) freed her from years of doubts, restlessness, and attempts to hide her real self from others as well as from herself. As she later told me, "No more secrets; no more hiding myself in some places and not in others.... I feel very integrated, very much in the same place. I had not really come out to myself.... I have a great love and respect for the women who have gone before me who have lost their families and lives because of their sexuality and political beliefs. I want to join the ranks of the fighters.... I want to be fully out with them." Her oldest daughter said it was about time she told them. Her youngest has since mounted a campaign to provide more support to bisexual and gay kids at her school. Marty's mother is eager to meet her new love, Anne.

Marty's path to self-acceptance and wholeness has opened her to love more fully. "I am very, very moved by ... [Anne] and am having reactions I've never had to anyone before. I have everything in this relationship I have ever wanted. First time I feel in love ... really in love. I live in love." Marty's love far transcends sex by, she said, at least 95 percent.

Anne, a single woman about Marty's age, neither thinks of herself as a lesbian nor knows Marty's past way of living out her lesbianism. She "gets a little off-center . . . afraid of thinking of me like this with others." What grounds Marty's love is their shared experience: similar blue-collar Catholic families, oldest of large families for which each had to assume parenting responsibilities, and similar spiritual rituals and healing values. What transforms such a communion of experience into love for Marty is Anne's "deep-heart connection with God" and Marty's "deep-heart connection with Anne." It is a connection that is an equal exchange of energy. "I feel as if when I connect with her mentally or physically or emotionally there is someone who is there coming back to me with whatever I am putting out. . . . We meet at the same place at the same time with each other. . . . She is very present, very present," which, of course, is what love is: being fully present in the presence of the other. No secrets; no closets in which to hide; no defenses to shield oneself.

Like Billie, Marty accepts her life as she has lived it, despite her crises. She feels that she is still growing, even stretching, though her path is starting to turn more toward fulfilling her "softer" side, as she calls it. She no longer feels driven to "advertise . . . [myself] quite as loudly as I used to or to have the following that I used to have. I had found some of my self-worth in people's reactions to me and I used to crave people to react dramatically to me. I don't need to do that anymore."

Marty also feels she has lived a fulfilled life. Optimistic about the direction of her life's path, she looks forward to creating residential, spiritually centered, healing centers for women. If her daughters asked her "What is there to live for?" she would tell them, "Life is a drama . . . you live for the experience of living. We live to learn that we can overcome; that we can have joy; that we can experience each other; that we can just have fun. I want to know how the story ends."

Sources of Marty's Resilience

While Marty continued to draw on her earlier sources of strength, two in particular contributed to her continued maturing: her emotional reconciliation with her parents and the integration of her lesbianism with her spirituality.

Reconciliation with Parents. Now in her mid-fifties, Marty is finally inwardly at peace with her father and mother. Her father's sobriety showed her she could conquer her own alcoholism. Her recovery from alcohol was the bridge to reconnect with him. As they became closer, they playfully kidded each other about their shared experiences. "We would sit here arguing who is the worst drunk. To his 'You never peed in the closet,' I would joke 'You don't have to pee in a closet to be a big drunk.' It was wonderful. . . . His favorite expression was 'Just do it.' I would say, 'I can't do it.' He then would say 'Make time. If you really want to do something, just do it.'"

Marty has also finally accepted her mother as the model of the strong woman she has always valued. She is most grateful that her mother "hung in there [after her father died] and that she found a way to get strong herself. . . . She just pulled her life together. Taking care of her house by herself. Always busy doing things. . . . She has a lot of strengths that she has gotten access to by herself. If she did, I can. . . . She is wonderful. I am so proud of her. I am crazy about . . . [her]."

Eroticism Integrated with Spirituality. Though Marty's eroticism persists to this day, it is being transformed and directed into a deepening spiritual life, which Anne models and supports. For Marty, "spirituality is about my connectedness to the spirit of the earth, the spirit of God in the earth and universe, and the spirit of other people."

"What do you mean by spirit, Marty?"

"The life force that is not containable. It is what happens between us, what we feel and can't describe sometimes. I feel very spiritual when I go into a deep part of myself and feel peace. It's a feeling of transcendence sometimes . . . a sense of connectedness of everything."

Marty is describing the ineffable sense of universal connectedness that is at the heart of mysticism, an experience of a boundless wholeness. Eroticism, as our life force that connects us with the world, then becomes the source of and a way to develop passionate ties and commitments. Marty graphically described her eroticism this way: "I still have a very, very strong commitment to the guts of everything. I love the visceral aspects of sex, of food, of walking in the mud, of loving the earth, and loving all that which I have always loved. I see the spiritual in everything."

Alcoholics Anonymous is Marty's natural connecting path to recovery. Of its twelve steps to health, the second and eleventh are her favorites. In her words, "There is a power greater than myself that can restore my sanity" and "through prayer and meditation, I can make contact with this higher power." For Marty, God is a "power greater than myself [that] is taking care of me and my life." Marty is no longer the goddess, the guru, the priestess of archetypal power. She has let go of the megalomania that almost possessed her.

Marty's twisting and turning paths through the brambles and thorns of her crises to wholeness have resulted in dramatic maturing and in the greater self-acceptance and serenity I felt in our greeting.

Not until Marty emotionally accepted her own lesbianism—her own empowerment as a woman as she defined it—did she bring her divided selves together. At last, she acts with integrity wherever she is or whoever she is with. Lesbianism integrates her feminist beliefs with her eroticism and spirituality. The consequence is a major spurt in maturity. Its signs are her capacity to love more fully, her released enthusiasm for new interests and commitments, and her transcendence of her alcoholic and sexual addictions.

When I again asked Marty the question I had asked ten years earlier—"What are your bedrock, strongest convictions and commitments, the ultimate source of your energy?"—she replied similarly but more simply: "Women. The women's movement. My spirituality."

I hope you have empathically walked with Marty on her path and not condemned her for having taken the path that she did to grow as maturely as she has. Don't dismiss what she has told us because of her treatment of Andy, her alcoholism, or her lesbianism. She is an extraordinarily honest person, with great integrity and compassion for her sisters. She has steadfastly and courageously searched for the path to wholeness as a woman with a deep-heart connection to God.

Andy's Path Through His Trials

Listening to Andy's tale about his last ten years brought Old Testament's Job to mind. A good and successful man of unimpeachable integrity and devotion, Job endured every miserable and sorrowful trial that the Devil inflicted. Though being sorely tried, Andy is no modern-day Job. Job ceaselessly complained, wailed, and moaned, demanding why God allowed the Devil to persecute his obedient servant so mercilessly. Andy has never complained, wailed, or moaned. I did, however, feel a twinge of resigned sorrow as he looked back over the past ten years and then forward to his next.

His brilliantly creative career is a major source of comfort, enabling him to endure his more personal crises. Typical of Andy, he is quietly proud of his achievements. Modestly—almost matter-of-factly—he told me a comment a visitor made about his program a few hours before our interview: "You are running the premier program in the world. I am in the presence of the world's expert." But he no longer thinks of his career as central to his fulfillment. "I feel I have had my career. It would not break my heart if I had to retire tomorrow. I wouldn't like it. I just feel I have done so much."

Rather the undercurrent of sadness I felt welling up came from two sources: his "extraordinary anguish" about his oldest daughter's health and current travails, and his progressive disability whose stabilization or reversal he rated as improbable.

Trials of His Oldest Daughter

Before he dies, the wish Andy wants to fulfill above all others is to help his oldest child regain her health as well as helping his children become more mature and happy adults. He and Marty are working closely with each other to help their adolescent daughters cope more healthily. Andy invites them to his home several times a week, takes each out weekly for a special treat, and is encouraging the oldest to get professional assistance. Marty appreciatively said of his efforts, "Andy has been extremely active in working with the girls and with me. We go to therapy together. We go separately. We go with the girls. He makes a lot of the contacts. He makes sure they get there. He took a dry run out to a new therapist. He is actually making changes in his own schedule. He can be very loving and caring with the kids. . . . He is now making these and other changes."

Spreading Paralyses

Andy is optimistic that he will fulfill his hopes for his children before he dies. He is not hopeful that he can maintain his health—his most important value nowadays. "With good health, I could do so much." It is not that Andy is in bad health. He rarely gets sick; his blood pressure and cholesterol are low; he still has a lot of sexual vitality. But his disability is insidiously encroaching on his freedom to move his legs and increasingly his arms. Andy now relies as much as possible on labor-saving devices and others' help to conserve his energy and limit his movements, which cause him pain. He uses motorized scooters; Betty helps him dress in the morning; he must rest his arm on supports to be able to eat. "My left arm is getting weaker day-by-day. . . . I have no great intense pain, not the pain of cancer in the bone. Just a chronic pain. Every time I use my arm it hurts. . . . With this weakness in my arm I cry myself to sleep . . . The sweetest thing would be to die. I don't want to end my life; I just want to end the pain."

Shortly after his marriage to Betty, Andy miraculously walked away from an accident—for which he was faultless—that totaled his car. Two days later, he was found in a coma. He has no memory of his first three hospital days. Other symptoms of brain impairment—such as incoherent speech and olfactory hallucinations—terrified his daughters. Misdiagnosis and inappropriate drug treatment, combined with his low energy level, delayed his return to work for three months. Andy now says of his body, "It feels old because it is infirm; my mind feels like I am twenty-nine or thirty-five."

Moreover, Andy's crises are taking a toll on his mental health and happiness. For the first time in the thirty-five years I have known him, telltale signs of a dark undercurrent are appearing: asides in the interview indicating concern about his mental health, increased moodiness and emotionality, and slippage in his ratings of his satisfaction with his life and happiness.

As his disability progresses, he understandably has begun to show signs of apprehension about his future. Andy kept qualifying his hopes with the words "If I am physically able." His first comment in the interview was, "Some things I can no longer do. I used to play the piano quite a bit and to do that requires bending my arm up and down. . . . Two years ago, I could play three hours; for me, that was a great satisfaction . . . a great release. I can't play any more." Contrast the tone of his associations to the same phrases I gave to Billie. Andy replied to "Mid- and late forties" with "Young, vibrant, healthy, intelligent, lively" and to "Mid-fifties" with "Apprehension, sadness, concern about finances, concern about health, wondering how I will fill my retirement years." For the first time, Andy referred to himself as becoming a quadriplegic—having limited use of all his limbs. In retirement, he would enjoy gardening, traveling, and playing music—"if I am physically able."

Despite these gloomy wellings from the darker undercurrent that I sensed, Andy rated himself to be quite optimistic and hopeful. I asked him how else he might live in order to feel he had lived a fulfilled life. He replied, "I feel I have lived a very fulfilled life, almost several times over. . . . [I have had] several life-threatening illnesses, three marriages, several families. I have struggled to find myself in a career and I've done it. I have developed interests in several areas; I have had success in securing grants for my research, in receiving awards, and in my publications. I have to say I feel very fulfilled." And a few minutes later, in response to a question about dying, he said, "I think about dying, being out of control, others sticking tubes down me. . . . I'm terrified of the process of dying but I don't fear death at all."

I turn now to the question, "What are Andy's strengths that enable him to now live an even more fulfilled life in his fifties—despite his Jobian crises that could devastate those of us less blessed with his strengths?"

Sources of Strength

As Marty did, so Andy did also. He drew on his earlier strengths as he coped with his crises. His parents continue to provide the love and support that he needs. But as he learns how agonizing parenting can be and anticipates the death of both parents within the next ten years, he appreciates them more both as persons and as parents. "I am very close to my mother and fond of my father. I feel they have done extraordinary parenting with me, helping me through my various crises."

Andy's androgyny and maturity also continue to be sources of strength. I pressed him to explain his remarkable creativity, productivity, and international reputation. Andy returned to the same answer he gave me in his mid-forties. Although he was not unusually intelligent or a "real superstar in one area," he has skills to do well in a number of areas. He traces his success to his superb educational preparation—"chance favors the prepared mind." Most important, however, has been the continuing integration of his androgynous strengths—his emotionality and his disciplined intellectuality. He has found a way to apply them to professional areas of special personal meaning to him, such as health and sexuality.

Stabilization of Masculinity. Andy's growth from his mid-forties into his fifties tapped increasingly into typically masculine strengths that were undeveloped. Setting up national and international conferences brought out assertive and leadership strengths that have enabled him to project his creative discoveries onto a national and international stage. The same strengths have allowed him to organize his clinics in ways that continue to bring him recognition. Committee and administrative positions also showed him how much he enjoyed exercising power and that he could stand his ground and defend his positions. Has his equilibrating principle been telling him that he might have overdeveloped his softer side to accommodate Marty's demands? He may have had to develop his more forceful and decisive self in order to grow more wholly—and be prepared to meet the impending physical crisis he senses is looming.

Maturity's Contribution to Vocational Success. More complicated to understand, however, is why Andy's vocational success has not been hampered or undermined by his unremitting marital, parental, health, and life-threatening crises. How can he continue to move from one vocational success to another? Because of his maturity. He continues to mature; he now scores higher on maturity than he did in his forties. Maturity provides the resources to adapt to crises. Successful adaptation contributes to greater strength. Andy feels he has become a stronger person the past decade.

Looking back now to my understanding of his strengths in his mid-forties, I underestimated his exemplary determination and command of his talents and energies. At first glance, he is no longer a superb example of all-round success and fulfillment. A second glance tells us that each of his crises was precipitated by forces not under his control: Marty's lesbianism, his daughter's problems, his expanding disability, and his second car accident. What is critical is how he is adapting to each. He is coping as maturely as the realities of his life permit. He is beginning to anticipate the ultimate test of his maturity: the smaller and smaller perimeter his growing disability is inexorably causing. But like other strong individuals, such as Stephen Hawking, Britain's brilliant quadriplegic physicist, I predict Andy will continue to make superb use of himself as long as he has his mind with which to roam the world. Already, he is teaching himself the Italian he has always wanted to master, with the hope that *if physically able* he can revisit his ancestral homeland.

Again, I posed the question I had asked ten years earlier: "What gives your life meaning? From what do you draw your staying power?"

Andy answered simply, "I have great faith in myself . . . a resilience and capacity to mobilize my and other people's resources. . . . I can make a difference and I have made a difference. That is within my reach. . . . I have the ability to empower myself and others and to give to others." Like Marty, who wants to create healing centers for women, Andy's vision is to create and fund a foundation to find cures for the neurological syndrome he discovered.

Recall Andy's answer ten years ago to my questions, "Where is your potential growing edge? Where could you be developing more?" He said, "I have lived life very fully. It has been a very rich life, full of a lot of pain and worry and setbacks, but what I haven't done very well is to integrate the pain and the triumph. I sort of see that as my next task."

Ten years later, has not Andy now succeeded in integrating his pain and his triumphs?"

I hope you have not dismissed Billie's, Marty's, and Andy's larger-than-life uniqueness as not helpful for understanding how to grow up to succeed and live a life of hope. Why not pause and reflect now and draw some lessons to remember from their lives? Then compare them with the lessons—both Roger's and mine—that I share with you in the next chapter.

Chapter 7

Eleven Insights into Becoming an Adult

Each us will take insights away from Billie's, Andy's, and Marty's stories that speak to us at this time in our lives. After quoting Roger's, because they nicely capture what I hope most readers will remember, I'll add several of my own.

1. Growing up is a lot more complicated than I had thought.

Yes. There are no simple *Reader's Digest* formulas to become more mature. There are no easy ways to change ourselves.

2. It's a damn slow process.

There are no quick fixes, "maturing pills," adult education courses, psychic credit cards, weekend self-help growth groups, or magical solutions for growing up that so many of us are looking for today. Miraculous conversions happen only to the few, like Saul of Tarsus on his way to Damascus; besides, their maturing effects probably endure for only a few of those few. Just how many converted non-backsliding Saint Pauls do you know? Billie and Marty tell us that we still can become healthy persons or find ourselves in our forties and fifties—if we work hard enough at our own maturing.

3. Learn how to endure and use the pain caused by uncertainty, misfortunes, and provocations of partners like Marty to adapt more effectively. Persist like Billie to find that balance between adjusting to others and fulfilling personal needs.

When we deny threats, flee into drugs, and withdraw to avoid frustration, anxiety, and boredom, we diminish the impetus to become more mature. To grow up to succeed requires the will to tolerate frustration and resist the temptation of self-indulgent escapades, as well as the great determination and persistence of an Andy.

4. *I'll never be finally "grown up" because there'll always be some new challenge to stretch me. Even ones I'll create for myself.*

I'd phrase Roger's insight somewhat differently: "I can continue to grow all my life. I don't have to say near the end of my life what Winston Churchill reportedly said of his, 'I'm bored with living.'" Billie says we can even look forward to our dying; Marty wants to know how her story is going to end.

5. *Many things can help me grow; but maturing goes fastest when I'm in a relationship with a loved one.*

Almost everything that makes us human comes from our relationships with others: our language, way of thinking, values, and attitudes about ourselves. Many experiences contribute to maturing. Because we are the social animals that Aristotle said we are, our relationships with others can be the most powerful generator of healthy growth. However, we have to be vulnerable to and educable in such relationships. Andy credited Marty's provocations for his emotional growth, which he believed had been indispensable to his vocational creativity.

6. *A lot can go wrong while growing up, but I have a self-regulating, psychic gyroscope that can help me grow healthily, if I could read its messages accurately and learn how to go in the direction it is pointing in.*

Definitely. Don't ever ignore your equilibrating principle.

7. *I don't have to be a permanent prisoner of what has gotten me to where I am now. Though it may take a lot of work, as Billie and the Millers have shown me, I can continue to grow despite my past. There's always hope.*

Yes, mature persons are hopeful; they have the psychic resources to alter their environment or themselves more effectively. Less mature persons don't. But even the most discouraged, messed-up person can still hope. The study's brightest man had been an alcoholic for nine years; he went down and down until he joined the homeless camped out under a bridge. I don't fully understand why, but one day he picked himself up to begin the long climb to where he was when I saw him in his late forties: happily living with his lover, economically flourishing, and vocationally satisfied. He died of AIDS with great dignity, so I was told by his co-workers, four years after I had seen him.

G. E. Vaillant and C. O. Valliant, studying how Harvard alumni changed over the years, pithily, and wisely too, said, "The things that go right in our lives do predict future successes and the events that go wrong in our lives do not forever damn us."[1] Billie, the Millers, and the remaining men and women of the study would qualify their advice by saying, *"if* we are mature and androgynous." That *if* is crucial.

I have three of my own reflections that may be helpful.

8. *A traumatic childhood, a crippling handicap, or severe stress is not necessary to grow up healthily."*

Children who experience a lot of stress *but learn how to grow from it*—I'd suggest because they are more mature and have a richer variety of androgynous strengths on which to draw—can turn out to be more self-directing and confident adults than children who serenely sail from one advantage to another in life. Why? The pubertal boy who fails to sprout apace with his friends, does not make the basketball shots as easily, and is mystified about why his friends talk so much about girls must find other ways to establish his competence among his peers. An unattractive, moody, unpredictable girl who struggles with her emotionality and relationships with other girls and boys must learn to develop alternative ways to get along with herself and others. Billie, Andy, and Marty are sterling examples of how we can bounce back from early disaster.

However, being abused by an alcoholic parent or losing the use of a leg is not essential to learn how to develop the strengths necessary to succeed. The study's 105 men and women tell us just the opposite. Those best able to cope with the problems of living generally came, as the Vaillants said, from favorable homes and had nontraumatic childhoods. Billie and the Millers are singular exceptions to what I found for the entire group. But then they were selected as singular examples of success.

9. While individuals take apparently idiosyncratic and diverse paths to maturing, their trek can be described in similar ways.

The paths lead to minds, characters, and selves that are reflectively aware, other-centered, well integrated, stable, and autonomous. They lead in the same direction for people of any age, gender, and cultural background, when they are free to follow their inner gyroscopes—their equilibrating principles. The circumstances of Billie's, Andy's, and Marty's lives and their seemingly different paths don't appear to be similar. But their paths eventually began to converge as they became more mature. They became more reflective and caring about others. They became more integrated, centered, and in better command of their talents and impulses. They began to be more whole persons of integrity.

10. The model of maturing identifies the critical strengths that contribute to how well we adapt to crises.

Living is seldom crisis-free. The kind of crisis that we face is not what really matters. What counts is how we go about resolving the crisis in ways that free us to continue maturing. That is what contributes to our success and well-being. When raising children, teach them the skills of living; when counseling or ministering to adolescents or adults, aid them to master the skills of coping (or problem-solving, in Billie's words) and adapting.

11. Becoming more mature is not the same as becoming more androgynous.

Though both maturity and androgyny contribute to success, they are not the same. Mature men and women are reliably androgynous, or, if you like, androgynous persons are highly likely to be mature. However, maturity is not equivalent to or exactly the same as androgyny. You cannot clone mature persons and then call them androgynous. While you would recognize some of the same strengths in mature and in androgynous persons, they would still be recognizably different. An androgynous male might be quite masculine in his competitiveness and typically feminine in his warmth and expressiveness but not be mature. Though maturity and androgyny go hand in hand in some individuals—like Billie and Andy—they don't always coincide. For example, they weren't integrated in Marty until she reached her fifties.

Maturity and androgyny more likely coincide in women than in men. If you are a mature woman, those who know you well would describe you as very androgynous. In their eyes, you would be seen as typically feminine, especially in your interpersonal relationships. Strengths like your understanding, sensitivity to others' feelings, and compassion would be obvious. They would also think of you as masculine, though to a lesser extent, because of your self-reliance, decisiveness, and willingness to stand up for your beliefs—all signs that research has shown describe a maturing autonomy.

On the other hand, if you are a mature man, you would not be seen quite so clearly by your peers as androgynous, though you would be thought of as typically masculine because of your assertiveness, decisiveness, and risk-taking strengths. Mature men are neither more nor less competitive, aggressive, dominant, or self-sufficient than less mature men. Acting like a fighting cock may prove your masculinity to other cocks—and even to some impressionable hens—but says nothing about how mature you are.

Exploring the relationship between maturity and androgyny is a prelude to how I will now try to tease out of the individual lives of 105 men and women the strengths *essential* to succeed as marital partners, lovers, and parents. What qualities do Billie, Andy, and Marty share that help us understand our own and others' familial successes? True, their paths are unique. However, their dilemmas are ours as well: adapting to the changing meanings of our femaleness and maleness, fulfilling our and our partner's sexual needs, and becoming satisfied and competent parents raising healthy children. What strengths do we need to adapt successfully to such changes and challenges?

Chapter 8

Becoming a Successful Marital Partner

Despite the excruciating turmoil of many contemporary families, men and women still rank succeeding in familial roles—their marital and parental ones—to be their most important sources of satisfaction. So the question to ask has to be, "What strengths are necessary to create successful marital and parental relationships and therefore stronger families?" Its answer depends on what we mean by "successful." Familial success was much easier to describe fifty years ago than today. Then, society defined it more clearly and firmly as a marriage and family that stayed together until death then did them part.

I remember my grandparents' golden wedding celebration, where they were toasted for their marital success. But my seventy-seven-year-old grandmother confided shortly before she died, "I've lived with your grandfather fifty-five years, and for more than fifty of them I wanted to get a divorce, but I never had the courage. No one has ever known. Thankfully, he never has." He lived to be ninety-four and never did. Divorce would have been a humiliating personal failure and disgrace; it still is for many. Marital researchers of the day would have identified both as exemplars of familial success. They had fulfilled their contract with society.

Fifty years later, society's definition of familial success is much less clear-cut. Society's laws and expectations about how we should fulfill our roles are less prescriptive; some have just withered away. The Census Bureau now counts cohabiting unmarried couples. More couples don't get a marriage license until their first child is on the way. Married women retain their family names. Some churches marry gays. Divorce has lost its stigma. Pregnant unmarried teenagers no longer must hide in homes for unwed mothers. Children born out of wedlock are no longer called "bastards". A minority of American children are now raised in traditional families. The majority of children will spend some part of their growing-up years with only one parent.

The changing meanings of *marital partner,* even of *parent,* reflect a fundamental change in how we think about successful intimate relationships. The largest national survey of Americans' mental health yet done, which originated forty years ago and was repeated twenty years later, showed just how much things have changed. This study found that success was no longer defined by how well we adjusted to society's expectations of how we fulfill our roles. Success was defined by how personally fulfilled we felt in our familial roles.

Andy and Marty mirrored quite well the changing cultural definition of successful familial relationships. Rather than continuing to adjust to societal norms about what a good marital partner and parent should be, they rejected these norms. Marty freed herself from what society, and she, had once thought a good wife should do: keep the house spotless and family fed with prize-winning apple pies, chauffeur the kids around without complaining, and follow her husband to Buffalo and then Great Falls. She vigorously rejected that she be 95 percent responsible for raising healthy, happy, and successful children. Andy assumed 50 percent of the responsibility for parenting, even though his colleagues sometimes resented his absence when he was home with the children. Marty created a more self-directed and fulfilling life for herself as a lawyer. Andy tried to alter what society said a man should be. By their mid-forties after years of painful labor, they had created a mutually fulfilling and intimate family life. While saddened that their paths have since diverged, I don't regret initially featuring them as a successful couple. Hazards and barriers can occur along the way that cannot be avoided or overcome—if one or both individuals are to continue to grow and become whole persons.

When our customs and institutions no longer support traditional roles, our personal resources contribute more critically to our success than ever. Adapting to increased freedom demands greater maturity. For many, the balance between adjustment and self-fulfillment in marriage has shifted from adjusting to what a wife and husband are "supposed" to do to primarily fulfilling our individual needs. Our character thereby becomes more crucial in determining how successful we are as partners. When our self-fulfillment rather than adjustment to societal expectations defines marital happiness and success, marriages are at risk when one of the partners does not find it fulfilling—the impasse the Miller's faced. It is not uncommon, for example, for men to feel more happily married and fulfilled than women or for men to believe they are better partners than their wives believe they are.

Karl and Jeannie Baker had a more fragile marriage than Karl believed. A consulting civil engineer, Karl traveled abroad about six months every year, while Jeannie remained home to care for their two adolescent daughters. He described his marriage in glowing terms and himself as a most successful husband, parent, and lover. Jeannie definitely did not. Listening to each describe their marriage, I thought they must be bigamists—I couldn't recognize each from the other's description. Jeannie told me that she was thinking of leaving Karl; after all, he had been leaving her for years. Karl had no inkling of the surprise she was preparing for him and dismissed my suggestion that he pay more attention to his marriage and to Jeannie's fulfillment. Four years later, he wrote to tell me I had been right. Jeannie had left him to search for a more fulfilling relationship.

If you wish to be a good marital partner, then learn how your partner views your relationship. You may feel that a scrappy argument quickens your blood and livens up your relationship; your partner may dread the spat. And while a hasty good-bye peck on your partner's cheek each morning may seem quite adequate to you, your partner could take it as a sign you don't really love him—particularly the one morning you dash out and forget.

Character Strengths Needed for the Ideal Marriage

A rich number of personal qualities, many of them attributes of maturity, are necessary to create a happy and fulfilling marital relationship, according to the study's men and women. These qualities include:

- Love and trust
- Interpersonal communication skills, such as sensitivity to a partner's needs and the ability to share feelings

- Shared interests and responsibilities, such as common work pursuits, and sexual compatibility
- Loyalty and commitment to the relationship, such as making time available for one another
- Sense of humor and other personal strengths, such as cheerfulness, self-confidence, and optimism
- Commitment to honesty and fairness

As the marital balance tips away from adjusting to society's expectations and toward fulfilling individual needs, these personality strengths become more and more necessary to keep a modern marriage alive. Adjusting to the societal expectation that we grin and bear each other "until death do us part" no longer keeps modern couples together—only our character does. Most of the divorced men did not know or could not tell me why their marriages had failed. Their easy reasons were the obvious ones that researchers had identified: arguments about money, children, and sex, or, in Andy's words, "incompatibility."

Today's women know the more intractable reason for marriage failure, however. Since almost all of the study's divorces were initiated by the women—nationally about two-thirds of contemporary divorces are initiated by them—we need to understand what women want from their marriages. They want men to communicate with them in their language. As poets sometimes do, Robert Frost spoke for both men and women in his poem "Home Burial." A wife sharply laments her husband's muteness about the death of their child. He can only talk about how his best birch fence has rotted. He asks why he can't say how he feels and why whatever he does say offends her. She tartly says, "You can't [speak] because you don't know how to speak." She means that he doesn't know how to speak in her language of feelings rather than in his language of impersonal things like his best birch fence. She then continues to speak for many women: "You *couldn't* care!"

But the tragedy is that he does care—in his way. His "best birch," his child, had rotted. Frost captures what we now know. Women and men often speak in different tongues.

The men and women were like those two proverbial ships in the night that silently pass each other by, only occasionally understanding the flashing code of the other. The couples could not communicate *in each other's language.* Like one of Marty's tapes, the women told me over and over, "He's like a computer." "He's afraid of his feelings." "I've lived with him for ten years and I still don't know what he feels." "He comes home exhausted at night and just grunts, while hiding behind his paper, when I ask him about his day."

While we may not have much control over who we "fall in love" with, we can deepen our trust in our relationship by learning how to communicate our needs and feelings more openly and honestly. Andy reminds us that a marriage that lasts nowadays doesn't automatically fall into our laps. We must work ceaselessly to learn how to speak to each other; even then, though soul mates, our relationship still may not endure.

The Personality of Men and Women Who Are Happily Married

We are now ready to answer the following question: "What are people who are happily married (one definition of marital success) *actually* like?" I can also ask a rarely explored second and more stringent question: "What is the personality of men and women whose *partners* are happily married?" Four themes describe men and women who report that they themselves are happily married. None will surprise you. Billie, Andy, and Marty have illustrated each.

Happily Married People Are Competent in Their Other Roles

The first theme is that maritally happy men and women are also *competent* and satisfied marital and sexual partners and parents. Competence in one role goes with competence in others. Why? Because all of our interpersonal relationships require similar strengths. Glance back at the list of virtues essential for a happy marriage. It includes communication skills, commitment, sense of humor, self-confidence, and honesty—qualities that Chapter Two identified as essential in *all* of our principal adult roles.

Of course, there are exceptions. Bill Spaulding was one. He built a successful marketing consulting firm, was chief executive officer, and was respected (though not loved) by his colleagues for his forceful leadership. He learned how to make the "tough" decisions—like firing two key associates, friends of his who had helped create the firm.

But his wife rated him as a dismal failure, not only by her standards but also on *his* criteria of the strengths necessary to create a happy marriage and be a competent father. He was the next-to-worst husband and father of the study, but he saw himself as much more successful. He succeeded in his work because he had a president's power to make others adjust to him. However, the aggressive entrepreneurial strengths that contributed to his firm's success got in the way of succeeding in his wife's living room and bedroom. A *Wall Street Journal* survey of successful businessmen found that bringing such strengths into the living room and bedroom created unhappy marriages. His wife—as a modern woman—knows she has a right to be happy and fulfilled; she is not about to kowtow to his presidential dictates. He was vocationally successful to the public, maritally unsuccessful to his wife. Trouble was obviously looming on the horizon.

Happily Married Men and Women Are Mature

Billie, Andy, and Marty told us how important maturity is to marital happiness and success. Others studying marriages agree. Persons whose marriages last are more self-confident and emotionally healthy; they are also more affectionate, warm, and cheerful than those whose marriages fail.

Happily Married Men and Women Are Androgynous

Again, Billie and the Millers illustrate what the larger group's results showed. Maritally successful men and women share strengths typical of each other. Men satisfied with their wives' companionship are more feminine; women satisfied with their husbands' are more masculine. To appreciate and enjoy being with a partner of the other gender, each must share some of the other's interpersonal strengths. If you are a man, do you enjoy talking with your wife about your feelings and relationships? If you are a woman, do you enjoy competing with and beating him at Scrabble and tennis? How do we understand and anticipate another's needs if we don't share the other's strengths to some degree? If we aren't maturely other-centered, we relate as an outsider, not insider, to the other's personal world. Our partner never feels really understood. Many women in the study felt that way about their partners: "He supports me but he doesn't understand me." One clue to Bill Spaulding's marital failure was that his peers rated him to be the seventh most masculine but fifth *least* feminine man of the study. He had not developed the interpersonal strengths necessary to enter his wife's world empathically, feel how she felt, and so understand her frustration as a wife.

Happily Married People Have Been Happy Since Adolescence

"Obviously," you may be saying. "Of course, happily married persons are happy persons generally." But wait. Not only were they happy in their marriages, but they have been happy at *every* stage of their lives since their teens. The roots of happy marriages reach back at least into our adolescent character. We prepare to succeed maritally long before marriage has even become an idea to romanticize or be scared about.

The Personality of People Whose Partners Are Maritally Happy

What is the personality of people whose *partners* are happy and fulfilled—my strictest test of how good a partner we are? What is an Andy like who made a Marty say, "I feel wonderful. I have such a supportive and loving partner. I have not just a safe place but a very real and honest relationship . . . that makes my marriage an 'exceptionally happy' one." And what is a Marty like who made an Andy rate the likelihood very high that his happy marriage would continue until his death? Their subsequent parting of the ways does not mean their basic personalities suddenly flip-flopped. Rather, Marty's lesbianism— probably constitutionally grounded—had become too high a barrier for Andy to want to get over and accept. But Marty was still willing to remain with him, as she had also during their first separation.

Interpersonally Feminine People Have Happy Marital Partners

Bruce Jackson, one of the study's three unrepentant male chauvinists, illustrates why so many contemporary couples are in trouble. He is a typical "macho" male whose wife eventually got fed up. He had been laid off as a division manager of an electrical equipment company and was looking for another job when I saw him and June. She found his constant presence at home unbearable. He was especially dominating during my visit, perhaps because he was hiding the pain he felt from being fired. He rudely interrupted June, squelched and dismissed every one of her opinions, and refused to help her set the table when asked. When their children tried to stand up to him, she loyally backed him up and went along with his ideas. (June confided to me that their oldest son, Tim—forced to go to a college not of his choosing—had dropped out and was living in the streets of New York. She hadn't told Bruce.) She also told me how much she still loved Bruce.

Three years later I got a call from Bruce, who had found another, less lucrative job. He was desperate, lost, confused. He kept repeating, "She's left me. She's left me. After twenty-five years of marriage, she's left me. We had such a good marriage. She's gone. I have nothing left." He had absolutely no insight into how his steamroller personality had so squashed June that to survive she had to get away from his physical presence. It is a tribute to Bruce's resiliency that he sought counseling, much to my surprise, and tamed his overbearing behavior enough to encourage June to return. But he since seems to have lost his spirit and vitality; he even looks defeated.

If you are a man, the odds are long that your partner will be happily content to live with you if you can honestly answer yes to each of the questions in the following paragraphs. Why not reassure (or disturb) yourself by rating just how good a marital partner you are or would be? Using a 5-point rating scale, give yourself a 5 for each question you unhesitatingly (honestly) agree with, a 4 if you hesitate momentarily, and so on until you have to give yourself a 1 when you almost draw a blank.

First and foremost, *are you an adaptable, cooperative, and yielding person?* According to my unbiased neutered computer, women want to feel that their partners are responsive and open and don't stubbornly resist and reflexively say no to their ideas. What most upset Marty about Andy was his persistent denial of what her alcoholism was trying to tell him: "Andy, I need your help."

Can you give several examples of how you've been sensitive to your partner's needs and desires within the past two days? If you answered yes, then cite several. If you have to scramble for a minute or two, don't rate yourself higher than a 2.

Next, *are you a nonjudgmental and self-accepting person and so more able accept your partner's frailties and gaffes?* If you unequivocally rate yourself a 5, beware that your great strength doesn't disguise Roger's fatal weakness. He was so self-accepting that he infuriated Beth—she sensed that layers and layers of self-centeredness hid his flickering soul. Such self-contentment really makes saviors angry.

Because interpersonal harmony is so central to women's self-worth, it is not surprising that maritally happy women have husbands whose character helps maintain that harmony: they are flexible, yielding, and sensitive to their needs. Their husbands definitely do not aggressively impose themselves on their wives, as I observed Bill Spaulding and Bruce Jackson do. We men need provocations (like rating ourselves on 5-point scales) to make us reflect about our relationships; women don't. Women tend to think about these issues automatically and to discuss them with friends. They have known for eons that their nurturing strengths are necessary to keep men happily married to them. The research only confirms that historic wisdom.

If you are a woman whose husband is happily married, then you are seen by your peers as *interpersonally feminine* but also virtuous in many other ways as well. How *warm, lovable, compassionate*, and *loyal* are you? Men value these virtues highly—in you. You also need to be *cheerfully, not moaningly, adaptable*, too. A sour and complaining wife grates on a man. Your husband doesn't have to be playful for you to be happy, but you sure must be if he is to be happy. Since men are not very expressive, particularly of their childish and affectionate selves, do successful wives have to be *playful* to help their spouses be more emotionally spontaneous? If you want to be maritally successful, you cannot be wishy-washy: You must be able *to make decisions that are true to your character*. And then there are twenty other angelic virtues you must have to make your partner happy—so my unbiased computer insists.

Women Must Be More Virtuous Than Men to Have Happy Marital Partners

Women who make their partners happy must have almost three times as many virtues as men who make their partners happy. Apparently, being a wife is much more demanding than being a husband. When I told Harriet about this result, she said, "So what's new?" It was new to me, though. Why must women have so many more strengths, particularly interpersonal ones, than men to make their partners happy? Their tenderness, compassion, warmth, loyalty, and flexibility are critical to their husbands' marital happiness. Without hesitation, Harriet interpreted the theme to mean that women have to be much more adaptable in a marriage than men. Rather humbling. My hunch is that since women's identity is so emotionally organized around their relationships, sometimes at their own expense, they are more fluid and no, not more adaptable, but yes, more adjustable to the quirks and demands of their husbands. Both Billie and Marty spent years as nurturing wives adjusting to their spouses. Historically, that is the role the "little woman" had to play: the self-sacrificing handmaiden that Marty rebelled against so furiously.

If you are like Marty or younger than the middle-aged men and women I'm describing, you may be questioning the validity of these findings for you or your generation. I too am uncertain. Roger tells me that younger women are forward, assertive, and aggressive. They more openly initiate contacts, even sexual ones, with men; they pay their own way, propose marriage to men, and initiate divorce more frequently. The study's middle-aged women said they had learned from their daughters what they could have been like. As women become more typically masculine, will they retain their femininity? Billie and Marty did, but then they had been raised for years to be nurturers. Will younger males be as happily married in the future to more assertive and less accommodating females? What is going to happen to those males—still the majority—who have been raised to expect women to go along with them, keep peace in the family, and adjust to their needs?

Are you upset that the more successful husbands are more interpersonally feminine than the less successful ones? All that that means is that the men had been rated by their peers to have interpersonal strengths typical of women. Successful partners were judged to be warm, affectionate, and sympathetic. This does not mean that some successful partners were not also self-reliant, ambitious, and strong individualists, but the judges did not *consistently* describe the successful ones like that. Such masculine strengths are not necessary to be good marital partners. One good partner might be ambitious, for example; another might not be.

Stereotypical males like Bruce Jackson and Bill Spaulding, who have not developed interpersonal strengths like empathy, are not emerging as successful in their close relationships. The stereotypically feminine female is doing much better, but will she continue to succeed as she becomes more typically masculine? What will happen to marriage in the future?

Why Marry in the Future?

When asked what marriages will be like in the future, I can make these guesses:
- They are going to be more "rocky."
- Women will not be as accommodating.
- Males will not change rapidly enough to develop the interpersonal skills modern women want.
- Because men need women more than women need men and men are less skilled in creating interpersonal supports, more men will suffer emotional isolation and loneliness.

The changing meanings of femaleness more than those of maleness are disrupting centuries-old meanings about marriage. Because the women's movement affected so many of the study's women— some, like Marty, in dramatic ways—I ask what I believe to be one of the most important questions of our century. "If you are a male, why would a young female these days ever want to marry, settle down with, and stay married to you all her life?" Men typically shake their heads and mutter in bewilderment, "What a stupid question." But women everywhere understand what I am getting at and nod in agreement.

Any relationship as problematic as that between a man and a woman who don't speak each other's language well must fulfill many different needs to endure. When one need is frustrated, other more fulfilled needs hold the couple together for the long haul.

What do I mean? Consider sex. Middle-aged men and women both want sex 2.6 times a week; when both work, they are washed out— not infrequently these days at different times. And now that women are less accommodating to men's timing, the couple probably is up for sex only on Sunday mornings. That leaves 1.6 orgasms unaccounted for. That's quite a lot of itchy horniness to carry around the next week. Ergo: frustration. If sex is the core of the marriage, what do you predict will happen? I agree. The couple had better have other needs they can mutually satisfy, or your prediction will become a foregone certainty.

When I ask women why they stay married to men, they tell me instantly. At least five bonds (security, children, status, sex, and intimacy) have *historically* kept them with the same men for a lifetime—and the length of women's lifetimes has almost doubled since the early 1900s, which can make living with men much more boring than it used to be. (That is Margaret Mead's comment, not mine.)

Marriage Meant Security

First in importance worldwide was that marriage provided the financial security necessary for a woman to have a family. She "needed to be taken care of," and a man learned to need to take care of her. No longer. As more women inch their way toward earning as much as men, security will become an archaic reason for marrying or remaining married when a couple faces rough times.

Marriage Meant Children

Second in importance worldwide was that marriage provided the opportunity to have children. Childless couples used to lose status; certainly an unmarried pregnant woman did. In the *Scarlet Letter*, Hawthorne put Hester in a stockade. "Bastards" were just that. No longer are these values held in many sections of the United States, as well as in some European countries. The 20 percent or more of American families headed by single women reminds women that males are only necessary to provide the first impetus. Fifty percent of women in the Los Angeles area (where most societal trends begin) told the Institute for Social Science Research in 1989 that they would consider having a child without a partner if they were near the end of their child-bearing years and were childless. In the twenty-first century, sperm banks and sterile needles will take care of the necessary impetus and give women many more choices about which genes to pass on. Since many men have not been educated to be competent fathers or are seldom home anyway, some women even now feel that males are obsolescent as fathers.

Marriage Meant Status

Probably third in importance for centuries was that marriage satisfied a woman's and her parents' need for status or social acceptability. I remember when an unmarried woman was called an "old maid" or "spinster." Parents of spinsters also lost status and didn't talk about their unmarried daughters. I don't know the origin of dowries, but surely some parents used them to bribe someone, anyone, to marry their daughters. No longer. Increasingly, in the United States and other countries, an unmarried woman does not lose status when she reaches thirty or forty. It has become her choice. Nor does a divorced woman nowadays lose status in many communities. Further, as women get equal opportunities to achieve in different vocations, whether as coal miners or lawyers, heads of Fortune 500 companies or taxi drivers, a husband's vocation no longer has to be her route to status in the community. In fact, the time is almost here when some men, like Margaret Thatcher's husband, will get their status from their wives.

Marriage Meant Legal Sex

Fourth, from society's standpoint, marriage is supposed to resolve all the frustrations that complicate male and female sexual relations. Ready accessibility to a sexual partner simplified things, left energy available for other societal purposes, and ensured some continuity in the caretakers of children who might appear one day. No longer. In many parts of the United States, as has been true of countries like France for years, a single woman can have a relatively unfettered though discreet and legal sex life and not be punished by her community. Husbands are becoming obsolescent for sexual satisfaction.

Marriage Is Intimacy

The only reason left for many women to marry is to have an enduring intimate or companionate and loving friendship with a man. But the meaning of intimacy for women is vastly different than for men, and women now demand intimacy on their terms. The best friends of most women in the study were other women. The best friends of most men were their wives. For women almost everywhere I have been, an intimate friend is someone with whom to share one's feelings about one's self, others, and the relationship itself. No "bottom line" or conclusion must be reached when women talk, as it must more frequently when men talk. For women, one meaning of a conversation is in the moment of being-in-relationship, not just in its content. Men talk more at others and women more with them. From the perspective of the women in the study, few of their husbands had an intimate friend. Marty and Andy were a rare couple; each viewed the other as a soul mate.

For most American men, intimacy means sex, so they can't use the word "intimate" in talking about their male friends. The men did not think of themselves as having "intimate" friendships—a good male friend is one with whom one plays poker, drinks, and watches the Tigers on TV.

So my next question is, "If women increasingly will marry men primarily for companionship, what qualities will men need to have to be able to form intimate relationships with women that endure?" Women know. Men will need to develop interpersonal strengths that make a woman happy in her marriage: empathy, understanding, compassion, and sensitivity to the needs of others. These are just the strengths that Marty felt Andy had been developing under her rigorous tutelage. Everything I have learned about male-female differences tells me that, generally speaking, males are not very mature in these typically feminine ways. When speaking about these issues, I say to women, "Be careful about leaving your partner; you most likely will not find a better one." The women look glum; the men smile for the first time and clap.

Some women despair, thinking that men are constitutionally built to be aggressively dominating and authoritarian antediluvians, but I'm more hopeful. American males are beginning to adapt. I think of a typical bastion of male virtue—a boy's school I studied, where teachers, parents, and trustees agreed that the school was athletic, competitive, masculine, ambitious, aggressive, and traditional. The school's teachers as well as students described the "typical boy" similarly. So where is the hope? In their wishes that the typical boy were different. The majority of the male faculty wished that the students were more considerate, caring, and sensitive to the feelings of others—typical feminine strengths. The boys agreed with the faculty in their wishes. Though not much has changed at the school since, at least the wish is there. Until parents and educators raise boys to be more interpersonally mature, to learn how to bring their feelings out of their black holes and label them, to speak more intimately, the future of American families is bleak.

If you are a male, have you also asked why you would stay married to the same woman until your golden wedding anniversary or beyond? Because I haven't heard younger males ask themselves this question as insistently as females have, I am less certain about their answer. I doubt that security or status is an issue for younger males. To marry to have children is not as biologically compelling a reason for men as for women. Younger males are not really that concerned about passing on the family name or property or expecting their children to provide for them in their old age. Staying married "for the children's sake" is no longer as persuasive a reason as it used to be when the primary marital relationship goes sour. Sex will always remain an insistent reason to marry and stay married, at least until desire and potency begin to wane, but our increased freedom to satisfy that in almost any way we wish without guilt reduces its marital adhesive power. I think we men still want our partners to take care of us: bake those special muffins, wash and iron our shirts, create an attractive and relaxing home, be a gracious hostess for our business colleagues, and anticipate our other needs. What's left? We want to have a loving, lifelong companion to whom we feel deeply committed. Do men have the feminine, interpersonal character to carry out their part of the marital bargain?

Because maritally happy men and women are also sexually fulfilled, I now explore how they view sex. I rely on Andy's and Marty's voices to understand what sex can mean. After describing the personality of sexually fulfilled men and women, I ask, "Is a good lover more than just a sexual technician in bed?"

Chapter 9

Finding Sexual Fulfillment

Tom Wolfe, the best-selling author, claims that Americans were less preoccupied with sex in the eighties than in the seventies. (If so, do you think it is because sex comes so easy nowadays, almost like a McDonald's hamburger?) When interviewed on NBC's "Today Show" about what he had learned from a tour publicizing a new book, he replied that Americans were more obsessed with the lives of the rich in the eighties. Other writers aren't quite so sure. Afternoon soap operas qualify for X ratings. My local video rental store has more sex couplings on tape in its curtained-off back room than computer scams, bank robberies, and Wall Street shenanigans combined. Grocery store paperback stands would erotically charge the Rip Van Winkles of the world, though not those of us sated by that graphic barrage. The paperbacks still sell, however. We are fascinated by the indiscreet antics of our politicians, preachers, and movie actors, just as the English are about those of their royal family. We even talk about condoms on TV and in the classroom.

   Is sex as important to us as pop writers and advertisers obviously still believe? Important, yes. As Marty says, "It's the way I play." But obsessively important, no. The adults I surveyed ranked it ninth in importance, though men ranked sexual fulfillment to be more important than women did. Except for those living in California, the men and women I studied didn't consider sexual fulfillment to be one of their top priorities. Sex was more important to those who weren't getting much—like the study's few restlessly roaming men. Though not *the* top priority that Freud assumed, sex still excites us. Advertisers know that. They will continue to find ways to use our dreams of being the ultimate lover to sell everything from silky lingerie and Calvin Klein's perfume, Obsession, to sleek Toyota coupes and corn flakes. Are they right about how to reach that pinnacle of lustful hope? Suggestive sexy stimulants? *Playboy* centerfolds? Kamasutran techniques? They obviously work for those who continue to buy the products, but in the long run, *character* rather than sexual accouterments and techniques make us the ideal lover.

Attributes You Need for a Sexually Fulfulling Relationship

The list below may seem old-fashioned to you if you believe that all a successful lover does is to hop in and out of a different bed every night engaging in laser-like lovings. But these qualities turn out to contribute most to a sexually fulfilling *relationship*. In declining order of importance, the men and women in the study said that the ideal lover
- Is loving, tender, and considerate
- Accepts his or her own sexual and sensuous needs
- Is patient and self-confident and has a sense of humor
- Shares his or her feelings openly and honestly
- Is sensitive to and skillful in fulfilling the partner's sexual needs
- Is uninhibitedly imaginative and playfully experimental in bed
- Is in good physical health and has lots of energy

With the exception of Andy's health, these qualities describe his and Marty's sexual relationship. Their extensive experience in workshops on sexuality prepared them more than most to accept and integrate their diffuse sexual needs into their love for each other. They didn't need the *Kamasutra* or "how to have multiple orgasm" books. I asked Marty what sex meant to her after she and Andy had gotten back together again in their forties. She replied, "I'm now enjoying sex more than I ever have. I enjoy the variety of it. I don't feel I have to have it daily, even weekly. I don't think it's the central part of my life. But it is the way I play."

Men found no topic more difficult to talk about than what sex meant to them, how their feelings about it had changed since their early thirties, and how it had affected their growth. Women felt much more comfortable and were more articulate by far in describing their feelings about sex. I think women's magazines and their special friendships prepared them better for my questions. The men talked more about sex than sexuality; the women more about sexuality than sex. Despite their education, almost all seemed quite naive about the meanings of sex, even Marty and Andy, the most sexually sophisticated and knowledgeable couple of the group. Marty said, "I realize now that I just never asked for what I wanted. It seems simple now. I just expected myself to be an expert right away and I never got what I wanted and so blamed Andy and all men."

Andy, the most knowledgeable and articulate of the men, added, "I never had permission to explore my sexual fantasies or feel comfortable and understand the male part of my sexual being. So, in a sense, I was intellectually informed but emotionally and spiritually naive, unsophisticated, and unaware of the gigantic area that so profoundly influences so many aspects of our behavior, and our roles and interactions, whether in bed or at work." He then continued to distinguish between sex and sexuality, a confusion that blocked many couple's mutual sexual fulfillment. For men, sex was sex; for women, sex was sexuality. Neither really understood the other's meanings. As Andy put it,

> There is an enormous difference between sex and sexuality. Sex refers more to genital and physical pleasure that has its ultimate end in intercourse or sexual release. Sexuality is a much broader concept that involves how one feels about one's self, a sense of personal identity, one's physical image, knowing how to sexually relate to other people of both sexes and ages, and understanding all of the dimensions of sexual relationships that have to do with giving and receiving, communicating and caring: all of the ways of expressing one's self sexually that have nothing to do with genital activity—ways like massages that release all of the senses.

I asked Andy, "How have you changed in your own sexual behavior?" He replied, "I've learned how important it is to pay attention to what Marty needs and wants, both in terms of genital sex and just in feeling nurtured and loved and respected. I've also learned to become much more comfortable discussing my own sexuality in large groups that I speak to."

Identifying Sexually Successful Men and Women

Other than inventing new ways to torture human beings, I can't think of anything that so excites our imagination more than dreaming up new ways to enjoy sex. Obviously, "sexual success" means different things. One male meaning can be found in adolescent fantasies (middle-age ones, too) of being a debonair Casanova, Don Juan, or modern James Bond "pillowing"—that marvelous Japanese term—a different woman every night. After knocking out the furious husband who bursts into the bedroom to discover our betrayal, we escape out the open window to catch a hovering helicopter's swinging rope to fly us to the arms of the next night's temptress. Ah!

Many young men measure their success by how many "conquests" they have made. Why else do they use words like "score" to brag about their adventures? Males admire the guy, like those famous basketball players, who claim they have scored with hundreds of different women; they wonder about the masculinity of the man who has scored with only one or two. I was not up to asking how many different partners the men had scored with in their lifetimes, let alone the past month. (Actually, compared to Kinsey's "norms," the men and women were almost impeccable examples of faithfulness.) So I opted to explore three different, increasingly more rigorous signs of sexual success. The first measured what Andy meant by "sex": sheer amount of enjoyable sex. The other two measured what he meant by "sexuality." The second explored beliefs about how mutually considerate, faithful, and enjoyable one's sexual relationship with one's partner was. The third assessed the character of what I call the "good lover": the person whose partner feels fulfilled in a mutually compatible sexual relationship.

The Character of Sexually Successful
Men and Women

I was surprised to learn that the character strengths necessary to enjoy a lot of sex and create a sexually compatible relationship differ for men and women. Apparently, men don't need any character at all to enjoy sex. Women do. They need one kind of character to enjoy having a lot of sex; they need another to have a mutually compatible sexual relationship. But both men and women need more of the same character to be good lovers to their partners.

Success as Having Frequent Enjoyable Sex

A typical male "performance" definition of sexual success is the number of times a person has sex each week or month. By this standard, the men and women in the study had become less successful after their first several "honeymoon" years. But they are not alone, as Kinsey told us decades ago. The decline is steeper the more educated one is, and the study's men and women had had a lot of schooling. In their early thirties, the men reported having sex with their wives 6.6 times a month; by their mid-forties it had declined to 4.5 times a month. Their partners agreed with their estimates. Both men and women wished that they could have almost twice that number.

Given what I now view to be a myth—that middle-aged women of the pre-eighties era were not really interested in sex—I am delighted to write that the women didn't differ from the men in any measure that I had of desire, enjoyment, excitement, and playfulness. Our Puritan heritage has conned both men and women into believing that women cannot feel as lusty as men.

The more sex we have, the more likely we are to believe that our partners are better lovers as well as all-round more competent partners. People who have frequent sex continue through the years to be strongly attracted to their partners, who in turn also view them as good lovers. Freely sharing their feelings and needs about sex and other feelings with their partners, they are spontaneously playful in bed. Considerate of the other's needs, they feel good about their marriages. One couple, who enjoyed sex five times a week, felt frustrated they couldn't have sex *every day*. Middle age is obviously creeping up on such greedy adolescents.

However, men and women differ in one perplexing—even provocatively significant—way. Finding out how frequently a man enjoys sex tells us almost nothing else about him, except that he'll be happily married, be judged to be a good husband, and can comfortably share his feelings with others. But how athletic he is sexually tells us nothing about his happiness, maturity, and personality, particularly his masculinity. A male can have little sex and still be happy or unhappy, mature or immature, and masculine or not. It is a male myth that having a lot of sex is a sign of one's maleness. Celibate priests can be very happy, mature, and masculine.

But how much a woman enjoys a lot of sex *does* tell us a lot about her, because sex is so closely intertwined with her personality. Although her partner thinks she's great in bed and a good wife, she won't necessarily believe her marriage to be as great as her husband does. Her peers describe her as a sensuous Carmen: assertive, forceful, aggressive, decisive, competitive, and strong but also playfully affectionate and an individualist. She and other women who enjoy sex have no feminine character traits in common.

I didn't expect these differences between men and women who enjoy a lot of sex and so am not sure what to make of them. After all, women can have sex even if they are not excited or don't enjoy it. Men are more vulnerable. They have to be excited enough to have an erection. They also don't initiate sex if it is not enjoyable—one reason few men rated the degree of their sexual enjoyment less than ecstatic or, in Roger's words, "glorious." I would have thought that men who were readily excitable and initiated frequent sex would share similar traits. The results say otherwise.

Fulfillment in a Mutually Compatible Sexual Relationship

Sex keeps its hold on us for decades. It can be addictively enjoyable. We savor the memory of a *good lovin'*; we think of a certain caress; we feel good about an intense attraction; we enjoy a wildly playful romp. But more is involved in enjoying sex, especially in long-term relationships. Masters and Johnson, the premier researchers in the sexual laboratory, told us years ago that those "glorious" and rapturous times in bed really depend more on our character than on our techniques. Four themes summarize their detailed clinical findings about couples who greatly enjoy sex: psychological maturity (for example, high self-esteem, stable sense of self); interpersonal maturity, especially understanding the feelings of the other; sharing similar values and being sensitive to the other's needs; and the marital satisfaction that results from creating an alive and enduring relationship.

Masters and Johnson were talking about what I call marital sexual compatibility or mutuality, or what Andy meant by "sexuality"—a more rigorous standard of *success*, I think, than just having a lot of sex or one-night stands, as enjoyable as they may be. By sexual mutuality I mean how enjoyable, considerate, well mated, and faithful the men and women believed their sexual relationship to be.

When the men were in their early thirties, their reported sexual mutuality, rather than amount of "glorious" rhapsodic sex, turned out to be as revealing of their personalities as a Rorschach inkblot and Tarot card reading. The men who had more faithful, mutually enjoyable sexual relationships were more mature; they had closer, happier marriages; and they had fulfilled their other adult roles more competently. Jumping in and out of bed with a different person every week, casually playing around with others, and splitting when the rose wilted and wine was gone did not describe the successful, happy, and mature thirty-three-year-old men. Marty and Andy only discovered that in their late thirties. Sticking it out, working through their conflicts, and making an enduring commitment not only reflected but also increased their maturity.

That I found the same pattern of results for *both* the men and women when they were middle-aged suggests that marital sexual compatibility reflects some stable underlying character strengths. Those who had been faithful, considerate, and sexually compatible with their partners in middle age had been happier and more productive since adolescence. They were also more happily married and competent in fulfilling their adult roles, as well as more emotionally mature.

However, men who claimed that they had created mutually compatible relationships and had not strayed did not share any specific *personality* traits, according to their peers. The successful women did; their peers saw them as loyal, conscientious, reliable, ethical persons of great integrity. Apparently, in women sexual faithfulness and mutuality are part and parcel of as well as buttressed by a strongly ethical personality, again revealing how well integrated sexuality is with a woman's character.

Some Reflections About Differences Between Men and Women

What are we to make of the consistent results so far that sex means something different to a man than to a woman? Is sex for a male really just a restless appendage for eliminating tension, needing only to be soothed, devoid of interpersonal meaning and so peripheral to more enduring personality traits and values? Is his erection only an Ollie North cannon running loose on the street, not securely anchored to more stable personality qualities? To use Andy's distinction, is sex just sex for men? Many women and mythology say yes. I now would agree. Sex does seem to be peripheral to a man's basic character. He doesn't even need to be forceful, aggressive, and competitive to enjoy sex. Despite widespread myths to the contrary, he doesn't have to be a James Bond—reassuringly!

For men, only when sex approaches what Andy described as sexuality and is embedded within a compatible mutual relationship do personality strengths, particularly those that make up maturity, begin to contribute to success. Any kind of man can have a lot of enjoyable sex. But only mature ones can establish a mutually respectful, enjoyable, and faithful relationship. Roaming James Bonds are to devoted husbands like Andy as sex is to sexuality. Do Casanovan pursuits of nightly adventures to bolster some macho ideal signal immaturity and an inability to make a loving commitment?

Typical feminine interpersonal strengths, which contribute so much to a man's marital success, don't stand out as essential to his feeling good about sex. This is true even for men who enjoy sex in a mutually fulfilling and compatible relationship. For males, sex as orgasm seems to be easily divorced from sexuality, even from intimacy. When I ask audiences what "intimacy" means to men, women answer immediately, "sex." No man has yet *publicly* disputed the women's equation and described intimacy as sexuality, the way Andy did.

The separation of sex from sexuality, perhaps more a biologically given fact about men than most women would like to believe, explains why men prowl sexually. Support anonymous prostitutes. Value being "on the make." Fantasize, as a 1950s fellow graduate student crudely boasted in class, about "raping virgins." Take part in date and even gang rape. Act as if "no!" is "yes." Use sex to take, not to give. "Make out," lose interest, and then drop out. Feel little remorse or guilt. Or not understand why their wives feel that "playing around" betrays their relationship.

One last question. Apart from biological factors, why do males typically isolate sex from a more intimate kind of sexuality? Could it be that sex is much more and sexuality much less safe for men? Intimacy requires vulnerability, dependency, and a willingness to yield and abandon self-control. Ian Fleming, James Bond's creator, tells us just how dangerous intimacy is in *Her Majesty's Secret Service*, when James falls tenderly in love and marries for the first and last time. Remember what happened when he left the church with his bride? Blowfield shoots her. The movie ends with James tenderly cradling his dead bride in his arms, hiding his eyes (tears?) from the camera. In this scene, Bond gives a depressing message to millions of males about what sexuality could be. The name "Bond" must equal sex, not intimacy; intimacy can hurt.

For women, sex has a different meaning. Enjoying sex draws on a woman's character in a way that it doesn't for a man. A woman who has a lot of sex and enjoys it thoroughly typically has many masculine traits like assertiveness and self-reliance but not necessarily any feminine interpersonal ones. Or conversely, a woman who has little sex and doesn't particularly enjoy it is not described by others in masculine terms. Neither woman, however, is more or less feminine than the other. A woman apparently does not have to be sensitive and empathic to enjoy or not enjoy sex. *Remember my cautionary warning?* Because sexually fulfilled women don't have any typical feminine attributes *in common* does not mean that some are not feminine. Also remember that all of us have both masculine and feminine characteristics.

However, when sex is part of a mutually reciprocal and intimate relationship, a woman's masculine attributes recede into the background as loyal commitment and other ethical strengths become necessary to sustain such a faithful relationship.

Do you think that these gender differences in the meaning of sex and sexuality reflect lingering cultural assumptions that sex and its enjoyment should be more the province of males than females? Demure, modestly feminine Daphnes aren't supposed to be sexual; seductively assertive, strong but feminine Carmens are. As women become more like Marty—less willing to subordinate their needs to those of men and more insistent on pursuing their own fulfillment—will we begin to see many more actively seductive Carmens on college campuses and main streets? Roger says yes. He claims that the last four women he has gone to bed with initiated the invitation. The chances are good that sexuality may become sex for more women in the future.

Are masculine, assertive, forceful, and competitive women better lovers from a man's point of view? Perhaps for a week or a month. But what about living with a Carmen for a lifetime? Or would women really want to spend a lifetime in bed with the James Bonds of the world? For the study's answer to that, let's turn to the third and most stringent sign of success—the good lover.

The Good Lover

I have only told you about how women and men view their *own* sexual pleasure and relationships. Now, I ask the more demanding questions that I also asked about marital success. "What are men like *whose partners believe that they are sexually compatible, considerate, and faithful to each other?* What is an Andy like who makes a Marty feel that they have an enjoyable and mutually compatible relationship?" Apparently, for a male to be a good lover, he must be yielding, cooperative, and sensitive to his partner. He definitely should *not* be assertive, aggressive, and dominant. So much for the macho John Waynes and James Bonds of the world.

"What are women like *whose partners enjoy sex and believe that they have a mutually compatible relationship*? What is a Marty like who makes an Andy really enjoy sex, want a lot of it, and feel that they are sexually compatible?" They are more typically feminine: compassionate, sympathetic, sensitive to a man's needs, tender, warm, affectionate, gentle, and loyal. Women who are superb lovers do *not* share any masculine trait. Remember the qualifying comment I just made. Individual women, like Marty, may be quite masculine, but to be good lovers, they must also be affectionate, sensitive to their partner's needs, and so on. Their masculinity has to be tempered, in other words, by feminine interpersonal traits. Men who want to have a sexually compatible marriage should, perhaps, try to marry the firm's typically feminine secretary rather than the typically masculine executive vice-president, *unless* she is also quite feminine interpersonally.

What a Catch-22 conflict for contemporary women! To enjoy sex they probably should be quite masculine, but such qualities may turn off men, unless they also come across as feminine interpersonally. The only way they can have their cake and eat it too is to be androgynous. Does this idea ring true for you?

Again, given the changing character of younger males and females, a host of questions arise about what sex will mean in the future. As males learn how to get along with and enjoy more aggressive women, will they still need loyal, affectionate, sensitive ones with whom to enjoy sex and create a faithful and compatible relationship? Are younger males becoming more like Andy? By coming to terms with their own "female parts," as Andy did, will they no longer be as defensive or uptight with more assertive women like Marty?

But what a growing survival problem for traditional men like Bill Spaulding, the tough president of his marketing firm but failed family man or for Bruce Jackson, the authoritarian executive who squashed his family, or for the Great Santini of the book and movie of the same name who treated his family like fledgling marines at boot camp. Are they in danger of becoming the sexual dinosaurs of the future? To survive, will they have to learn not only how to relate to stronger women but also how to become more interpersonally sensitive if their wives are to feel fulfilled sexually? If they don't grow up in these ways, who will they have sex with in the future? I can't see them settling into an enduring marital relationship with the emerging modern woman. Andy's path will not be an easy one to learn how to take. If a Bruce Jackson can get in touch with a quieter, softer, yielding side, perhaps he will feel more comfortable with a more initiating, assertive June, as Andy did with Marty.

I also wonder if the more sexually assertive women of the younger generations will discover that they don't need those sensitive, caring, considerate men to really enjoy sex and to have a sexually compatible relationship with. If women follow men's path and segregate sex from sexuality, will they adopt the kind of impersonal in-and-out, hit-and-run, sexual behavior so typical of males for centuries? Marty didn't; her femaleness saw to that. But maybe younger women have now gone past the Martys who were their leaders several decades ago. Maybe as they integrate more typical masculine strengths into their personalities, they'll stand up to the Bill Spauldings of the world and even enjoy sex with them for a lifetime.

Our traditional meanings of maleness and femaleness are increasingly maladaptive. The growing divorce rate testifies to this. So does the problem of sexual harassment. Men's centuries-long teasing, propositioning, and rubbing up against and touching women—so unconsciously a part of being male—is now being recognized as sexual harassment, subject to legal challenge. Understanding "sexual success" is, always has been, and probably always will be a complicated though tantalizing quest. What have we learned so far?

First, sexual success has several different meanings. It can mean enjoying a lot of sex. It can mean having a mutually faithful sexual relationship. It can mean being a good lover who makes his or her partner feel well mated in a faithful, considerate, and enjoyable sexual relationship.

Second, women who have frequent sex that they enjoy are typically masculine. Men who enjoy and have a lot of sex share no particular personality traits.

Third, women who enjoy sex as integral to a mutual relationship are mature, loyal, ethical people. Men who create sexually compatible relationships are also mature, but not necessarily any more or less masculine or feminine than men who don't.

Fourth, good lovers—particularly women—who are considerate and faithful and create mutually enjoyable sexual relationships are interpersonally feminine. How masculine they may be is *irrelevant* to how good a lover they are. Men who are good lovers share some feminine interpersonal strengths, such as being yielding and cooperative. They definitely are not domineering or aggressive.

Social commentators claim that the modern American family is in crisis, suffering from instability, violence, weakening "family values," and neglected and abused children. A healthy family requires three strong foundations: an enduring, mutually fulfilling, and companionate relationship between the parents; mutual sexual compatibility that binds a couple; and mature adults called to be competent and fulfilled parents. The next chapter introduces you to Harry Barnett, a successful and happy man who, with his wife Eloise, created just such a strong family. He illustrates a father called to be a competent and fulfilled parent.

Chapter 10

Harry Barnett:
Called to Being a Good Father

When I got married I just assumed I would be a father; it was no big deal; everyone became parents, if they could. I also had no idea how demanding being a father was going to be—even in those days, when women stayed home to be mothers without as many complaints. When I recall my first public talk to parents at my son's nursery school, I realize I must have felt overwhelmed by how many virtues I lacked as a father. I titled it "Parenthood: The First Requirement for Sainthood."

Raising children today demands much more of adults. Not knowing how to prepare them for a more uncertain future, deciding who is going to take care of them, and keeping our sanity while struggling to help them cope with sex, drugs, violence, and our divorces make parenting infinitely more troubling and challenging. No wonder thoughtful adults now agonize for years about whether to become a parent.

In spite of these uncertainties and disturbing demands, adults in their thirties and forties still value being a good parent. They rate their parental role to be more important than any other except their marital role. Although a national survey found that adults in the 1970s valued being a parent as much as adults in the 1950s had, it also found that college-educated men had become less satisfied with being fathers in the intervening twenty years. Apparently, more men have become less emotionally fulfilled in their relationships, not only with their kids but also with their colleagues at work and possibly with their spouses, if they too are working.

More young people, like Roger, moreover, may choose not to become parents in the future. When I ask why, they tell me, "I'm scared to have kids. I wouldn't know what to do when they cry," or "I don't want to go through what my parents went through with me," or "I'm too selfish to give up what I want to do and be a slave to kids."

Modern parents feel that they don't know how to raise a child. They are right. No instinct tells them how to change diapers, help their baby sleep through the night, or make their kids share their favorite toys with their friends. The truism that even as basic a maternal skill as nursing is instinctual is just false. Harriet compared mothers who successfully breast-fed their first baby with those who did not. The successful mothers differed from the unsuccessful ones in only one major way: They had access to accurate information about how to breast-feed, which suggests that we must learn such skills to become competent parents.

Marty and Andy tell us that the fundamental issue is not the "mechanics" of parenting, like learning how to train a child to use the potty or deciding who is to take the children to school today. They could not settle these issues until they had resolved what parenthood meant to each of them. Andy only learned in his late thirties that he enjoyed being a father and had the character strengths to be a good one.

According to numerous measures and peer judgments—the same standards that I used to select Billie and the Millers—Harry Barnett is the study's most all-round successful and happy man who *also* feels drawn to be a good parent and contributing citizen to his community. Like Andy, Harry was not the perfect husband, ideal lover, best father, most satisfied breadwinner, or most ethical idealist. He also was not the happiest and most fulfilled, most mature, and most androgynous man, either. But if you knew all sixty-five men and I asked you to select the two or three who most successfully fulfilled *all* of their major adult roles—including their parental and citizen roles—I think you would have selected Harry as one of them. He illustrates the principal strengths and familial background that, according to the study, help make men fulfilled as well as competent parents. Like the Millers, he too had his ups and downs. As we'll see, the difficulties were not with Eloise, his wife, but with his children—especially with Rusty, his oldest. What kind of father was Harry when I revisted him in his mid-forties? And how had he changed as a parent by my next visit, ten years later?

Harry as a Father in His Forties

Harry's Parenting Crisis

Harry had not changed much since I had seen him thirteen years earlier. He was a little heavier, had a little less hair, was a little grayer—not unexpected for a forty-four-year-old. His stocky five-foot-ten-inch frame vibrated with his energy; I caught my breath keeping up with him as we raced to his new Jaguar, which he was inordinately proud of. On the way to his elegant but simple home, spaciously surrounded by acres of privacy, he invited me to go flying with him. (I took a dip in his pool, instead.) He found flying his own plane relaxing and used it to visit some of the more distant nursing homes that he owned. He relied on Eloise, a research scientist at the region's principal hospital, for advice about medical policies—and politics.

Harry and Eloise had been happily married for twenty-three years and had two adolescent children, an older son, Rusty, and a younger daughter, Sally. His kinetic energy and conscientiousness in his vocation and community activities—he was president of the Chamber of Commerce, served on several boards, and had received state recognition for his contributions—did not carry over into his relationship with Eloise. I asked her what the best things were about her marriage and what one thing she wished she could change about Harry. Without hesitating, she said, "Our companionship, closeness, affection, and children. But I want him to be more compulsive about getting things done."

Surprised, I asked, "Compulsive? You mean about his work?"

Eloise replied, "No. Here. He doesn't get things done around here. He assumes I'll do them. He is very organized and he is very relaxed. He doesn't run a compulsively organized business the way some people do. He's very effective [deep sigh, almost of resignation]. But if only . . . he's very patient and very flexible. No . . . not flexible but very willing to go along with what I want if I take the lead. He's a very good father, concerned about the children." On her criteria of what made a good parent, she rated Harry to be higher than her on patience, consistency, self-confidence, and loving qualities; she saw herself as more unselfish.

When asked how much of the time he enjoyed being a parent, Harry checked "Nearly always," and to the question of whether he had ever wished he could be free from a parent's responsibilities, he replied no. His fondest wish to see fulfilled before he died was, "to see my children happy and successful."

"Why?" I asked. Harry replied this way:

> I suppose because of a deep feeling that I have about the kids. The sense of their worth and ability and the tremendous obligation I feel to provide what it takes for them to use their abilities. We both feel very lucky to have two very bright and able kids.... I think what would probably blow my computer most would be if ... it's my selfish side ... for them not to be successful and happy. That would be one of the hardest things for me to be able to cope with. Gets back to those feelings of their potential worth. How much that means to me. I'd feel a certain personal loss and responsibility.

To my question, "What are you trying to do about fulfilling such hopes?" he unhesitatingly said, "Our approach has been to try to set as good examples as we can, to give them a standard to at least have as a reference. And to provide what direction we can and the responsibility. It is a tough line to draw when we have the money and yet we want them to have some feeling of responsibility for what they have."

The depth of Harry's feelings for his children also emerged in the picture and story he projected onto a blank card like the one Marty had written her story about playing with children on.

> Here we see a man in a plane, flying through the clouds with a dog and one of his children. They are off where they can see no other human or any sign of civilization. The father and child are enjoying the solitude and isolation, and the ability to talk and communicate with each other without any interruption from anyone else around. Very happy and very deep feeling for each other. I see it as a break from the usual more hectic existence. It is a rare

opportunity for them to be together and enjoy each other, their dog, and nature all around them.

In the interviews, Harry kept returning to Rusty, then fourteen. Sally, his youngest, "doesn't do much wrong and is a fantastically good student and so it is easy to ignore her needs." But Rusty was different.

> He's a real problem. He's been very challenging. Very strong, decisive but somewhat insecure. Being the first child, his unpleasantness here in the home reverberates down to Sally. Rusty is caught between his insecurity and push to be independent and rebel against us. And he's so outspoken and aggressive.
>
> We have sought counseling about him and learned that in our attempt to have an open communicative relation with him we may have blurred the generational boundaries. He really rakes Eloise over the coals. It has been a hard time for her. He "matured" early and when thirteen wanted to try his wings. We didn't think it was time yet. Well! We got into these huge spiraling conflicts. Nothing got accomplished. All of our ideas went up into smoke.
>
> It's a tough time for kids. Drugs, alcohol, sex. Just their safety. And the tremendous peer pressures that Rusty is under. It's a tough time for parents, too. And the school didn't help. Tough, rigid, unforgiving. Several faculty had been in the Marines. Their discipline had no love, no warmth. Made everything worse.

I felt some hurt in Harry about Rusty's orneriness. I wondered if Rusty's rebellious groping for independence was a predictable and healthy effort to become his own person, particularly given how decisive and strong Harry and Eloise were. I counseled patience, of which Harry claimed he had little. Harry admitted later that he and Eloise were perfectionists and may have been too tough in their demands, which they had not made with much "finesse." Both parents saw themselves as "tough disciplinarians." Harry told me:

> I think parenting is the most demanding, challenging, frustrating job one can do, if you really are critical and sit back and think, "What could I have done better?" Virtually im-

possible to be perfect. It is so . . . it requires you to be objective about things which you can't be because you are so enmeshed in them yourself. It is so much easier to be understanding with those you are not so close to. So many demands and challenges that are always changing. You just have to walk that thin line between too much and too little.

Amen!

Harry was a loving father, as Eloise told me. He also valued and respected his children's talents and individuality and accepted responsibility for helping them to fulfill them. However, as he told us when he said "it's my selfish side," he was aware that his hopes for their success and happiness might be his, not theirs. He also held them to firm expectations. Like most parents, however, he was challenged to walk that "thin line" between holding them to his expectations and being either too authoritarian or too permissive in ways that might blur legitimate generational boundaries.

Being a loving and democratic but firm parent to today's adolescents is, as Harry said, the most demanding and frustrating job we can have. As the opportunities for them to go astray have multiplied, parents since the mid-fifties have enjoyed being parents less. But not Harry. He made being a good father a genuine commitment. His loving, respectful, and firm attitudes sustained him as he explored how to be a good parent. (Harry's story tells us, though, that even good parents can have troubled children and be baffled about how to help them grow up healthily.)

Harry's Own Parents

Our own parents' attitudes about parenting and their personalities are our earliest, most vivid models of how to be a parent. How did Harry remember his own parents? He felt that his parents loved and respected each other; they were demonstrative in showing each other their love. They also accepted and enjoyed their parental role. Because his parents had had clear values and expectations, the atmosphere of Harry's childhood home had been consistent and predictable. Speaking for Eloise as well, he said, "Our parents were disciplinarians; they both were pretty tough. We had to work for things, obey certain rules. We had our curfews and expectations. Eloise and I are trying to have a more open communication, more give and take, be more willing to listen than our parents did with us."

Both his mother and father had been in good physical and mental health. He recalls them as active, energetic, affirming persons not absorbed in their own lives but interested in their children's. Feeling close to and loving them, he respected and valued them both (though his father more) as role models. He could count on them. Actively concerned about Harry's development, particularly his intellectual growth, they made themselves available when he needed help; both helped him with his homework. He never felt that they rejected him. His mother, with whom he felt more temperamentally compatible, was a warm and expressive person. His father, sterner, even authoritarian, held him to higher disciplinary standards. Harry stubbornly rebelled against these standards—just as Rusty was resisting Harry's expectations.

Parents have the joyful or regretful opportunity to learn how their children turn out as adults. Certainly one index of having been a competent parent is the future success, maturity, and well-being of one's children. Harry and Eloise not only believed they were good parents. They also felt their children had the maturity to turn out okay as adults. (They described their children as quite mature, ranking above two-thirds of the other children in the study.) Ten years later, how well had Rusty and Sally coped with their children's' adolescence and early adulthood? What was Harry's commitment to being a father to his *adult* children?

Harry as a Father in His Fifties

Five years after my visit, the Barnetts moved to a major metropolitan area, where they became extremely successful vocationally. By the time I interviewed Harry one evening in December, 1993, he had become the chief administrative officer of one of our country's foremost health maintenance organizations. Eloise was recognized as one of the world's premier researchers in her field, had been named president of a research organization, and had received a coveted national prize in her field.

Rusty and Sally

As many adolescents do when they leave home, Rusty and Sally got themselves together. Both children completed college without misadventure, are now successfully rising in their careers, and are beginning to explore their paths to marriage. Harry expects that they will fulfill his three most important wishes: become professionally successful, be happily married, and make him a grandfather.

Thinking back over his fifty-five years, Harry rated his years guiding his children through their adolescence as the most difficult of his life. Speaking of these years, he reflected that they had been

> very hard on Eloise and very hard on the family. I don't think that as a professional, I was quite as productive then as later. We should have gotten more help for my wife so there would have been less strain on her. There was no way we could have handled Rusty differently. Just had to endure it. Perhaps we should have tried professional help in retrospect, if we had known it would have taken as long as it did. . . . I wish I could have done better.

Reminiscent of his comments about parenting ten years earlier, Harry continued, "Parenthood is most demanding. You become an expert only when it is over. Very difficult to be expert while going through it. They are the first product off the assembly line."

Harry's Calling to Be a Parent

Having survived Rusty's adolescent turmoil—though with lingering regrets that he had not been more patient—Harry has since deepened his commitment to his calling as a father. Signs of his commitment returned over and over throughout his tests and interviews. When asked what his happiest experience had been or of what he was most proud since my previous visit, he immediately replied, "The accomplishments of our kids. . . . It is a double relief to have endured . . . [the turmoil] and to come out with things having gone so well."

Like Billie, Andy, and Marty, whose careers had also absorbed their energies from early adulthood to their mid-forties, Harry has begun to come to terms with his career aspirations. Feeling vocationally fulfilled, he values his family relationships more. Despite his distinguished career, his two greatest current satisfactions are his relationship with Eloise and his relationships with his children. His comment about why they are so important reflects the depth of his need for people and the kind of family out of which successful and healthy children come. About how important Eloise is to him, he said:

> I'm a person who needs affection and companionship. I never would be a loner. . . . I don't enjoy it, I hate it when she is gone. I don't like to eat alone. I don't like to sleep alone. . . . I take great pride in what she has done. She has been a terrific role model for my children. Sexually she is very important. We have worked very hard to sustain a meaningful relationship and we take great pleasure in being together. . . . Our family has really jelled. We went through those conflicts . . . [which are] pretty much gone. Our family is just delighted to be together. Very supportive of each other. We look forward to having the kids here. If we are away, they support each other. We have fun. They are merciless in giving us the needle. They bring their friends home. We have been really successful as parents.

"You rate yourself as very fulfilled and competent as a father. Why?" I asked. Harry described the same kind of strengths that the study's other successful men and women also saw in their own parents.

> They have always known that I have loved them and was there to help them. . . But at the same time, I have been a pretty good disciplinarian and set high standards for them. I expected them to produce to their abilities. If their report cards were not good I didn't spare letting them know about it. . . . I communicate to keep their respect and not take advantage of that respect. . . . I try my damnedest to be positive . . . and with Rusty, in particular, I can understand at the time when he needs understanding and when he needs a kick in the ass. I say to him, "Suck it up and get on with it." I can't do that with Sally. Girls don't respond in the same way.

If Rusty and Sally asked him, "What is there to live for?" Harry—like Billie and the Millers—would answer, "Life is fabulous. People are interesting. If you are willing to look around you and accentuate the positives and just look for them and not allow yourself to spiral into negatives, then life is a great experience. A fabulous opportunity."

Keep Harry in mind as we explore the meaning of parenting further. In the next chapter I ask what light the larger study can give us about two questions: What kind of personality do men and women who enjoy being parents have? Which core strengths contribute to parental competence—that is, what strengths do parents share whose children turn out well as adults?

Chapter 11

The Character of Fulfilled and Competent Parents

Harry found it "unbelievable" that some people regret having children. Others like Billie's father look forward to the day their children will permanently leave them. One said that he wished he could donate his adolescent son to society and write him off as a charitable gift on his tax return. Then there are those who, like Harry, so love their children that they exult in their successes and suffer their failures; they look forward to accompanying their children on their paths to fulfillment as long as they live.

The Character of Fulfilled Parents

Do parents who enjoy being parents differ from parents who don't? Yes. Can we really talk about the character of *the* fulfilled parent? Probably yes for mothers; probably no for fathers.

Men and Women Who Feel Fulfilled as Parents

Mothers and fathers who enjoy being parents are in fact competent ones. They also succeed in their other principal adult roles. Why? Because their maturity enables them to adapt well to the strains and difficulties of being parents. Their maturity also gives them the strengths to adapt well to their other familial roles. Parents who enjoy being parents are like Billie; because they believe they can cope with whatever may arise, they feel good about themselves.

Rusty tested his parents' maturity for years. Explaining how they responded to their trials, Harry said:

> We both persevered. We are both strong. We both did our best . . . to try to understand what Rusty was going through . . . [The counselor] reassured us that there were no deep and dire problems. My wife and I supported each other. We never allowed him to split the two of us. The kids now make fun of us for being a team. They say, "Of course you'll support mom." They did their damnedest to divide and conquer.

Harry drew on a long history of maturity to cope with Rusty without becoming disenchanted about being his father. He was more mature than 97 percent of the study's other men when he and they were Rusty's age. His high school counselor saw him as "fundamentally serious and a responsible worker but also a playboy, very diversified in extracurricular activities, and just very outstanding." Harry's college advisor wrote that he was a "sound and hardworking" man of "good character." He rated his emotional stability and determination excellent, his intelligence and personality good, but his originality only fair. In his mid-forties, Harry was the fourth most mature man of the study; he has continued to be very mature into his fifties.

Because no other shared or common strengths describe *both* the fulfilled mother *and* father, being a parent most likely means something different to women than to men.

The Character of Mothers Who Feel Fulfilled as Mothers

If you are a man looking for a partner who really enjoys children and will feel fulfilled as a parent, look for a woman who is adaptable and not a "stuck-in-a-rut" person. She should be sensitive to children's needs and willing to try anything that might help them grow up healthily. She should also be an emotional person who is warm, compassionate, cheerful, and loyal.

The Character of Fathers Who Feel Fulfilled as Fathers

However, if you are a woman who wants a partner who enjoys being a father, you will have to rely much more on your intuition than on what I found. Males who enjoy being fathers later in life come in many different packages that have almost no common colors, shapes, or wrappings. It's as if no "father character," no strong core of traits, is necessary to feel fulfilled as a father. Only a bare handful of traits describe the fulfilled fathers. They are adventurous, willing to take realistic risks, and, like fulfilled mothers, are willing to try new things.

These traits made me feel better about myself as a father. If you knew my son, you'd know why. He has really tested how adventurous a risk taker I can be. I never anticipated that when he was thirty-two he would decide, in his words, to "play for one or two more years" before "settling down." He bought a twenty-five foot Vertue sailboat and taught himself how to sail and navigate by the sun and stars. One night he called from Juneau, Alaska, where he had been working, to tell us, rather off-handedly, that he planned to sail around the world alone for several years. If you are a parent, you may empathically understand my reaction to what I called his "extended vacation." I asked him, "What if you don't arrive in Auckland when you plan? What should we do?"

"Oh, just forget about me."

Well! Easy to say when you've never been a parent. As Rusty taught Harry, so my son has taught me that the riskiest thing a person can do is to become a parent. Could this be another reason why today's youth may be leery about having kids?

So if fathers who enjoy being fathers are adventurous risk takers, and not stuck in ruts, that makes me a satisfied father—except for the realistic part. I risked sailing with him from Tahiti to Bora Bora: forty-two hours to go 110 miles by his reckoning, being battered by huge waves, apprehensively watching him dance around the deck, changing sails and tying up ropes; I laid flat on the heaving deck, gripping the gunwales as if my life depended on it—which it did—as the tumultuous waves swept over the heeling cabin; I upchucked despite Dramamine and my vow not to and wondered if Harriet was about to lose both of us. I proudly discovered my son on that trip: his self-taught competence and serene self-confidence. But *realistically* adventurous? I didn't tell him that I swore if ever I got back on ground, I'd never sail again. Instead, I'd be more sane and hike with him on land.

I did twenty months later. This time he chose Sri Lanka, which was in the midst of a brutalizing civil war. For a day, we dodged trees felled to block the roads, saw generators knocked out so that large areas were plunged into darkness, and avoided buses and trains, which were systematically being blown up or whose operators were being shot. If not on sea or land, then maybe in the air next time. How about free-fall parachuting with him over Kenya? (He insists I exaggerate both on sea and land—but it's how I felt.)

Parenthood as a Calling

The study's results puzzled me, though. Why aren't satisfied fathers more sympathetic, warm, playful, and a host of other good things as well? Why weren't they like Harry? Why is a father's personality seemingly so irrelevant for feeling fulfilled as a parent? To discover what being a parent meant to men and women, I turned to the meaning of work. Work can either be just a job that has to be done or a real calling—the original religious meaning of *vocation*. If you have a strong number one self, you may sense what being "called" means. If not, think of Marty, called to be a feminist. She has a mission, a commitment, to do what she is meant to do, to have a consuming goal or way of life that focuses her best talents and energies for some transcendent purpose. Think also of Harry, called to be a loving but firm parent. (I sometimes think my son's calling is to be another Columbus or Neil Armstrong—an adventurer challenging destiny.)

Might not we talk similarly about parenthood? We could view parenting as just a *job* and therefore resent how much time and energy we have to spend on our children. When the children reach late adolescence we could tell them, as Billie's father told her, to leave home. Like him, we would never visit them as adults. Or we could view parenting as a *calling* as well as a route to self-fulfillment. It could give us the opportunity to continue growing and fulfilling some of our strongest nurturing and affectional needs. Harriet feels this way. She dropped her appointments, even our special weekend together, to drive four hours to be with our daughter and Benjamin when his temperature reached 102. She couldn't resist the call of her surging grandmotherly needs. At 104, I would have gone with her.

So why did satisfaction with being a father seem so irrelevant to the men's personalities? Of the thirty attributes of parenthood about which we can be satisfied (such as the amount of time and energy that parenting demands), eight measure how much parenting is fulfilling, meets our strongest needs, utilizes our best talents, is central to our identity, and is compatible with our temperament—signs that parenting isn't just an impersonal job but is deeply meaningful to us. For mothers, six of the eight attributes predict their overall satisfaction with being a parent. Women who are the classic mothers really enjoy being mothers. For fathers, only two contributed as much to fulfillment. Perhaps this difference means that a man's paternal role and strengths are peripheral to his identity and personality. American boys are not raised to think of themselves as fathers or to develop the strengths necessary to be good ones.

How might this difference in the meaning of parenting show up in real life? If dad comes home tired one night wanting some fun in bed before going to sleep and the baby in the next room cries, what happens? Mom immediately loses her desire and feels compelled to leave their warm bed to go comfort *her* baby. Dad, impelled otherwise, irritatingly tells her to wait a minute or two. She may oblige, but guess what she's thinking of? Or if a child is sick, who frets and feels called to stay home to take care of it? When I describe motherhood as a calling rather than a job, women know immediately what I mean. Of course, fatherhood can be a calling, motherhood a job. But the odds are long that it will not be men but women, like Marty, who will feel more sharply divided between taking care of their children and making the committee meeting.

A woman for whom being a mother is just a job

1. Complains constantly about how much time her children take
2. Leaves her child to watch TV much of the time
3. Looks forward to vacations without the children, who she parks at grandmother's
4. Makes no special effort to be home when the children return from school
5. Nags her husband when he doesn't take over when there's a problem

What other signs can you suggest?

One or two of these signs are not enough to tell us that parenting is a job rather than a calling for us. Parents need to get away together or be alone to keep their own special interests alive. Mothers who must work can't be home when their children return from school. And they may be too tired to patiently read McCloskey's *Time of Wonder* for the eighth time before bedtime.

Our underlying attitude, however, can create a pattern indicating that parenting is a job, not a calling. Today's perceptive kids know the difference. Risk asking them which of their friends' parents is a "natural"—someone who really enjoys kids. And ask them why they think so. Or pose an easier question: "What are parents like who are not really committed to and excited about being parents?"

I now believe that parenting has a different meaning for the typical woman and man. Although the two perspectives may be converging in younger generations, the differences still cause much conflict between fathers and mothers.

If you are a woman, you may think I am sexist. But the following question seems logical to ask: How much does a woman's biology influence her emotional commitment to her child? I believe it plays much more of a role for her than a man's does for him. We are learning how mother and child become emotionally bonded. Feeling life in one's womb for months contributes to this bond. We also know that the fetus learns to recognize its mother's voice *in utero*—another step in bonding mother and child. Such bonding probably creates a more intense identity conflict for career women than for men. Eloise and almost all of the other career mothers of the study were conflicted about their calling to be a good mother and desire to do well in their careers.

Marty has told us just how painful the conflict can be. She was less satisfied with every attribute associated with parental "calling" than she was with every comparable item indexing vocational "calling." Being a top feminist lawyer fulfilled her more than being a good mother. She told us who her number one self was when she spontaneously said, "I can be successful in my work and feel good about myself and have some of that rub off on the family relationships." She did not say, "I can be successful in my family relationships and have some of that rub off on my work."

Andy enjoyed being a father more than Marty did being a mother. She sensed this, mentioning several times how "relieved" she was that he enjoyed being a father. That he enjoyed it and was such a good father made her feel less guilty. But Andy also felt more fulfilled by his work than by fatherhood. Harry's troubles with Rusty did not diminish his satisfaction as a parent to the extent that he became noticeably less fulfilled as a parent than as an administrator.

Since enjoyment of parenting and fulfillment as a parent can be increased by becoming a competent parent, what parental strengths contribute most to our competence?

Competent Parents Are Loving, Democratic, and Firm

Don't despair that the participants of the study believe that sixty-three strengths contribute to being a competent parent. I can boil them down to eight basic ones. In rough declining order of importance, they are as follows:

- Patience and other personality traits like sense of humor, high energy, self-confidence, and calmness
- A loving, affectionate attitude
- The ability to create a predictable environment for children that is consistent, firm, and fair
- Good communication skills like listening, understanding, openness, and empathy
- Respect for a child's individuality
- Playful involvement with and enjoyment of children
- Acting like a teacher who has expectations and goals for raising a child
- Taking a problem-solving attitude toward childrearing and using such skills to help a child learn how to adapt

While all these strengths are necessary, the most competent parents consistently differ from the least competent in three key ways. Competent parents

- Are loving
- Are democratic—that is, they respect their children's individuality
- Have firm expectations of their children

Feeling loved gives us the security to explore and risk. If we are afraid to take risks, we don't discover anything new about ourselves or our world. Being loved also provides us the model of how to love others. Feeling unloved and rejected can destroy us. Charles Dickens wrote in *Dombey and Son*: "For not an orphan in the wide world can be so deserted as the child who is an outcast from a living parent's love."

Feeling that we are genuinely listened to and respected affirms our sense of worth and autonomy. Parents who are not democratic, who walk roughshod over our needs and temperament, can undermine—or squash—our individuality and self-confidence.

Parents who provide flexible but firm guidelines about how we should behave help us to control our efforts and talents by ourselves. Parents who too quickly give in to our screams can aggravate our petulance and self-centeredness and reduce our will to persist and learn how to cope.

Fulfilling Lives discusses the specific parental traits that contribute to a child's future success and well-being in detail. Here, I highlight just a few themes that apply to both mothers and fathers. I then examine each of their special contributions to their children's future success as marital partners, lovers, and parents.

Parents' Personality, Not Childrearing Techniques, Contribute to How a Child Turns Out

Two parents may restrict TV viewing to Saturday mornings, but that technique may have radically different effects. One child may interpret the TV rules as punishment by a rejecting and hostile parent; another may feel the rules are being imposed by a loving and accepting but firm parent. The first child becomes sullen and sour or resistant and negativistic; the other complains and argues but does not withdraw or become hostile.

Competent Parents Share Feminine Interpersonal Strengths

The more competent fathers were like Andy and Harry. They were androgynous, scoring high in understanding, gentleness, and sensitivity. Competent mothers are seen by others to have these and numerous other interpersonal skills.

Competent Parents Produce Healthy, Adaptable Children

The children of competent parents are more mature and adaptable than those of incompetent parents. Emotionally stable, physically and mentally healthy, and happy mothers raise mature children. These mothers are also loved by others, are conscientious, are open to trying new things, and so fulfill their potential more than mothers do whose children are less mature. Likewise, the fathers of mature children are mentally healthy, mature, open, warm, not overly demanding but decisive and adventurous.

Competent Mothers and Fathers Contribute to Their Children's Adult Success Differently

Mothers much more than fathers enable their daughters and sons to succeed in their familial relationships. However, neither parent apparently influences the quality of their children's adult friendships.

Mothers Who Contribute to Their Daughters' Future Familial Success. A woman trying to balance completing graduate school and taking care of her children said of her own mother, "Everything I know about relating to my children I learned from my mother. I just brought it up to date in some ways. All I learned about how to respect my kids, how to talk with them, confront them, demand respect and integrity from them . . . it all comes from a certain tone of love and firmness that was so much my mother. It's a tone that is a big part of me, and I can pass it on."

Sue Schwartz was one of the study's three most fulfilled and competent working mothers. She was also one of the most happily married women and her best friend gave her an almost perfect score for being a close friend. Sue loved being a mother; she had no desire to be freed of her responsibility for her children, who, she said, had never created any problems for her. Her husband agreed with her judgment. Their two children were the fourth most mature and healthy of the group.

Sue believed that her maternal attitude and competence stemmed from her mother's influence. When I asked, "For what are you most grateful about your mother?" she stressed, "For her example. Many ways. Not everything, because she wasn't perfect. She did everything she thought best to be a mother. She made mistakes because she was so overzealous as a mother. Too unselfish in many cases; that's what I am not grateful for. She loved to teach us things; she loved to love us. She had no favorites; she loved all four of us."

Is it any wonder that Sue rated her feelings toward her mother as warm, close, and understanding? She spontaneously replied to the incomplete sentence, "My mother and I . . ." with the words, "loved each other a great deal," and to the fragment "When she thought of her mother . . ." with "she smiled with affection."

Sue's mother modeled many traits of the computer's portrait of the ideal mother who contributes to her daughter's success as a wife and mother. Daughters who, as adults, create successful intimate relationships had warm, affectionate, and outgoing mothers who were emotionally involved with others. Open to sharing personal secrets and feelings with their daughters, their mothers maturely and clearly affirmed their belief that their daughters should achieve academically, be ethical persons, and create warm and loving relationships with others. They were neither rigid dogmatists nor long-suffering, defeated martyrs. As a consequence, the successful daughters respected and loved their mothers and wanted very much to be like them. Identifying with mothers so mature in caring and communicative strengths was a major reason why the women succeeded as wives, mothers, and lovers.

The women who failed in their intimate familial roles came from homes that had few of these strengths. Their mothers were more self-absorbed, cold, even hostile, severely disciplining, and didn't give as lovingly of themselves or as openly and freely as mothers like Sue's did. Such mothers tended to provoke their daughters to resist and rebel stubbornly against them.

Fathers Who Contribute to Their Daughters' Future Familial Success. I can't say much about the fathers of women who grow up to be good wives, lovers, and parents. Sue spoke for many of the women when she answered my question, "What's your greatest disappointment about your father?" Sadly, she said, "My father could never tell me he loved me or that I looked nice or pay me a compliment until three days before he died."

"What did he say?"

"Thank you sweetheart. I'll never forget what you've done for me." Sue then commented, "I nearly fainted. He leaned over and kissed my arm. That's the most wonderful thing that ever happened to me. I was so glad. It took forty years, but I no longer feel bitter. He just really felt he could never tell me."

The fathers of daughters who succeeded as wives, mothers, and lovers had been emotionally present in their daughters' early lives but only quietly in contrast to the overshadowing presence of their wives. They had not withdrawn from family disputes and arguments. Unlike Sue's father, they had freely shared their feelings and ideas with their daughters. The girls' fathers had supported and encouraged them—for example, in athletic activities. But they weren't as emotionally involved in their daughters' lives as their wives were. So they didn't have much impact on their daughters' later familial success.

Parents who want their daughters to enjoy intimate and fulfilling relationships with their adult partners and children, should:

- Talk very openly and freely with each other in front of and with their adolescent daughters about what they think and feel
- Expect that their daughters should develop loving and caring relationships with others
- Be sure that their daughters clearly understand where they stand, particularly about how they should get along with others

Mothers Who Contribute to Their Sons' Future Familial Success. I have no doubts about who contributes most to boys' later ability to create close relationships with their partners and children. Their mothers!

Men who create happy marriages, mutually fulfilling sexual relationships, and who are good fathers have had mature and mentally healthy mothers when they were growing up. Their mothers were outgoing and emotionally involved with others. Though accepting of their sons, they held them to high expectations, particularly academic ones—but not in ways that eroded their sons' basically good feelings about them. By being affectionate and creating close and loving relationships with their sons, they helped them learn how to relate intimately with family members as well as with others.

Harry's mother fits most of this picture better than Andy's does. Harry felt close to, respected, and loved his mother. A warm and affectionate woman, she was devoted to him and others. To Harry, however, she had not walked that thin line very well of balancing respect for his needs and ideas and her own too-firm ones about how to raise him.

Men who did *not* succeed in their primary relationships felt rejected by their mothers when young. They in turn did not love their mothers, who they recalled as distant, authoritarian, dominating, even hostile. We have seen that success in our intimate roles requires typical feminine interpersonal strengths. Growing up with a rejecting, cold, or hostile mother may impel a boy to reject his own interpersonal potential and to overdevelop masculine traits in order to assert an independent identity. Bruce Jackson illustrates the effects of a coldly rejecting mother. He failed maritally because he needed June to be the mother he never had, but a mother whom he could tyranically control the way his mother had controlled him.

The results are convincing. Mothers whose sons later become good marital partners, parents, and lovers are loving, accepting women who respect their sons' individuality but who expect them to meet high standards.

Fathers Who Contribute to Their Sons' Future Familial Success. Fathers contribute little to their sons' subsequent success as marital partners, parents, and lovers. Men like Harry, who succeeded in their intimate relationships, had fathers who accepted them. Sons like Bruce Jackson, who failed in such relationships, had fathers who rejected them. Rejecting a son turns out to be the most demoralizing thing a father can do to his son. Feeling rejected by a distant, uninvolved father sows the seeds for later discordant relationships, particularly inclinations to be stubborn and rebellious. Perhaps you are as uneasy as I am that fathers seem to contribute so little to their sons' later success in their personal relationships. I am not sure how to evaluate this finding. Two stories suggest how early in life fathers may create templates in their sons of how *not* to get along with others. Two-year-old Georgie was pointing out trucks, cows, and trees in his picture book as he slumped, cradled in my arm, on the living room couch while I waited for his father to come home to begin the interviews. When his father came in the door, Georgie immediately ran toward him, with his arms outstretched to hug him. His father shook his hand instead. Georgie's mother told me that her husband had never hugged either of them, told them he loved them, or remembered their birthdays. What a model of intimacy! What interpersonal seeds was he sowing in Georgie? Which ones would sprout? Rather, which potential seeds wouldn't?

A five-year-old black boy in an inner-city school came up to me scowling and with clenched fists as I walked past his kindergarten room at dismissal time.

"Get your dukes up! I'm going to fight you," he screamed.

Momentarily taken aback and thinking he was being playful, I raised my fists. He wasn't being playful. He charged into me, flailing. Fortunately for me, at that moment his mother swept by, and, without breaking her step, swooped him up under her arm, and sailed serenely off down the hall as he squiggled and squirmed, still screaming "Get your dukes up! Get them up!" I inwardly cried for him. Not just for his mortification but for his future. I could see a hurt, defiant "father" inside him urging him to put up his dukes to protect himself by attacking first all strange "whiteys" who were out to hurt him.

Why do fathers contribute so much less than mothers to their sons' close relationships? I draw some hunches from men's male friendships, to which I return in the next chapter. Typical American male friendships are quite superficial; they're primarily social rather than personal. The fathers could not teach their sons much about intimacy, because they themselves did not have the skills to be intimate with others. Like Andy, few of the men had been close to or good friends with their fathers, who were part of a generation of males, so man after man told me, that had only worked to fulfill their duty as breadwinners.

How does a son learn the self-disclosing skills that intimacy requires if he has a father like Mark's? Mark's father was dying of colon cancer, just as Mark's grandfather had fifteen years earlier. He, like his father before him, never uttered a word about it and avoided all of Mark's determined efforts (as his grandfather had resisted his grandmother's) to talk about it. Be a man. Be strong and silent. Grin and bear it. But this is not a good father.

If fathers are unable to talk with their sons about how they feel—even about the most important of all topics, such as their impending deaths—how are sons to learn the skills of being intimate with their spouses, lovers, and own children? Being open, expressing feelings, and sharing experiences are some of the most precious gifts a father can give his son. He should allow his son to know him from the inside out.

I asked the men what their greatest disappointment was about their fathers and later about their goals for raising their children. Many said they regretted never *knowing* their fathers and that they wanted to be a different father with their own children. Harry's story about a man flying alone with one of his children and a dog—described in the preceding chapter—captures what I heard over and over from the more competent fathers: They wanted to have a more intimate relationship with their children. Since such fathers are more mature and have more competent and mature children, perhaps they are sowing seeds that will enable their sons to become more successful marital partners, parents, and lovers.

Harry's father was typical of those whose sons turned out successfully in their marital, parental, and sexual roles. Andy's father was less so, more because of his New England taciturnity than his active rejection of Andy. We'll never know just how much his father's reserve pushed Andy to join support groups that taught him how to be more emotionally expressive. But Andy felt very good when he first hugged his father, who responded so warmly that Andy looks forward to similar hugs when they meet. Moral? If you are a son, don't give up on your father. He may just need some loving prodding. (Bruce Jackson would need a lot of bulldozing.)

With only one exception, all the men had grown up with fathers present in the home. This is no longer the case for millions of boys. I am frequently asked, "What about boys who grow up in single-parent families where no father is present? What happens to them?" Since no one has yet thoroughly studied how such boys turn out as adults, I answer, "I'm not sure." A few studies report that boys survive divorce much less well than girls, particularly if they subsequently live only with their mother. They are more aggressive and less socially mature. Boys living only with their father are more mature and cooperative and feel better about themselves. However, such boys have not been followed into adulthood to discover the character of either single mothers or fathers whose sons later succeeded.

What may be most important for a boy's future healthy growth may not be just having a man at home but a father who really wants to be a good parent. He should be a competent but loving, interpersonally mature man who cares about and is actively involved in his son's development. Boys whose fathers are rejecting, emotionally inaccessible, distant, and cold may be better off, in the long run, not having them around. Growing up with fathers like Bruce Jackson, who reject them, and worse yet, hostilely so, could undermine their future intimacy, social, and vocational success. Such boys need to develop a sustained relationship with other males, like older brothers, friends, teachers, scout leaders, and grandfathers, who provide the loving, respectful, and firm presence essential to healthy development and adult success.

As I've pointed out earlier, succeeding as a marital partner, lover, and parent depends on our character, maturity, and feminine interpersonal strengths. Andy's and Marty's struggles show us that it is not easy to change our character, but that it can be done. They demonstrate that we can create happier, more fulfilling marriages and learn to enjoy being parents. Most of us would like simple "self-help" books to teach us how to argue more constructively with our partners or deal with a stubborn two-year-old. In the long run, however, no technique works unless it reflects our character—our attitudes, values, and ways of getting along with others.

What about fathers and mothers in the twenty-first century? My hunch is that more will struggle with the issues, as Marty, Andy, and Harry have, and will follow more in Andy's than Harry's footsteps. Like Andy, younger males will still view their vocational self as their number one self. But they may enjoy their children more than their own fathers did, for whom being a father was a number three or four self.

Now that women are freer to choose what they want to be, I expect more will choose not to have children. In making that choice, they will not lose status or the respect of others. But they may not escape the regretful comments of their own mothers who would like to have grandchildren to mother again. More of those who do decide to have children will view being a mother as their calling, which bodes well for their children's future healthy growth and success. I am much less hopeful about those teenage mothers and fathers who have not chosen or have chosen unwisely. The rate of unwed teenage pregnancies will most likely not decline until society—especially through its schools—educates children more wisely about sex, babies, and their development.

The key question that advocates for building strong families must ask is, "How do we resurrect the idea that parenthood should be a calling?" One way to encourage greater commitment to parenthood is to appeal to today's emphasis on becoming healthier and more fulfilled. Both fathers and mothers grow more healthily than childless adults do. The evidence is dramatically clear that fathers become more mature than nonfathers during their twenties and thirties. Being a mother is one of the top three determinants of a woman's maturing in her thirties and forties. Children disturb us, provoke us, educate us. They tell us much about who we are. They make us more caring and less selfish. They prod us to grow up. If being a parent is more than just a job, children capture our hearts and bring much joy.

Given the gender differences between American men and women in the quality of their familial relationships, do such differences also occur in their same-sex friendships? Is there a core set of personality attributes that describe men and women who succeed in having close friendships? The next chapter explores these questions.

Chapter 12

Succeeding as a Friend

Roger, my spokesperson for the generations after the one I studied, insists that men, "when they're serious and not trying to appear macho," really desire friendships with other men like those that women have with other women. He may be right. But the men were more inept in their friendships than the women, so I shall focus primarily on describing their relationships with other men.

Four themes describe the men's and women's friendships with their own gender: Men and women do not differ in what they want in their intimate friendships; men and women differ in the quality of their same-gender relationships; men who have close male friendships are androgynous and have feminine interpersonal traits; and men's and women's ability to form intimate friendships doesn't *consistently* tell us much about their other successes, though it does suggest that their maturity may contribute to the quality of their friendships.

The Ideal Friend

Above all else, both men and women want friends with whom they can be vulnerable, trusting, self-disclosing, and mutually affectionate and loving. They also wish that they could be with each other more often to share their mutual interests and activities. However, spending much more time with friends, while desirable, is not crucial. The people in the study prefer to keep in touch primarily by phone; few wrote more than several letters a year to their friends. Few want any sexual feelings to complicate their relationships.

Male and Female Differences in Quality of Friendships

Widely held opinions that men and women differ in the quality of their same-gender friendships are true. My evidence is too clear to need more than a bare-bones summary. Compared to men, women

- Believe it is more important to have a close friend
- Feel more fulfilled in their friendships and so less lonely
- Are more intimate with and closer to their friends
- Feel more affectionate and loving toward their friends
- Are more open and self-disclosing in their relationships
- Feel more comfortable sharing their greatest insecurities, failures, and feelings about their own parents

Why are friendships between American males so inexpressive and emotionally thin? Traveling in Asia and the Middle East always reminds me of how American males rein in their feelings and guard their inner selves in their relationships with each other. Turkish, Indian, and Nepalese friends walk arm in arm, hold hands, and lean on and hug each other publicly; Chinese male friendships are known for their depth and loyalty. When I compared American with Turkish and Italian friendships, young American men felt more discomfort and anxiety expressing most of the qualities that describe an ideal friend. Many American men resist reaching out to give another support, affection, and love. One man spoke for many when he ruefully remarked, "I don't know how to tell a man that I like him and would like to be his friend." Some men felt that sharing their feelings even with their partners was unmasculine and a sign of weakness that they equated with effeminacy. A few men had never hugged their wives away from their beds. A few had never told them they loved them. A few had never given their wives a birthday present or spontaneously brought them a special gift or called them in the middle of the day to let them know that they had been thinking of them.

For at least 200 years, American society has not valued enduring, same-gender, close adult friendships (especially between males) as highly as other societies. Tocqueville told us this was true of American males in the early nineteenth century. He observed them "always considering themselves as standing alone, and they are apt to imagine that their whole destiny is in their own hands."[1] Speaking of the effect of democracy on an American male, he said that it "separates his contemporaries from him; it throws him back forever upon himself alone and threatens in the end to confine him entirely within the solitude of his own heart." [2]

The lonesome American cowboy still remains a romantic hero. Strong, alone, self-contained Clint Eastwoods and John Waynes restlessly moving on from one adventure to another are enduring motifs in the American male psyche. Robert Redford and Paul Newman's friendship in *Butch Cassidy and the Sundance Kid* tells us that modern Americans wish their cowboy heroes were not so lonesome. These outlaws' inseparable friendship was sealed by shared activities: robbing banks, visiting prostitutes together, loving the same woman, traveling to Bolivia and dying there together—but they did not talk openly about themselves with each other. Not until they faced capture and death did Butch admit to Sundance that he had never fired his gun to kill a man.

I can bring nineteenth-century American males up to date with a few modern vignettes. A ten-year-old fourth grade boy began his poem with the words, "I'm a space man, a great man, a high paid man, and lone." He went on to talk about all the themes that have described the typical American male as a brave, heroic, adventurous explorer. He concluded with "circling . . . around the moon and seeing every distant star."

And my son's ambition to circle the earth alone in his twenty-five-foot Vertue sailboat.

And by a national survey that reported that fewer than 25 percent of adult males in the United States said that they had a close friend. When asked what "close friend" meant, they said sharing similar activities together, like participating in sports, playing cards together, drinking, and talking about women.

And by Stuart Miller's three-year odyssey, almost a calling, in search of what he called a "true male friendship." Interviewing hundreds of American and European men in their thirties and forties about their male friendships, he wrote a poignant book. One chapter, titled "The Death of Intimacy in Our Times," captured what he discovered: Few men felt they had a deep friendship with another man. Miller himself had never created one either. He speculated on why had he failed in the book's last paragraph: "This reflexive cringing from all true engagement is a curious emotion. Probably it is part of human nature, the instinct of self-preservation asserting itself, a deep suspicion of involvement with others, of involvement with anyone outside of myself. A reaction known even to our most ancient poets. To meet such fears, only courage will do." He concludes by quoting Pindar's prayer, "Oh Gods! Let me have the strength and the courage to love my friends!" [3]

Or by the "close friendship" of Martin Brown, which was not what it seemed. Martin talked warmly and animatedly about his "close" friend, with whom he said he'd had long, "personal philosophical talks" for the past several years. His wife, a social worker sensitive to such relationships, had worried about how alone he had been ever since she had known him. Now she was happy that he had found, in her words, a "soul mate." When interviewed about his friendships, Martin replied, somewhat disconsolately, "I've noticed what I do with my close friends over the years is that I tend to lean on them to get enough support. Sometimes I push them to do more for me than what they want to do. They then set limits, and after that, I find I'm not as good friends with them. Now, for the first time in my life, I have had a really close friend for several years. We talk and talk about the most personal things."

When I wrote his "close friend" to get his view of Martin and their "friendship," he returned the materials uncompleted with this comment: "I can't complete the enclosed ratings. I don't feel I know him very well. We have talked several times about my work; he usually just listens. I know almost nothing about him. Sorry."

Martin was the study's fourth most alone and friendless man. No wonder just a few sporadic long talks with another man had given him the feeling of "closeness." From her feminine perspective, his wife had assumed their relationship was like hers: a deeply intimate and self-revealing friendship.

Martin's "close friendship" is a caricature of the persisting friendships that many men claimed. Few had what their wives would call a "close" friend. Predictably, after I had concluded each interview and was talking with the couple about the study, the woman, more curious than the man, would ask her husband whom he had selected as his closest male friend for me to obtain information from. With few exceptions, the wife's impulsive reaction was, "You call him a close friend? He's just a casual acquaintance." Only 22 percent of the men—one of whom was Martin—claimed that they had a very close friend. On the other hand, one claimed he had twenty-four close friends! That's a lot of intimacy.

The Personality of Successful Friends

You've probably already guessed the character of the men and women who create close friendships with others. The character of a close friend is like that of a good marital partner. The men and women who created intimate friendships—as they and their friends described them—were androgynous. Their peers also described them as cheerful, emotionally stable persons who cared for and were sensitive to others' needs. They accepted and felt in good control of themselves. No wonder they trusted themselves to be playful and could risk trying new activities with the other. Their commonly shared portrait makes a lot of sense. Friends don't have to appear what they aren't with each other, even when their guard is down, as when they are playful.

The other strengths that describe good friends are more clearly etched for the men than for the women. The men who make good friends are more typically feminine in every interpersonal strength on which their peers rated them: from being affectionate, understanding, and sympathetic to being loyal, warm, and yielding. While also seen as stereotypically masculine—athletic, decisive, and leaders—the successful friends do not share a single one of more typical masculine traits, such as competitiveness, aggressiveness, dominance, or forcefulness. These traits can potentially divide and separate, if a friendship is not bonded by other strengths. The Andy Millers and Harry Barnetts rather than the Bill Spauldings and Bruce Jacksons of the study have close male friends.

I'm not sure how well I have examined the question of who succeeds as a friend. The meaning of success in male friendships may be more complex than my measures have captured. Since male friendships have not been well studied— particularly of men from different social classes and educational backgrounds—I cannot check how true the study's findings are for other men. My findings don't describe the friendship of Butch Cassidy and Sundance. I can't guess how they would have answered questions about the attributes of an ideal friendship and rated theirs. The movie makes it clear, however, that their masculine strengths cemented their friendship; perhaps this is true of many men today.

Men need many more strengths than women to succeed in their friendships. Remember that women who had happy husbands had many more virtuous qualities than men did who had happy wives; women had to be more adjustable to keep the marriage going. I'd make the same interpretation about men who succeed in creating close male friendships. Good male friends have about three times more virtues than good female friends have. Men are not raised to be proficient in intimate relationships—to be accepting, to yield, to cooperate, to soothe hurt feelings, and to bolster friends' good feelings about themselves. So numerous strengths are necessary to sustain a close relationship over time with another male who may not have perfected such strengths.

What Success in Friendship Predicts About a Person

The last of the four themes—that people's success as friends tells us little about them—suggests some implications we need to reflect on. The women and their friends generally viewed their friendships as either very intimate or perfect—only 15 percent of the women rated their close friendships as less than quite close. Their best friends also inclined toward rating the women as perfect on the different attributes of an ideal friend. Are most women really paragons of the ideal close friend? I doubt it. They did not talk that way in their interviews; about 20 percent had trouble giving me the name of a close friend. Since women are commonly believed to excel at understanding and sympathizing with others, is it too threatening to a woman to think she does not have close friends? Could it be that the women's friends did not want to hurt their feelings by rating them less than perfect, even though they had been assured that I would never let their friends know their ratings? Furthermore, when Martin rates his friendship to be more intimate than Andy does his, could this suggest that men are confused about the meaning of intimacy? For American males, words like *intimate* and *close* carry too many mixed meanings. Homophobic reactions to these words may cause some to undervalue the intimacy of their friendships.

The character of *both* men and women who succeed as friends is easy to describe. The closer you feel your same-gender friendships are, the more likely your colleagues will judge you as well adapted vocationally. Your partner will be happy that he or she has married you. Your closest friend will say that you excel on the six attributes you feel describe a close friendship. Everyone will rate you as ethical and typically feminine in the way you get along with others.

That a man's maturity, which consistently predicts so many adult successes, does not predict well the quality of his friendships troubles me. Perhaps the men's images of friendship were so diverse—more like juicy oranges for Andy, nuts for Bill Spaulding, and cauliflowers for Martin—that my computer became confused.

However, women who have close and intimate friends with whom they share their personal feelings about most everything are indeed more emotionally mature. Furthermore, women who succeed as friends are likely to also be competent and happy wives, mothers, and lovers. So a woman's intimate relationships with other women predict her maturity and success in her other personal relationships better than a man's.

I have now completed the book's major section about intimacy in our marital, parental, and sexual, as well as friendships. We are now ready to step back from the details of each role to understand the character strengths that men and women who succeed in all their personal relationships have in common. What are the irreducible attributes that men and women need in order to succeed in *all* their personal roles—as marital partners, parents, lovers, and friends?

Chapter 13

Ten Prescriptions for Building Strong Families and Relationships

"Family values" is a catchy and appealing slogan for the political agenda of the nineties. However, its vagueness—like that of an inkblot—permits politicians of every stripe to project their biases and hang ups onto it and so obscure the underlying issue: How do we create the strong families that are the foundation of any healthy community? To answer that question, we must first ask, "What is a strong family?" It is like the Leighton's and Barnett's. It is an enduring companionate relationship in which the partners are mutually sexually fulfilled and are called to be parents like Harry. It is a family founded on the character strengths and values that the study has identified.

Successful Personal Relationships

Five themes capture most of what we now know about successful relationships.

Success in Personal Relationships Has Many Different Meanings

We must be clear about the kind of success we want if we are going to achieve it.

Success in One Familial Role Predicts Success in Others

This is not 100 percent true, but it occurs frequently enough to suggest that a core set of strengths contributes to our success.

Men and Women Successful in Personal Relationships Are Mature and Androgynous

The model of maturity identifies the primary strengths necessary to cope with the day-to-day stresses of living. Living closely with partners who speak a "foreign language," growing children, and aging lovers inevitably provokes strain and argument. So it is not surprising that mature men and women adapt better to their familial roles than do immature men and women.

Obviously, the more numerous and diverse strengths we have, the better equipped we will be to successfully fulfill our different roles. Our familial and friendship roles require interpersonal strengths that typically describe women. Although it is not an earth-shaking result that good marital partners, parents, lovers, and friends share such strengths, this is the first time that good evidence supports those who have advocated that American society permit its men to be more androgynous.

Successful husbands, fathers, and lovers, as well as close friends, don't share any strengths most typical of males. Assertiveness, aggressiveness, forcefulness, dominance, competitiveness, and self-sufficiency are either irrelevant or can get in the way. Success as a hard-driving executive may not mean success as a marital partner or lover, unless one has also developed a warmer side to one's personality.

That interpersonal traits typically called feminine contribute to strong families forces me to think differently about how we raise males in the United States. We expect them to be assertive, competitive, and self-sufficient, but not to also be empathic, caring, and sensitive to others' feelings. Are we preparing them to be dangerously obsolescent in their future relationships with modern women? Are we not at risk, as a healthy society, if we don't alter our meanings of maleness to develop the strengths necessary to create healthier families and a sounder, kinder, and gentler America?

Why do so many American males still fear appearing to be emotional, affectionate, sensitive to others' needs, gentle, and yielding? Why do we regard such strengths in a male as wimpy, weak, sissy, gay? No wonder contemporary families are falling apart when such strengths are indispensable to forge strong families.

Just because a man has feminine interpersonal strengths does not mean he is not a virile male. The successful male partner, father, and lover is masculine, self-confident, self-reliant, independent, and respected for standing up courageously for his beliefs. Roger was right when he wrote me, "Because the person I see in the mirror is okay, I can be gentle and giving to others. I can expose my heart. That's something all the tough guys in the movies aren't tough enough to do!"

We need to be more critical about some religionists' and politicians' personal meanings about family values. If they gain ascendancy they can actually undermine and destroy the character on which strong families must be built. Not until religionists like Jerry Falwell and Pat Robertson, and politicians like Dan Quayle and Jessie Helms, lead New York City's next Gay Pride parade will our country begin to develop the healing cultural values necessary for developing strong families. This is not as irreverent or frivolous a statement as it may seem. Fearful of being thought of and labeled as fags, teenage boys ruthlessly suppress their softer strengths to assume the straitjacketed masculine role of keeping their chins up, controlling their emotions, competing with other boys, and dominating and sexually harassing girls. (*Schools of Hope* cites the evidence that supports these ideas about boys' peer relationships.) Our cultural climate must permit the 95 percent of heterosexual males to not be scared of their tender and softer sides. Then these men will be able to communicate with the emerging modern woman as empathic companions. Leading a Gay Pride parade will not increase the number of gays—most likely genetically and constitutionally determined in any case—but will release millions of heterosexual males from their irrational fears of just the kind of interpersonal strengths on which strong families are built.

To create strong families, therefore, we should make the development of mature and feminine interpersonal strengths a high priority, especially for boys.

Some Personal Relationships Have Different Meanings to Women Than to Men

For a woman, being a mother is more integrative of and central to her personality than being a father is to a man's. For a man, sex seems to be more peripheral to his core personality than it is to that of a woman (at least to a contemporary middle-aged one).

These gender differences are so deeply ingrained in our characters that they silently color and disturb male and female relationships, not just within the family but also in the marketplace and political arena. John Bobbitt can force his wife to have sex—as men have done for centuries in many cultures as their marital right—but Lorena Bobbitt views that as rape and cuts off its instrument. A mother staying home to take care of a sick child is viewed by her boss as slacking off, as unreliable, and therefore as ineligible for a promotion. An inquisitorial Senate committee of late-middle-aged males grills Anita Hill with apparently no understanding at all of how women view sexual harassment.

For both women and men, however, when sex is integrated with their relationships, feminine interpersonal strengths describe the lovers' character.

Men and Women Desire Similar Kinds of Friendships, But Women Succeed Better in Forming Them

Just as men have become less satisfied with their relationships with their colleagues and (for college-educated men) their children in recent decades, I expect that more men will feel unfulfilled in their relationships with their partners and close friends in the future. As in the familial role, to approach their hopes for a close relationship, men need to risk becoming more interpersonally skilled and not let their typical strengths—aggressiveness, competitiveness, and dominance, which are appropriate in achieving other goals—take over.

We will encounter many of the same themes when we ask about the personality of men and women who succeed vocationally. But we will also discover that typical masculine strengths come to the fore as the critical character strengths necessary to succeed in our work. Androgynous men and women can succeed in both their interpersonal and vocational roles.

Building a Strong Family

Of the many influences that help children to grow up to succeed, parents are one of the more important ones. But so are schools. So are peer relationships, especially during adolescence. However, parents can interpret, mediate, support, or try to counter these and other influences, such as TV and church. The following ten prescriptions for building a strong family draw not only on what we have learned so far but also on later chapters. They are based, too, on other findings—particularly schools' predictive effects—reported in *Fulfilling Lives*. (*Schools of Hope* identifies the type of school that contributes to children's later adult success.)

1. Be loving, democratic, and firm parents. Enjoy raising your kids.
2. Love and respect and don't try to dominate each other. Share your feelings and ideas openly with each other and your kids—when they're ready. Create an intellectually and culturally stimulating home. Be a teacher to your kids. During meals, don't look at TV but talk about politics, budget deficits, the Supreme Court, and the museum's latest art exhibit. Define words. Explain. Value your kids' minds. Teach them how to study and go about solving problems.
3. If you are a woman, stand up to your friends for your calling to be a mother. Remember that it is mothers who value interpersonal skills, such as caring and relating to others ethically, who most directly help their daughters and sons succeed in their intimate relationships and become ethically principled adults.
4. If you are a father, never reject your kids, particularly your son, even if you do separate from your partner. Be actively involved in their lives. Include your daughter as well as your son in camping and sports activities. Teach them both what it takes to survive outside the home. Help your daughter become as strong and autonomous a woman as you expect your son to be a self-confident and self-determining man. Don't put down either child for developing traditional strengths of the other gender. Be available when they need you, again especially your son. Hug them every day and tell them how much you love them.

5. Value your children's work in school but not at the expense of their extracurricular and community activities which contribute more than their grades and test scores to their adult success. Encourage them to take leadership positions. Above all, don't pay them for getting A's, and never even hint that they will be failures the rest of their lives if their Scholastic Aptitude Test (SAT) scores are undistinguished. Since boys who have high SAT scores are at risk of failing as adults, encourage them to develop the interpersonal skills they need to succeed in their familial relationships.

6. Remember that your kids' adolescence is a potentially high-growth time, during which they can more firmly build on (or rebuild, if they have to) their identities. They will have to explore and test themselves in numerous ways. Keep in mind that successful, healthy, and happy adults are not stuck in ruts, are optimistic, and feel in control of their lives. So raise your kids to take judicious risks, to hope, and to assume responsibility for their own maturing.

7. Remember that you can best help your kids grow healthily into adulthood by making their teenage years high-growth years for yourself and each other. Grow with them. They will "disequilibrate" you—either unthinkingly or deliberately—to test what you feel is important. They will test just how saintly you are. Be a firm but respectful and loving parent. You will need the greatest parental virtue in abundance: patience. The second most important virtue is a sense of humor; the third, a lot of energy. And then there are sixty others. Reread Chapter Eleven about fulfilled and competent parents once a week and plan some specific steps you can take next week to enjoy being a parent a little more.

8. Keep growing and stretching yourself. (If your thirty-two-year-old daughter decides to sail around the world alone in a twenty-five-foot Vertue sailboat, go part way with her.) Be models to your children of how mature and healthy adults continue to grow. Help each other continue to grow.

9. Be sensitive to how traditional gender roles affect your children's maturing. Fulfilling them well during adolescence contributes to success in traditional adult roles. However, value and encourage those opposite-gender strengths that also contribute to future suc-

cess and well-being. Remember that the process of maturing is the same for boys and girls, though each may need to develop more in some ways than others at different times. Help your girls to become more healthily autonomous and your boys to mature interpersonally during their teenage years.

10. Remember that despite some help from our genetic make-up, parents, schooling, partners, and children, we still create our own success, mental health, and happiness. We are our own psychological Horatio Algers.

Jane Allen is a superb example of an economic Horatio Alger. What does her life tell us about the strengths necessary to succeed in our vocations?

PART THREE

Succeeding at Work

Chapter 14

JANE ALLEN:

SUCCEEDING AS AN ENTREPRENEUR

What is the first word that comes to mind when I say "success?" Is it money? It is for many Americans who dream of high-paying jobs, making it big, and becoming millionaires by their early thirties. Surveys of today's teenagers suggest that even a million may not be enough. Some want to be billionaires—like Bill Gates, founder of Microsoft. Seventy-two percent, the highest number found in the last two decades, say their primary reason for going to college is to learn the skills to make a lot of money—though Bill Gates never graduated from college.

Vocational success means many different things: doing well in our work, making a great discovery, pioneering a new fashion, being regarded by our colleagues as outstanding, getting a promotion, achieving responsibility and power, having a job everyone envies, enjoying work, and, like Marty, finding our number one self in the work to which we feel called.

Just because we succeed in one of these ways does not mean we will succeed in the others. Do you know that a decade ago, when half of our country's lawyers were in their thirties or younger, 45 percent of them were bored and discontented with law? Why? Drawn to law because of the income, status, and power they thought it promised, they discovered that they really didn't enjoy their work. Remember Dave Corcoran, the well-adjusted lawyer I told you about? He was extraordinarily competent, respected, and wealthy, but unfulfilled. Another man in the study is a playwright but has to grub around to get enough money to survive to do the work he loves. Eloise Barnett is a world-renowned medical scientist who has published countless articles. Yet when I saw her, she dreaded going to the lab each morning, because, as she wrote me five years ago, "Doug, I hope my children learn early what will make them happy; I still don't know what I want to be." She was forty-eight. She is much happier now that she is president of her organization.

I found no relation between how much money the men and women made and their satisfaction with their work. My surgeon discovered that for himself in his mid-fifties. He charges $3,000 for an hour's operating time, yet he told me that he hated his work and wished he could retire. Adults know that money is not the be-all and end-all. They rated it to be twelfth in importance, but competence in a satisfying vocation seventh in importance. They also rated being leaders and possessing power next to the bottom in importance. Because leadership and high income go together and draw on the same character strengths, I combine the two and refer to those high in both as successful entrepreneurs.

The Sources of Jane Allen's Entrepreneurial Success

Some persons succeed in creating a vocation that integrates their interests and talents in a calling that they enjoy, do well in, achieve respect for, and earn more than enough in. They have everything. Jane Allen was such a person when I first met her ten years ago. After Billie and Marty, she scored highest on a combined measure of income, judged leadership, her vocational fulfillment, and her colleague's satisfaction with how well her vocation fit her personality—the four measures of success I will use to identify the character strengths needed to succeed vocationally. As you read about Jane, try to figure out why she succeeded so magnificently.

Jane fulfills the classic American entrepreneurial tradition. When she was twenty-nine, she started her own business distributing sporting supplies and equipment to schools and community groups. She did not fit my stereotype of a successful businesswoman selling sports equipment. Instead, I met a slender, warm, responsive, attractive brunette with a fierce passion to succeed on her own.

Her first words in the interview were,

> I started and couldn't stop. I created a monster; it kept growing and growing. I started with $600 of my own money. Four years later I am distributing nationally, have a paid staff of ten, am grossing over a million dollars a year, have just started my own advertising agency and a monthly newspaper which I edit. I now have a full-time art and graphic staff. It's a drive I can't really explain. Such a hunger to succeed. I have had a taste of success and will never let go of it.

When asked what goals she would like to fulfill before she died, Jane immediately replied, "to build a multimillion-dollar business," which she was certain she would succeed in doing—and which she had several years later. "I always wanted to succeed in life. My biggest dream has always been to be a millionaire. Not to marry one but to make it myself. I feel I have to do it by myself. When little I had no one to depend on. I never would ask anybody for anything. I'd starve first." Jane had indeed married a millionaire, lived in a spacious mansion that had a huge swimming pool, sauna, Jacuzzi, and all of the other signs of opulence, including morning and afternoon "nannies" to take care of her two children.

But how had Jane made it on her own? She started by rebelliously defying her tyranically abusing mother, who tried to control her every movement when she became a teenager. When she was fifteen, Jane fled home permanently, dropped out of tenth grade ("I couldn't sit still long enough to bother with the books"), married a twenty-seven-year-old man, became pregnant seven months later, and vowed to herself to divorce him when she reached legal age, which she did. Supporting herself and her son, she did so well in sales that she won numerous sales campaigns. When she was twenty-two, she met Vince, her future husband, who was rebounding from his recent divorce. Several years later, while inspecting a store with him that he was buying, a robber entered. In the fracas that resulted, the robber killed a customer and shot her, temporarily paralyzing her right leg. This accident was a turning point in her life.

> Before the accident I had always been very moody, malcontent, unhappy. My mother had never allowed me to have

a good friend, to even laugh, to totally enjoy myself. I had to go into therapy because I was reliving the accident day and night. After therapy, it was all of a sudden . . . everything suddenly snapped. My whole life changed. I was able to like myself, which I couldn't do before. After that, I could pursue my career. For the first time I really feel very happy with my life.

Mother's Contribution to Entrepreneurial Drive

When asked what she felt the sources of her drive to succeed were, she said her mother, but in what she called a "perverse bullheaded" way. Her mother was an exceptionally strong, dominating, and authoritarian woman. "To deal with her, I had to be strong too. Otherwise, I'd be in an insane asylum today. I always felt as if I had been adopted. Though I felt much closer to my father. I loved him and wanted to be like him, probably because we were so temperamentally similar. But I never felt they were my real parents. I don't mean I felt rejected. I just felt I had to depend on myself."

Ten years later, Jane still harbored bitter memories about her mother when I asked what her greatest source of disappointment about her was. "Just that I don't have a mother. I never felt like I did. I remember when she had a tree switch to use as a whip. She would cut my legs. . . . I didn't have a happy childhood at all. . . . I remember when I was twelve she came at me with a yardstick and was going to beat me, but I was big enough to stop her."

Jane believes that she inherited her "soft side" from her father, who she really liked. She felt "tremendous pain" when he died, but she suppressed her need to cry, fearful of becoming, so she claimed, too emotional and aborting her pregnancy.

Envy as Motivator

Another source of her hunger to succeed was envy. At the age of seven, she visited an aunt's beautiful home and immediately made up her mind that this was the way she wanted to live. "I have always envied people that had things. . . . I've always wanted to make enough money to help other people." About the same time, she decided she wanted to become a doctor, not just to help other people, but also because it was a "tremendous status symbol . . . the ultimate one. I would want to be the best; I'd probably have to be a surgeon. I'd still like to be a physician."

I asked, "Would you want to go back to school and begin that career? You are still young and money is no problem."

"No way," Jane said. "It would be a waste of time and energy. I don't now feel that I could do it."

"What about nursing?"

"No! I couldn't work under the doctors. I'd end up taking a scalpel to them. It would be denigrating. Doctors are very chauvinistic. I could be a doctor but I couldn't work with one."

Women's Movement

A third source of her urge to be in charge of her own life was the women's movement, whose themes had preoccupied her in therapy. Like Billie and Marty, she had learned how to get in touch with her more assertive self. "I have become a stronger person. I can understand what the feminists are talking about. Now if I think something is wrong, I speak out, like when the bank first refused me a loan because I was a woman. My business has made me a little harder, tougher, less feminine. It's like, 'Welcome to the real world.'" To succeed in such a world, she had found that she had had to become "almost brutal." Imagine a feminine-appearing woman doing the following to survive in a competitive, male-dominated business.

> Intimidation is the rule of the day in my business. I had no idea of how rough New Yorkers could be. They are streetwise and very coy. They understand only one type of language and that is toughness. When I first started out, they would say, "Yes," and a month later I still had not received my supplies. So I drove a truck up there, parked in their doorway, and said I wasn't going to leave until I got what I wanted. I have never had any more trouble. They'll chew you up if you let them. A man has authority with other men. A woman has to earn it their way. I'm no longer gullible. I don't take any nonsense. I have a backbone now.

Clarity of Purpose

I felt her singular clarity about what she wanted was critical to her success. By the age of thirty-three, she was well along the road to becoming a millionaire; she had become a respected leader in the local business community; she loved her work, which her colleague felt suited her very well.

And what of her marriage and family? When I first met her in 1982, she was happily married, felt very supported by her husband, and felt fulfilled as a parent. "The whole realm . . . the whole picture is finally together . . . the whole puzzle completed." She was one of the three happiest people of the study. Her peers agreed that she was a happy and fulfilled person.

Ten Years Later

Now, forty-three-years-old, Jane's "whole picture" has some gaping holes and new pieces that still do not quite fit together. Her sporting business or "monster," as she proudly referred to it, doubled in size within a few years; it was driving her faster than she felt comfortable going. "It had gotten beyond me. I started to burn out. . . . I have only one life to live. I want to live to the fullest and . . . [my business] was not a primary possibility." Having achieved her dream to create a multimillion-dollar business, she had become restless to move on to new challenges. Successfully selling her business, she invested the proceeds in twenty-some rental houses, which she rehabilitated and rented to earn a steady income. She also secured her realtor's license, and, as she had done in her twenties, soon broke a national realty company's local records for home sales. "If I touch something, it mushrooms. I go very quickly." Bored by her success, she is now deliberating whether to set up her own business consulting firm.

The center-piece of her picture—her marriage to Vince—cracked shortly after she sold her business. Awed by Vince's brilliance, college education, and business acumen, she had always felt inferior and deferred to his opinions, especially about managing her business. She was hurt that he had never read her story in *Fulfilling Lives*. Explaining why she divorced him, Jane calmly and matter-of-factly reflected,

> The last time you and I met I had low self-esteem and I didn't recognize it. . . . As I became more and more aware of my capabilities in the business world and began feeling better about myself, Vince started to pull me down. He would tell me that I was inadequate, stupid and that there was no way the business would make it, especially if I left him. . . . He did everything humanly possible to beat me up with verbal abuse. I didn't recognize it as verbal abuse. . . . He threatened and degraded me in front of people. . . called me awful names such as cunt and bitch. I wanted to crawl. My self-esteem was going. . . . One day he called me stupid in front of my staff.

Vince's persistent effort to control her by putting her down, a court trial initiated by the Internal Revenue Service for his failure to pay income taxes, and the likelihood that their assets might be attached permanently broke the marriage after several attempts at reconciliation.

Therapy's Contribution to Success

During this period, Jane again sought therapy to better understand her tie to Vince. She claimed it changed her life, as it had earlier during her recuperation from the gunshot wound that temporarily paralyzed her leg. As I sensed with Marty, I also sensed on first meeting Jane at the airport that she was different: more composed, articulate, and self-confidently assertive. (I pushed my feet into the floorboards several times as she maintained her speed weaving through heavy traffic and road construction detours on the way to her home.) Therapy created three interwoven effects that set Jane on a different path and also illuminated other reasons for her success as an entrepreneur that I had not clearly recognized earlier: increased self-understanding, healthier self-acceptance, and a redirected drive to grow and succeed.

Increased Self-Understanding. Throughout the three-and-a-half-hour interview, Jane returned again and again to the theme of how much more she understands herself now. Some of her more prominent learnings were:

1. She is attracted to people who, like her mother and Vince, seek total control of her life. (Vince was the study's most masculine man; he dominated and dismissed her opinions. She had yielded and entered therapy to understand why.)
2. "I found I am only in control of my life and of no one else's. I can control what goes on with me but I can't and don't want to control others. They have a right to have their own feelings and desires. If I can't live with them, then I have to make a change. That is what I mean by becoming aware of problems." (Jane had prevented her mother from seeing her grandchildren for years; as a result of this insight, her children can now make their own decisions to see their grandmother.)
3. "My weakness is my relationships. I recognize a problem before it starts now. At least I am aware so they don't become uncontrollable."
4. Jane became more aware of her more feminine strengths and how much more sensitive she had the potential to be in her relations with others.
5. "I understand. . . love, and it is a key to making you grow."
6. "Because I understand myself so much better, I am a better parent; I have come in touch with my own feelings."

Healthier Self-Acceptance. One of Jane's strengths that I had earlier underestimated that contributed to her vocational success was her belief in her own masculine entrepreneurial strengths. Ten years ago, flush with her early business success, Jane had rated herself to be more masculine than Vince, her colleague, and her closest friend had described her; for example, they saw her as much more compassionate than she saw herself. Jane still rates herself as more masculine in her relationships and way of approaching problems than Billie, Marty, Andy, and Harry rate themselves—each also entrepreneurs in their own ways. But like Billie, she has learned that she can be soft-spoken and feminine and be more effective than when assuming a gruff voice and being assertive. "If a woman is confident and competent she can be . . .[men's] equal."

Jane's view of women reflects her estrangement from more typical feminine ways of relating and is 180° opposite to Marty's. "I still have little respect for women. Basically I don't think they are honest.

Women are very devious. They are not truthful with men at all. I see it every day. They are not themselves and that is why my relationships with men last forever. I don't have any relationships with women that have persisted. I could care less about women. . . . Women are supposed to cater to men. I can't be like that." At least to that, Marty would agree. Jane infinitely prefers being with men, with whom she feels comfortable. "I was a tomboy. I liked to climb trees, build treehouses, and be in the woodworking shop. . . . I understand . . . [males] for I speak their language."

Jane also asserts that she thinks and controls herself like typical American males do. Despite her changes, she asserts that "I haven't lost the more masculine point of view," by which she means analyzing a problem, making decisions on the basis of its logic, not the emotion or sentiment, of the situation, and getting to the bottom line quickly, whether about a business or personal issue. Emotionally she wished to keep her family with Vince intact; logically, she felt she had no other choice than to divorce him. Speaking of her divorce, she said it was "totally logical. I couldn't let the emotion [take over] and get to the surface . . . [or else] I would vacillate. Just like when my father died. I wouldn't let myself cry. I just suppressed it."

Her equilibrating principle—the guardian of her mental health—has since taken its sweet revenge. Her first words in our most recent interview were "I probably fell in love for the first time in my life. It was an enlightening experience and I didn't know what it was. I didn't know what the feeling was . . . it was just an incredible whirlwind."

I asked, "Is this the first time you have been in love?"

"Vince was my best friend, but I didn't know what love was. My parents never told me about love. They also never touched each other in front of me." Though she had to abandon her first love for a married Catholic man who could not divorce his wife—to give him up "seemed to be the logical thing to do"—"the love is there and I'll keep it forever. I understand it and it is a key to making you grow." Her second fondest wish she would like to fulfill before she dies is to have a "loving and understanding relationship," which she believes she will have.

Jane's equilibrating principle is also leading her into other feelings she has long pushed out of her mind as a result of her image of being a tough, no-nonsense, logical, pay-attention-to-the-bottom-line entrepreneur. She is on a self-conscious program to become more feminine. "I would like to stay home and bake cookies. I would like to support my future husband's career. He has to have a dynamite career. I entertain beautifully. I can be a real asset. . . . I see myself fitting into that niche. I feel really good about it."

Accentuating her physical attractiveness is another feminine strategy. Her bathroom contains countless (to me) make-up jars of every shade, color, and scent. She feels that she is a late-blooming twenty-year-old, ready "to enjoy life to the fullest. Whatever I do I can be happy and not feel I am over the hill. I feel better, look better. I think I look better than I ever have." I agree. She looks youthful, is femininely attractive, and bubbles with delightful energy—again very much like Billie.

Jane is also encountering her softer nurturing self as she now transforms her career into being a superb mother of Vince's and her eleven-year-old boy. Her fondest wish is to be a good parent. Her wish is so compelling that she considered sacrificing her current love to move to another state so her son could have the advantage of a most expensive education. She acknowledges that she had not been a good parent to her sons. "Not until recently did I understand myself. So how was I going to raise children? I didn't understand feelings. How empty my oldest son felt. Been a void there. If I wasn't able to love and understand love, there has . . . [to] have been a void in their lives. . . . The oldest is the toughest because he was probably the most abused. . . I just was not a good parent to him especially."

Jane may be riding a swinging pendulum seeking its resting place or centering point. While a strong, assertive, self-reliant woman, she is learning how to give voice to her inner father's softer side—how to yield from strength and to be aware when she may overwhelm her eleven-year-old son with too much hovering.

Redirected Drive to Grow and Succeed. A key source of her vocational success (one I also did not emphasize enough ten years ago) is her hunger to grow, become better, and succeed in whatever she touches—nowadays finding what she calls a "soul mate" who has a dynamite career she can contribute to. To my question, "What are your strongest commitments that anchor your life and that give your life meaning from which you draw staying power?", she answered without hesitation, "Being true to myself and to my abilities. I have a strong desire to achieve, to succeed... Anything that I do I want to do well." She has the confidence to know that she can achieve well on her own. She survived as a teenager with a baby by hard work; she married far above her educational and economic status; she became a millionaire by her own efforts; she repeated her previous sales success as a realtor; she has now abandoned her secret desire to be a "world shaker" to accept her femininity and is determined to succeed not only as a parent but also to find her soul mate.

Like Billie, the Millers, and Harry, she does not believe the myths about middle-agers: that "life is over"; that the future is all down hill; and that one must have a mid-life crisis. Jane fervently said, "I am getting better, like a vintage wine.... That people feel they have to have a middle-age crisis is just not wanting to grow. Then growth does stop. You just have to continue to grow and be better." She is optimistic about the future. When I asked how she would respond to her son's question, "What is there to live for?", she replied as Billie, Andy, Marty, and Harry had. "Everything. I just do it. It is just such a great experience to live. Something is always changing and it's more an adventure than anything else. Every day, minute, is an adventure. You don't know what is going to happen next." Like the others, she accepts that her past was what it had to be. I asked her what new experiences or types of growth would she like to have to be able to say, if she were near death, "I have lived a fulfilled life." She replied as Billie, Andy, Marty, and Harry had: "I can already say that."

I don't know if Jane's story inspires or discourages you. It can inspire us, because she is another example of a strong person who has the talent and character—especially the determination and willpower—to overcome some incredible handicaps to achieve her dreams. Her story can also discourage us. We may compare ourselves with successful people and feel depressed, particularly if we've had no real handicaps to blame for our inertia or middling success. Keep in mind that I am describing people identified as exceptional examples of what it takes to grow up to succeed. As I draw the group portrait of the successful entrepreneurial leader who makes a lot of money, keep either yourself or Jane in mind so you will have a real-life person on which to drape my computer's more impersonal analysis.

Strengths Needed to Succeed Vocationally

The strengths the group identified as necessary to succeed as managerial leaders and professionals were, in rough declining order of importance:

- Adaptive intelligence skills, such as analytical and organizational abilities and good judgment
- Motivational commitment to work hard
- Ability to understand and manage interpersonal relationships
- Communication skills, including empathy
- Disciplined knowledge and competence
- Caring concern for and patience with others
- Adaptive work attitudes and habits: reliability, objectivity, and decisiveness
- Imaginative perspective
- Mature sense of self: self-confidence, mental health
- Honesty and integrity

An imposing list of strengths is required to succeed vocationally. Intellectual skills, disciplined knowledge, and competence now come into their own, but not at the expense of character strengths such as commitment, empathy, compassion, decisiveness, understanding, and integrity.

Today's youth, singularly motivated to get the "big buck," know the importance of intellectual skills and knowledge for their future success. However, few speak as if they know how important their character will be to their success. Maybe you will find James Ferguson's prophetic comments to a National 4-H Congress in 1983 useful. Since he was chairman of General Foods, was rich, and probably enjoyed his work, he should be credible.

> The future is not going to be a comfortable time for people who cannot adapt and be flexible, or who don't have imagination and a willingness to take some risks.
>
> I'm disturbed by the trend these days—all too prevalent, in my view—of young people to narrow their sights too early, and to tailor their education or their career planning or their interests to one narrow specialty. Because it stifles that capacity to grow and change. Whether you go

to college or not—stay as broad as you can, as long as you can! Because business fundamentally is a matter of relations among human beings. Success in business means successfully dealing with and motivating people. And the higher a person goes in most companies, the less important it is that he or she have facts, figures, and specific expertise. And the more important it is that he or she have flexibility, inventiveness, judgment, and the capacity to deal with change, and with other people.

Specific vocations not only require specialized knowledge and competence but other strengths as well. Consider physicians. According to one observer, the most critical qualities they need to adapt to the stresses of modern medicine and be effective healers are psychological maturity, social competence, and the willpower to moderate their aggressive and competitive Type A personalities!

Personality of Successful Entrepreneurs

America has always been seen as the land of opportunity where one can make it on one's own. Millions of immigrants still believe that. Though our image may be tarnished for some, they know that some of their relatives and friends are succeeding in creating new lives for themselves. Some immigrant Vietnamese fishermen are succeeding as shrimpers along the Louisiana coast, numerous Koreans are flourishing as shop keepers in Los Angeles, more and more Indians are making it as motel owners, and a number of Chinese students are surpassing white Americans as academic achievers. We have long accepted the folklore that anyone who worked hard, was enterprising, and did their best would not just survive but could fulfill their dreams—even become a millionaire, and thus happy—like Jane.

Such virtues may no longer be in fashion for those who look for the shortcuts to wealth and status. Tom Wolfe, the best-selling author about sex and greed, may be right after all. We are fascinated with those who "make it big" and with how they did it. The media are obsessed with the outlandish salaries of some business executives, Donald Trump's eight-story yacht and the $100,000 a year he spent for its flowers, and the planet's eighty-nine male and three female billionaires that the editors of *Forbes'* located one year. While it takes a billion dollars for real status nowadays, I think most of us would agree with Jane. A million or two would do. So we buy our daily lottery ticket, play the slots in Las Vegas, and keep pasting those stickers on American Family Publishers' $10 million sweepstakes certificates.

Though wistfully envious of the instantly rich and powerful, many Americans still hold onto some old-fashioned values. We agree in ranking a happy marriage, parental competence, and vocational fulfillment far ahead of wealth, leadership, and power. Until this past decade, even teenagers ranked their goals similarly. Entrepreneurial owners of small businesses, like Jane, say they value other goals more than they do money. Most important to them is the quality of their product and service. They next value the freedom to make their own decisions, flexibility, self-reliance, and good customer relations, and only then, a lot of money.

Is there a successful entrepreneurial personality? Yes, though successful male entrepreneurs have more strengths in common than successful female ones do. Jane is almost a pure example of an entrepreneur, possibly because she is so masculine—the indisputable strength that vocationally successful men and women share. They are judged by those who know them best to be strong persons who are

- Adventurous
- Willing to take risks
- Willing to stand up for their beliefs
- Courageous
- Assertive
- Forceful
- Self-reliant
- Independent
- Self-confident
- Ethical
- Fulfilling their potential

While a good portrait of Jane, the group portrait of the vocationally successful women says it is incomplete. Surprisingly, in contrast to successful males, successful female entrepreneurs are also judged to be aggressive and dominant; they definitely are not soft-spoken. They have thick skins and function well under stress. Must entrepreneurial women act more masculine than men? Jane thought so for many years, until her equilibrating principle told her that by ignoring her femininity, she was stretching herself too far out of shape. "I remember how masculine I was at one point . . . and felt I had to be masculine in order to get things done because I was in a totally man's world. I thought they only understood if you said it in a gruff tone of voice and you were assertive. . . . It is not necessary any more to crack the whip. You can get things accomplished just as well if you use a different tone of voice."

That women who are leaders who earn a lot of money are judged to be consistently masculine provokes a sobering thought. Women make less money and occupy fewer positions of high responsibility where they could make more money than men. They are the backbone of the low-paying, nurturing professions of teaching, nursing, and social work. It is fashionable to assert that the income disparity between men and women reflects discrimination (which is true), unequal access to the "old boy network" (also true), and games played by men's rules on their turf (also true). But the results suggest another, possibly more telling explanation. Many women may find the path to comparable pay to be too foreign to them, given the ways that their character has been shaped. May not interpersonally sensitive and nurturing women avoid or grow weary of the daily competitive, aggressive, even intimidating struggle of which Jane spoke? It requires masculine strengths not readily available or palatable to many.

For some women, a different tone of voice is not enough, however. Joan Meredith was such a woman. The study's most feminine woman, she is an artist of considerable talent. Her home overflowed with paintings that even my untrained eye could see were exceptional.

"Joan, why are you hoarding so many good paintings in your apartment?"

"I know I should take them to show at different galleries. But I just can't seem to get myself to do it. It's just that, well, I'm just not aggressive enough. I've never been. Anyway, they're not good enough. They couldn't compete with what I've seen. Besides, I'd feel devastated if none were sold."

Not having developed self-confidence, assertiveness, competitiveness, and a tough skin means that her talent, like that of Emily Dickinson, will never receive the recognition and rewards that it deserves while she lives. Unfortunately, Joan is not poor enough to be driven into the street to show her work. Fortunately, her more assertive daughter will inherit the bonanza.

Obviously women can succeed vocationally as well as men. They can be as entrepreneurial as Jane, as disciplined and creative as Eloise, as outspoken and influential as Marty, and as superb an administrator as Billie. All of them are androgynous and share similar masculine strengths.

Men who succeed as leaders are also androgynous. In contrast to women, they are judged to have numerous interpersonal strengths typical of women in addition to the masculine ones they share with women like Jane. They are not the loud, harsh, dominating, cigar-stomping, insensitive Edward G. Robinsons that Hollywood stereotypically depicts. Those who succeed are soft-spoken, seldom swear, and are warm and affectionate men who are sensitive to their colleagues' and subordinates' feelings—and they love children.

That successful male entrepreneurs are thought by others to have interpersonal strengths typical of women but the successful female leaders are not so viewed is another provocative finding. Apparently, the entrepreneurial man is more at home with his personality strengths than the woman is. Like Harry, they are mature, feel good about themselves, are judged by others to live satisfying and happy lives, and feel competent in their principal adult roles, especially in their marital relationships and as citizens contributing to their communities. They are also vocationally fulfilled and are so judged by their colleagues who know them best. Successful female entrepreneurs show *none* of these strengths or achievements. While male and female entrepreneurs are androgynous, especially masculine, apparently women's entrepreneurial strengths are not well integrated with the rest of their lives.

Entrepreneurs who overdevelop their masculine strengths to the extent that they exclude interpersonal ones like warmth and understanding have two vulnerable Achilles' heels. Vince Allen is one prize example. Bill Spaulding is another. Remember that Bill had built his own marketing consulting firm from scratch. I had to warn him in an awkward and tense post interview session that his future success both as a CEO and as a spouse-father might be in more jeopardy than I felt he realized.

Among his peers, he ranked second after Vince in masculine character traits like leadership, forcefulness, and competitiveness which he had used so well to build his multimillion-dollar firm. His vulnerability came not from such strengths in themselves but from their singular severity. They were not integrated with the strong people skills to which James Ferguson referred in his talk to the 4-H teenagers. His three peers rated him to be one of the five *least* feminine men of the study, and, more crucially, in the bottom 15 percent in interpersonal skills like sensitivity, understanding, and sympathy. He could brusquely fire his two close cofounders without one sleepless night. Decisiveness not integrated with sensitivity can push a leader to self-destruct. Although one of the study's most vocationally satisfied and competent men, his colleague and wife, who knew how good a CEO he was, rated him barely above average in vocational fulfillment.

His success as a husband and parent was, as I mentioned earlier, his other Achilles' heel—at least as his troubled and unhappy wife viewed it. She rated him on each of her six criteria of what made a good marital partner and parent to be one of the study's two worst spouses and fathers. He saw himself to be a much better husband and father: affectionate, sympathetic, understanding, and compassionate. Inaccurate self-perceptions of this magnitude make him vulnerable to failure in any activity whose success depends upon understanding his interpersonal strengths.

The dangerous gap between his and others' views of his strengths could have made him resist my warnings. Fortunately, he heard one warning, even musing, "I wonder if that's why headhunters have refused to suggest me for the presidency of a large firm that has been looking for someone with my expertise and experience." He was more skittish about talking as humbly about his family life.

We have learned that women who succeed in their traditional gender-related familial roles have numerous strengths in common but men, especially as fathers, share fewer. Now we learn that men who succeed in their traditional power and breadwinner roles also have numerous strengths in common but women don't. Have we stumbled on a social evolutionary insight? Centuries and centuries of socialization as males and females have produced the character strengths necessary to adapt to our prescribed gender roles. Andy and

Marty have told us much struggle may be demanded to develop the personality required to fulfill each other's traditional roles with competence.

Parental Contribution to Entrepreneurial Success

Just as parents influence how their children get along with others—remember the five-year-old boy challenging me to put up my dukes—so also do parents shape their children's ideas about themselves as workers and what they want to be when they grow up. I must tell you a story about a six-year-old—a story I did not believe until I verified it with the head of one of our country's more prestigious schools. While interviewing Bobby for admission to the school's first grade, the head had asked him why he wanted to come to the academy. Soberly and with great self-assurance, Bobby said, "Because it is a top school and will help me get into Harvard, so I can become a doctor and make a lot of money." What a somber vision of one's future to have when six. Who did he get his vision from?

Perhaps it is because centuries of cultural conditioning so powerfully shape and fix so early males' identity as future breadwinners, I could not detect by their mid-forties any continuing contribution that their own parents' values and personalities made to their entrepreneurial success. By that time they are on their own psychologically. This was not true for women like Marty and Jane. Successful female leaders share a distinctive pattern of maternal and paternal traits. Their cultural encouragement of their entrepreneurial strengths may be less encompassing and so leaves considerable room for parents to still influence their daughters into middle age.

Fathers rather than mothers shape their daughters' future vocational success. Middle-aged women who are leaders and earn a lot of money describe their mothers to have been tense and physically and mentally unhealthy. They possessed few positive qualities that would inspire a daughter to emulate them as models. So over time, they became less and less relevant persons in their successful daughters' vocational histories.

Billie, Marty, and Jane described their mothers in this way. They and some others frequently expressed hostility, certainly disappointment, about their mothers in the interviews. One told me, "My mother could have been so much more than what she had become—just a housewife and mother." Their mothers had not provided them with a model of how to resolve the conflicts that many successful women now feel between their careers, family responsibilities, and personal needs.

Women who earn a lot of money and hold leadership positions have a unique relationship with their fathers who they describe as warm and affectionate men who valued caring for and loving others. But when they were children, their fathers firmly (and even sharply) held them to high standards, actively spurred their academic achievement, and disciplined them for failing. Their daughters reacted predictably. They ambivalently loved but rebelled against their fathers. I don't think that they abandoned their more masculine identification, which they may have overemphasized in order to please their demanding fathers. Instead, they became stubbornly rebellious and may have learned how to convert it into the independence and self-reliance necessary to fashion a nontraditional female career in a male vocational world. Might not ambivalence toward a loved and respected but demanding father be the cauldron from which aggressive, competitive, and rebellious energies can be drawn to make it in the typical world of money and power?

Marty's and Jane's fathers now begin to measure up a little more to the computer's portrait of the fathers of entrepreneurial daughters. Both viewed their fathers as warmer, more expressive, and more lovingly supportive than their mothers. No wonder they felt closer to and loved their fathers more than they did their mothers.

Ten years ago, Jane's career was that of an individual entrepreneur. Now she views work differently—as something to be shared with a successful husband-to-be as his helpmate. So I introduce you in the next chapter to Chen Lee who has a lifelong calling to be a successful and renowned scholar. He and his wife, Lin, like the Millers, were the other of the two most all-round successful couples in the early eighties.

Chapter 15

CHEN LEE: MAKING WORK A CALLING

For most of us, a *healthy* number one self needs to be more than just making a lot of money and exercising power. Has our compulsive American pursuit of money and extravagant consumption made us any happier and more satisfied with our lives? Are reports really true that *ten* times more of the affluent eighties' baby-boomers are depressed than people in my Depression-wracked generation? Since the mid-fifties, the suicide rate among adolescents has skyrocketed. Drug addiction, alcoholism, and violence never seem to abate. Japan and Germany are also wealthy countries. But a Gallup poll found that of sixteen different peoples, the Japanese were least satisfied with their lives, and only 10 percent of Germans claimed to be very happy. Isn't it a peculiar paradox that the citizens of the three wealthiest countries on our planet are so discontented?

The equilibrating principle may be catching up with us. The young lawyers who are bored may be learning that they shouldn't have gone into law just for its money, status, and power. The youthful bond and commodity traders making thousands of dollars a week are discovering that their stressful long hours interfere with their social and family lives. One out of three teachers say they want to leave teaching because it doesn't pay much. However, *Schools of Hope* reports that a more basic reason is that they feel they can't continue to grow and reach their full potential. Is preoccupation with making money obscuring deeper reasons for our discontent, which we may not be able to express clearly even to ourselves? Once a person's basic survival needs are met, people who make a lot of money are no more likely to be satisfied with their jobs than those who make less. Money—as long as we have enough to live reasonably well on—contributes little to our personal fulfillment.

Why? What are we forgetting about what makes a healthy and happy vocational self? I recently asked students what the religious meaning of *vocation* is. They didn't know. When I said "calling," they looked at me blankly, as if they had never heard the word. (One smart guy yelled out, "a cat in heat." I looked at him blankly. The students went wild. But I looked it up later. He was right. Is it a sign of the times to think of a vocation as a transitory urge rather than an enduring commitment?) Anyway, these students were not exceptional. A recent commentary on changing American attitudes claimed that we adults have substituted money and power for our lost understanding of work as a "calling." Work has now become just a job to get money and status. A "calling" is a way of life, formerly a divine summons—"what one was meant to be," which in religious terms leads to committing one's self to some transcendent purpose, like Marty to feminism or Harry to parenting.

Remember the scandal of Mary Elizabeth Cunningham? A Phi Beta Kappa and a graduate of Wellesley College and then of Harvard Business School, she became executive assistant to William Agee, president of Bendix, and then shortly afterward his lover, though both were married to other partners. Shortly after that, she became a young vice-president of the company, and shortly after being forced out of Bendix, she was named an executive vice-president of Seagram & Sons. Surely she was an enterprising woman who succeeded financially and held responsible leadership positions of great status and power. She learned, however, that her work was just a job, not a calling. In her words, it was a job, not "what I was always meant to do." She left her job and began her calling by founding a nonprofit organization that helps young women get through their pregnancies and create viable lives for themselves and their children. She says of her calling, "It's like arms have just enfolded you, like a religion." [1]

Called To Be a Scholar

Chen Lee is a fifty-seven-year-old, world-renowned scholar of Chinese cultural history and literature. His life tells us what a calling is and shows us how its roots go deep into our character. He has never strayed from what he "was always meant to do"—be a scholar and write books. ("Even when I was a child, I dreamed I'd like to become a scholar.") Nor has his personality changed since adolescence. Nor has he ever regretted his thirty-four years of marriage to Lin—"My wife is the central figure in my life. . . . We are better as a couple than each of us would be as a single person." Nor has he ever felt he has not been a good parent to his two daughters, one of whom has been hospitalized since birth because of brain damage. Nor does he have the personality of an entrepreneur who makes a lot of money like Jane Allen.

However, like Jane, he is extraordinarily conscientious, even driven; he single-mindedly devotes his energies to whatever current scholarly project consumes his attention. And again like Jane, he must have a project ready to begin when he finishes his current one—which is another book and, I expect, then another and another until he dies. Also like Billie and the others, he accepts his past without regret, believes he has never experienced a mid-life crisis, is optimistic about his future, and feels he has lived a fulfilled life but looks forward to more of life to live before he dies. If his daughter asked him what is there to live for, he would affirm (though less ecstatically than Marty) that "life is for living and everybody that is living should make the most of it, of the opportunity to do one's best. Not to waste it. You have two choices on this earth. You are determined to make the most of your life or not to. . . [it is] much more satisfying to think positively about those things."

Chen's professional career began to follow that of a typical academic thirty-five years ago after graduating from Haverford College. He entered graduate school at the University of California at Berkeley to specialize in East Asian studies, especially sociopolitical affairs and literature. After securing his Ph.D. in the short time of four years, he stayed on as a teaching assistant, published his first book four years later, moved to another university (where he received tenure in two years), and published several internationally acclaimed monographs. These led to his election to the presidency of two different specialized professional organizations. Following another move to one of the country's more prestigious university departments, he reluctantly accepted the president's request that he head his department. He held this post so successfully for several years that he was asked again to chair one of the university's largest departments. Despite these honors, he viewed such administrative jobs as distractions which he felt obligated to fulfill. In 1982, he told me that "being chairman is a drag. I find myself spending three hours every day doing administrative drudgery . . . [which] can be a waste of time. . . . I could be so much more productive. So far I have not regretted being an administrator, but it has slowed down my creativity. I would like to write a few more books before I am finished."

When I interviewed him again in the fall of 1993, I probed further about his leadership strengths. In Chen's typical self-effacing way, he said, "As an administrator I was adequate. If I am asked to do it, I will do it. I didn't enjoy it. I did it for ten years out of a sense of duty, a sense of obligation. When the president asked me to do something, I could never say no. So I ended up being asked to do things. . . . That's my personal weakness. . . in my old age maybe I should be more self-assertive."

Since 1982, Chen had, of course, published more books, three of them in Asia. Founding a journal in a subspeciality of his field and increasingly invited to lecture and give courses abroad, he became so well known and respected that he was the first foreign-born scholar elected as president of one of the academic world's most prestigious professional organizations.

Again, typical of Chen, he modestly claimed he didn't understand why he had been elected. "I don't really know what they saw in me. My publications. My standing. I don't know. That was a surprise to me for a foreign-born scholar to even be nominated. I had no expectations that I would be elected. . . I thought all these honors should go to much more senior people [in their sixties]. I had no expectation I would be elected, but for some reason I was."

When I pushed him to identify his strengths that led to what he now sees as having been his greatest achievement, Chen explained,

> I try to do things differently. . . Somehow I came to be known as . . . [an interpreter of a country's] culture. Things like its ideology, prejudices, emotions, national character, symbols, assumptions, images.
>
> I am much more interested in what goes on in people's

minds.... Someone on the nominating committee said they were looking for someone doing something unique, different, original. Different from what most other people did.

When pressed further about his strengths, Chen talked of his

> graduate students who I have helped become scholars.... I am known as a humane teacher, though maybe not a terribly good one.... I work very closely with students. They do some very good things. Whether because of my influence I am not too sure. At least many of the people who have done their dissertations with me have done some significant work. I have been very happy with that. When they go out into the field they would be recognized as my students.

Shortly after his presidency, he was called to join America's foremost department in his area. Given his prominence, I was not surprised to learn of his extensive contributions to numerous committees and boards, including a national commission to set minimum standards for what today's students need to master in his field of expertise, a Library of Congress committee, and state institutes in varied fields of the social sciences.

Chen is as exquisitely clear about his identity as a scholar as he is about his academic values. When I asked how he would most like to live the rest of his life, he replied simply, "I am very bookish. I would be happiest if I could be surrounded by books." And when I pursued him to defend how fulfilled his life has been, he said,

> Because of my own self-definition as a scholar I would have fulfilled my life if I could have made a contribution to scholarship in my field... that would be remembered.... I have rather modest expectations about the books I write.... I write books because I enjoy writing books.... If one person reads one of my books then I feel I would be satisfied. If one person gets something out of the book and if that changes his or her life in a slight way, then I feel I have not been totally useless. I don't know if that is a Chinese, Confucian, or Quaker value but I have that sense.

Sources of Chen's Calling

Chen's calling draws on at least three wellsprings: his family tradition, his ethnic background, and a complicated but maturely integrated personality.

Family Tradition

If Chen was not born a scholar, his family background certainly destined him to be one. His grandfather was a scholar specializing in and writing about Chinese literature. His father was a journalist who traveled extensively and was away from home for years at a time. He wrote books which he later encouraged Chen to do also. In mid-life, his father changed careers to become a professor of politics, settled into doing serious academic work, and wrote books on political and cultural issues—a way of life Chen explicitly says he took from his father. Furthermore, Chen married into a scholarly family. Lin's father is a creative and internationally distinguished philosopher whose judgment about his writing Chen values highly. Reflecting on his own standards of academic excellence, Chen said his father—his mother, as well—taught him that intellectual achievement and excellence were important. "I have to think what I write may be read by my father and my father-in-law. I cannot afford to be superficial. . . . When I do some perfunctory work I feel very disgusted with myself."

It is not atypical for sons of achieving and distinguished fathers—and grandfathers—and sons-in-laws of similarly distinguished fathers-in-law to not dare to compete with them. They rebel against their father's values to search for a distant, noncompetitive career. Sometimes a son's drive to create his own vocational identity is so intense that it leads to compensatory development of talents or a way of life not as compatible with what he "was meant to be" or live. Erratic success and inner strain may be signs of being at odds with one's true self. How did Chen escape this fate?

He agrees that his family destined him to be a scholar and that he did not revolt against its expectations and values but instead worked hard to fulfill them. Why? His father's prolonged physical absence during most of Chen's critical growing up years diluted day-by-day father-son irritants and reminders of his father's achievements. Also, at seventeen, Chen won a competitive scholarship to study at Haverford College and has seldom returned to Taiwan since. Another reason may be the Confucian value of not dishonoring one's father by rejecting him and his values, though Chen is unsure how much his Confucian heritage has contributed to his success.

Finally, a less conscious reason may be Chen's reaction to his parents' departure for Europe when he was six years old. For three years, his grandparents raised him. During this time he never saw his parents, who, he says in his understated way, he "missed very much." Fifty years later, he still regrets that they did not take him with them. Parental separation at the age of six sometimes is felt as abandonment. It can create resentment and retaliatory fantasies of such intensity that they demand prodigious energy to control, deny, and compensate for. I have mentioned the path that children sometimes take: become like the person they have lost, regain their presence, and so moderate the intensity of their anger. Another unconscious path some take is to convert resentment and defiance into their opposite: a strict conscience, gentleness, deference to, and acquiescence to authority—for example, to presidents of universities.

Chen is aware he took the first path; he may not be as aware that the second path may "explain" his primary weakness—his inability to assert himself and say no to authority.

While not formally religious, Chen thinks of himself as highly ethical and committed to universal values that unite the international scholarly world and that sustain the moral basis of his calling.

> I have basic values like honesty, integrity, conscientiousness that have not changed over the years. I don't know where they came from. . . . [They] are very important to me because all of us judge others and ourselves and one has to have some moral or ethical framework to value other people. We cannot evaluate other people unless we evaluate ourselves. And honesty becomes very important . . . [also] to be open to different lifestyles, different kinds of thinking, to understand other people who are not necessarily like one's self. I am not always practicing what I preach. . . .
> I do have a commitment to scholarly integrity and aca-

demic freedom. What one does ought to be free from politics, state interference. . . . If you do something well, you should be able to communicate with others in other countries and engage in a dialogue free from polemicism and politics. I think that is my faith and basic commitment.

As a student of cultural values moving to transcend his own East Asian and American identities, Chen reemphasized the universalist values underlying his scholarly identity.

> I do have the view that the world is dominated by anti-intellectuals, those who are very materialistic or jingoistic and chauvinistic. It is necessary that small circles of people in all countries transcend these tendencies. . . . My big dream is to be one of those people working to strengthen these circles.
>
> It seems to me there is a growing intellectual barbarism in the world: people spending time and energy on armaments, war preparedness, fighting, killing, and other anticivilized actions. I have told my daughter there is meaning for those people who refuse to participate in those kinds of barbarisms and to maintain civilization. We are heirs of mankind's accumulated wisdom. Those of us who can and have the determination and inclination to maintain civilization must continue to do that. I tell my daughter she ought to be proud of being part of an elitist minority and not to feel embarrassed about talking about elitism. We are in a dark period of human history and we need elite minorities who can do other than prepare for wars.

Ethnic Background

Though Chen expressed uncertainty about how much his ethnic and Confucian heritage or Haverford College's Quakerism influenced his values and world view, I feel his ethnic background contributes more to his scholarly success than he admits. He feels comfortable when with other Chinese. He writes about China from, one might say, the "inside out" and must self-consciously criticize his own views to eliminate less conscious nationalistic biases or prejudices that he may have. His bicultural identity contributes to his creativity. It provides him with the experiential basis for standing outside of American and Chinese culture to secure an outsider's and insider's perspective on each.

No one strength, such as his conscientiousness, but a pattern of strengths that seem to be drawn from Asian cultural traditions suggests that his ethnic background contributes to his success. His deference to and respect for his seniors, unfailing modesty—even self-negation—and understatement, and interpersonal harmonizing skills necessary to be an effective administrator (especially of university prima donna faculty) let me know I am not in the presence of a stereotypical American. He may object to what may be unfounded biases, but let us keep them in mind when I describe the computer-drawn portrait of the vocationally fulfilled American male to see how he may differ.

A Complicated But Maturely Integrated Personality

According to tests, like the Rorschach inkblots, Chen was far more inwardly complicated than what he appeared to be outwardly in his middle years. Like Marty's inner world, his was also populated by rich, vivid, emotionally intense, and conflictual images that puzzlingly contrasted with his gentle, calm, acquiescent, and polite manner. But unlike Marty's erotic fantasies, Chen's were basically aggressive: fierce and ferocious wolves, daggers, blood from an accident, glaring eyes, fighting dogs, lobster's claws. Unlike Marty at the time, Chen had the disciplined and realistic controls to not be possessed by such powerful aggressive energies. Instead, his maturity enabled him to draw on them for high-level critical analyses and creative ideas that went against conventional views in his field. Ten years ago I predicted his scholarly work would take him along paths different from those his colleagues might take—which, in fact, has turned out to be true. He has stubbornly stood his ground against fads in his field, such as quantitative analyses and computerization, and against younger critics' charges that he is superficial because he ignores class struggles, Marxist economic insights, and, recently, more politically correct ideologies.

In 1982 I found him to be not only an inwardly passionate but also a warm academic because of his potential emotionality and empathic sensitivity to others, which could contribute to his administrative success. When I asked how he, as department chair, had survived faculty who could be tough and self-centered, he reminded me I had said ten years earlier that he probably took the role of a "doormat" on whom he allowed others to step. Lin tells him he is much too accommodating and should be more assertive and say no more frequently. "So how did you remain sane?" I asked him. He replied as Harry did. "They got to me from time to time. But I can forget about them once I get to my studies or library.... I try to shut them out once I am reading or writing. I could compartmentalize, which was the only way I could maintain my sanity.... I can switch from one preoccupation or mood to another very easily. I may be very upset or distressed about something, but I can switch it off and begin to work on other things."

Mature persons have enough self-discipline to be on top of their talents and not allow personally upsetting conflicts to disrupt their efficiency. Chen and Andy were the two most mature men of the study. Lin, his closest friend, and his most knowledgeable colleague also rated him as the second most androgynous man. Such rich and varied intellectual and character strengths undergird his complete satisfaction—he wondered if he were too complacent—with his vocation.

Chen's familial destiny, ethnic heritage, and personality prepared him to be a scholar. A Haverford College professor he affectionately respected opened the path to international sociopolitical and cultural studies. Chen's calling was set by the age of twenty-one; it beautifully brought together his familial background, cultural identity, and personality so that he could dedicate himself to the ideal of scholarship. Lin has stood by him every step along his path. "She understands my strengths and weaknesses. She supports me in my professional duties. She has helped me in my profession. She encourages me. We have the same values about research."

The Personality of Persons Called to Their Vocations

Is your work—whether as student or physician or engineer—just a job or a calling? Why not rate your own satisfaction with each of the items below. If you are very satisfied with an item, give yourself a 4; quite satisfied, a 3; moderately satisfied, a 2; somewhat dissatisfied, a 1; and very dissatisfied, a 0. Then add your scores up.

1. Your salary or wages
2. Self-fulfillment you get from your work
3. How good you are at your work
4. Your opportunity to achieve at your potential level of ability
5. Amount of time you spend on your work
6. Opportunity to continue your growth most of your working life
7. Effects of your work on your family and social life
8. Your work uses your best potentials
9. Your personal relationships with your colleagues
10. Your work satisfies your strongest needs

If you scored 40, then you are called to your work as strongly as Chen. The higher your score, the more likely you feel called to your work. If you scored about 25, you are similar to the typical professional or manager. Satisfaction with the even-numbered items more directly contributes to fulfillment and happiness than satisfaction with the odd-numbered attributes. Why? Because when our work fulfills our strongest needs, then money, the clock, even the needs of our families, become less immediate. Absorbed in our work, which is really play for people like Chen, we don't notice that it is time to eat; we tap into energies unfettered by doubts about or resistances to our work; we don't care if others think we are odd. The result is that we don't feel as unhappy about our salaries or the amount of time we put in. Our morale soars much higher than that of people who watch the clock, worry about their status, and dream about their next raise. The best protection against burnout is to be called to our work. Marty's calling was to be a feminist lawyer rather than a mother. She was more satisfied with every one of the even-numbered items as a lawyer than she was with the comparable items as a mother.

To feel that our work—whether as a scholar, parent, feminist, or adventurer—fulfills our needs, gives our talents their full scope, and channels our deepest interests is what becoming more fulfilled is all about. Remarkably, the same meaning of vocation as a calling occurs in fifth graders in Saudi Arabia, eighth graders in Tokyo, and college students in New Jersey. No wonder our maturity is the best predictor of our vocational satisfaction. The more mature person risks seeking new ways to grow; the less mature individual seeks only the security of the known. We don't grow if we fear taking risks, even with our income and status. Billie, Andy, Marty, Harry, and Jane all know that truth. Many of today's youth, including six-year-old Bobby aspiring to go to Harvard, young MBAs pursuing the fast track, and the rest of us who believe that money buys fulfillment have yet to know that truth.

Of course, satisfaction with the odd-numbered items—such as with our competence, relations with our colleagues, and salaries—contributes to how good we feel about our work. But they are more peripheral to growing more wholly. At best, they enable us to fulfill our basic needs and grow through our work. If we are highly competent in a task that we don't believe is central to our needs and talents, then satisfaction about our competence is not going to increase our satisfaction with other aspects of our work. Our relations with our colleagues are not unimportant. They provide the emotional working conditions, climate, and models that in turn can enhance our growth and so our sense of fulfillment. An adequate salary can free us from preoccupations that divert us from concentration on our work.

We cannot reason ourselves into a calling or commitment. It emerges out of our character as we get ourselves more and more maturely together. Many years of tracking how men and women succeed and become happy confirm over and over how much of what we achieve is only the *visible* projection of our *less visible* maturing character. That is also why we cannot buy success and happiness.

When our work is a calling, not just a job, our colleagues are just as aware of it as we are. Chen, Lin, and Chen's closest friend, and colleague had no doubt that he was called to be a scholar. So I explored the meanings they attached to vocational fulfillment or calling further. Men and women called to and fulfilled in their work, as they and their peers judge it, are, not surprisingly, more mature. Mature persons have the strengths necessary to create more fulfilling work as well as familial lives for themselves.

However, two perplexing puzzles now arise: Men's, *but not women's*, vocational fulfillment predicts other competencies; vocationally fulfilled men, *but not fulfilled women*, share a large number of character strengths. Just as the meaning of being a parent differs for the two sexes, so the meaning of vocation differs for men and women—at least at this point in time.

Men's Vocational Fulfillment Predicts Other Successes

Vocationally fulfilled middle-aged men are generally satisfied and happy persons who, like Harry and Chen, have been so since their teenage years. They are happily married and satisfied fathers; their children are emotionally healthy and mature. They are also more competent in their other adult roles as well. Because they are nondefensive and open in their relationships they are able to create comfortable intimate relationships with others. They are also more mature and have high self-esteem. Harry and Chen match this portrait exactly. Andy would have in his mid-forties. He was vocationally fulfilled and happily married. In Marty's words, he was a "supportive and loving... strong and caring partner." He was also in the top 10 percent of successful fathers. To phrase this important finding differently, men like Bruce Jackson, the laid-off electrical division manager, who have trouble at work are likely to also have trouble at home with their wives and their children, as he did.

That I had obtained these same findings when studying the men in their early thirties tells us how true they are. And that George Vaillant, studying middle-aged Harvard graduates, found a similar pattern suggests that being able to adapt to different and demanding roles is due to stable, underlying strengths that describe one's maturity.

Vocationally Fulfilled Men Share Similar Personality Strengths

Vocationally fulfilled men but not women are typically masculine. Strong, self-sufficient, and confident, they function well under stress. They impress their peers as being energetic, aggressive, and independent, in control, and willing to take risks. They make decisions easily and defend them readily. Dominance, forcefulness, and competitiveness—the core of the very masculine male—are *not* commonly shared traits of men satisfied with their work. Try acting like Bruce Jackson when working for Microsoft, AT&T, or your local hospital, and see how far you would get.

Vocationally Fulfilled Men are Androgynous

The men happy in their work are also androgynous, which means that their maleness is mellowed by interpersonal strengths, such as understanding, gentleness, and eagerness to soothe hurt feelings—strengths more typical of women's way of relating. However, their masculinity is more visible. Though Chen's culturally determined interpersonal style is more prominent and contributes to his marked androgyny and administrative success, he also ranked higher than 75 percent of the other men in masculinity. Recall his ferocious wolves and fighting dogs, whose aggressive energy he channeled into long hours of critical, analytical, scholarly work.

Because men called to their work share so many similar character strengths (their peers reliably agree in describing them on four times—40 percent of 100 traits—more strengths than the women's peers agree that they have), they are more easily bonded into an unspoken fraternity or brotherhood. If the successful businessmen, journalists, and engineers accidentally met at Heath's bar one evening, they would immediately feel comfortable with each other. (More introverted and less sociable men like Chen would feel more like outsiders.) They would intuitively understand each other's "deals," conflicts with the IRS, exasperating colleagues, and partner's complaints.

Not just shared experience but common personality strengths cement the "old boy network." This is one reason why women feel like outsiders or emotional strangers to men's groups. Women who feel excluded from the office lunch group or the late-afternoon "beer gang" may be deliberately ignored, but there may be deeper reasons. They may not give off the same vibes, express themselves similarly, share the same unspoken experiences that had earlier formed the men's character, or appreciate the meaning of male competitive bragging, backslapping, playful punching, and on and on. The men's shared character bonds them in unconscious but simpatico ways. Jane, with her entrepreneurial character, experience of the rough-and-tumble business world, and ability to speak men's language might feel more comfortable if the men didn't exclude her for other reasons. Marty might also feel more comfortable, if she could check her passionate feminist distrust that men who succeed do so on the backs of submissive women.

Women Are More Conflicted about Vocational Fulfillment

On the other hand, a woman's work apparently means something different to her than a man's does to him. Remember that I am describing what is more likely to be the case for many, certainly not all, women. This may be truer of middle-aged than younger women these days. While a man's success and happiness as a worker, spouse, and parent go together, the study suggests that a woman's vocational success does *not* predict success in the other areas of her life. Few married mothers with careers in the study felt really happy, fulfilled, and, most critically nowadays, guiltless. Billie, Marty, and Jane were exceptions, but then the tests identified them to be exceptional: Billie because she had the strengths to be one of those rare Superwomen; Marty, because she had redefined for herself what a good wife and mother were to be, had made her career her primary calling, and had had a husband like Andy who accepted being an equal parent; Jane because her driving ambition to create a multimillion-dollar firm was her primary calling. Jane had always worked, could afford to pay for help with the children, and had a casual, even laid-back husband who supported her until she started to succeed on her own. Before that, Jane had told me that she would have been in severe conflict if he had not supported her.

Why can husbands fulfilled in their work succeed in their familial roles more easily than their wives? Why is it more probable that in a two-career marriage, the vocationally satisfied husband will more successfully balance his roles than his vocationally satisfied wife will hers? It was no mystery to Marty, who had fought that battle. Men still have only one calling—their work—and two jobs—their marriage and parenthood. Neither they nor others, until recently, expected much of them as husbands and fathers. We can feel more easily satisfied doing well in a job than a calling. Men focus their energies and talents on making it, "getting ahead," not on developing the strengths needed to be better husbands and fathers. The maturity of the vocationally satisfied man also makes it easier for him to juggle his work and the competing demands of his wife and children.

Nowadays, some women want three callings—children, marriage, and work—or three coequal number one selves. They focus on their relationships with their husbands, children, children's teachers, grocery clerk, in-laws, friends, neighbors, and everyone else who they meet and must smile at, please, and adjust to. And if they are working, they must also focus their talents on "getting along," let alone "ahead." That is why, for example, women must have more varied strengths to make a marriage work. I think Marty would go on to say that a woman's nurturing identity, so deeply imprinted in her psyche, emotionally hears the cry of her baby before that of any other person, even of her husband. She is also more aware of those at work who need her. Juggling three callings is inherently conflictive. Remember William James's quote about not being able to be a tone-poet, saint, and bon vivant living "in the same tenement of clay." Except for those rare individuals like Billie, something has to give.

Alice Matthews was fighting—and losing—the battle of balancing three jobs. She was a mother of a three-year-old boy and a six-year-old girl. As a pediatric physician on the staff of a major teaching hospital, she could not fully control her hours; she depended on Jerry, her husband, who was a social worker, to adjust his schedule to fit hers. Like Andy, he had a deep egalitarian commitment. He willingly altered his work so he could take the children to school every morning, make dinner, and generally be available when Alice couldn't be. But as he ruefully said, "I've come to feel that there is a special bond between a mother and her children; when they really hurt, they reach out to Alice. There's little I can do at such times." Though they had resolved the logistical problems, like having help, Alice admitted that she always felt torn when she left for the hospital before her daughter had left for school or came home late at night after Jerry had put the children to bed. She could barely hold back her tears when she talked of how she had to walk out on those mornings when the children were hurting. And how guilty she felt that Jerry was taking the full brunt of her career, even though he had never complained.

On the basis of Alice's tests, I felt—and she agreed—that the personal cost for her mental health of juggling three jobs was too high and might actually work against filling any of them successfully. She had known this inwardly but had not wanted to admit it to herself. I said, "I will say three words. Don't hesitate. Just pick one of the three: career, children, Jerry."

"Children," she instantly replied.

She heard the question. She heard what her calling was to be. When Alice finally faced that truth, her inner clouds evaporated, at least temporarily. She and Jerry have since gone their separate ways.

Billie had heard "problem solver," which included career, wife, and mother. Marty and Jane had heard "career": Marty to be a feminist, Jane to make a million as a creative entrepreneur. When push comes to shove, a calling means hearing one voice louder than others and following it as long as we are called. We then must make room as best we can for the other voices without guilt. Marty and Jane show some of the ways it can be done. In the long run, unless one is like Billie, trying to have three callings risks paying some damaging emotional costs.

Women may view their careers differently than men for another reason. Though women who are called to their work tend to be more mature, they, unlike their male counterparts, share few specific personality traits. For example, they are judged by their spouses, friends, and colleagues to be assertive, adventurous, courageous Jane Allens not stuck in ruts. They are also viewed as honest, undefensive Martys fulfilling their potentials. But that is about all. Not being raised to have shared formative vocational experiences in childhood and adolescence does not create shared personality strengths. So if the women who were satisfied with their careers got together at Heath's bar to talk about their work, they'd feel more like strangers to each other than the men would. Not feeling similar vibes or having shared growing-up work experiences or thinking similarly when solving problems, they'd feel more strain around each other and notice how diverse rather than how similar they were. They would, for example, have more trouble than the men agreeing about forming a Rotarian group or deciding to have a night out on the town together as a group. They would really come together, however, if they talked about their children and husbands.

A simpler though similar reason may explain why women who feel good about their vocations share so few common strengths. For men, their vocations are their identities, and they have been since they were three when their fathers asked them what they wanted to be when they grew up: a space man, a football player, or a police officer like their daddy. For women, their vocations may or may not be at the core of their identities. Some women worked because their husbands expected them to; others, like Eloise, were in fields that didn't fit them but didn't know what they might prefer; some, even professionals like Alice, were reluctantly torn and ambivalent about succeeding too well; and some, like Jane, felt consumed to succeed. A number were satisfied just to "muddle along" because their work was not that important to them to expect more of it. Might not the women's diverse meanings of vocation cloud finding any shared strengths among those believed to be fulfilled by their work?

Understanding why men and women succeed is never as easy or simple as surveys and my kind of computer analyses suggest. I wondered if women whose vocational identities were similar to their traditional nurturing ones might not share more common character strengths. I was right. Female elementary and secondary school teachers who view their work as a calling that they enjoy describe themselves differently than those who are dissatisfied with their jobs. They are more androgynous, and, as I expected, their interpersonal femininity is most pronounced. Compared with women who are less satisfied with teaching, they are more sensitive to the needs of others, more compassionate, more understanding, and so on. The nurturing demands of fields like teaching, social work, nursing, and other traditionally feminine vocations are good examples of how the special demands of different professions can override some of the more general character strengths required to succeed vocationally.

Are women and men called to nurturing vocations more likely to succeed in familial roles which require similar nurturing strengths for success than those called to more typical masculine vocations? Do teachers, for example, create stronger families than engineers or businessmen? I don't know. As women increasingly enter traditional masculine vocations, will their familial success diminish? The pressing societal question is what future path will lead to stronger families without stealing from women their right to self-fulfillment?

Parental Contribution to Children's Vocational Fulfillment

Women's different interpretations of vocational fulfillment made it impossible to identify the kind of common familial or childhood pathways to success that were found for entrepreneurial women. Though men called to their work share many character strengths, the direct contribution of their parents and of early childrearing become less and less important throughout the years. Fathers, not mothers—as Chen's story tell us—are the keys to men's calling to their work. Men who had become vocationally fulfilled by their early thirties had fathers who were energetic and in excellent physical health. They had been available and accessible when their sons needed their help—for example, with homework. The men also remembered their fathers as warm, affectionate, and loving persons who made it clear that their sons should care for and love others in turn. Harry had described his father this way.

Sons who did *not* grow up to feel called to and fulfilled in their work by their early thirties had fathers who were authoritarian and severe disciplinarians when they were little. The fathers were excessively firm, not democratic. As a result, the sons had felt rejected and stubbornly rebelled against their dads. Failing in college or being fired from a first job may be the only way some sons can safely get back at fathers who had despotically squashed them when little tykes. Was this why Bruce Jackson's son dropped out of college and lived on New York City's streets? What a beautiful way of silently not fulfilling an overpowering father's high hopes without defying him openly.

Twelve years later, however, when the men were middle-aged, their fathers' contribution to their vocational success had become almost invisible. The only lingering influence that successful men reported about their fathers was their acceptance of and emotional involvement with them when young. The unsuccessful middle-aged men still felt rejected by their fathers. They probably will always feel that pain. As Andy, Harry, and Chen tell us, men make their own vocational success by middle age.

It is now time for another capsule summary of what Jane, Chen, and the study's remaining men and women tell us about the steps to take to succeed vocationally. Given so many people's conflicts between their familial and vocational responsibilities and hopes, I will conclude with some thoughts about the study's implications for fulfilling them both with less stress.

Chapter 16

NINE STEPS TO SUCCEED VOCATIONALLY

What lessons do the lives of the study's 105 men and women—especially Jane and Chen—teach us about how to succeed vocationally? What steps might we take as a youth or adult to succeed in our work?

Step 1: Be clear about *how* we want to succeed in our vocation. Clarity about our purpose and direction and certainty about our priorities enable us to see further down our path, to avoid enticing diverting ones, and to focus our energies more effectively. Do we want to be a millionaire like Jane? Write books like Chen? Create a more just society for women like Marty? Be highly respected by our colleagues like Andy and Chen? Be called to and love our work even if we must forfeit wealth and power like Mary Elizabeth Cunningham?

Step 2: Actively search to understand ourselves—our mind's favored talents, most important needs and values, preeminent interpersonal skills, leading self-attitudes and strengths—to discover "what we are meant to be." Eloise Barnett's research productivity and international reputation, while gratifying, were not fulfilling; not until her early fifties did she discover that her leadership talents were her route to fulfillment. Roger's success as a history teacher did not quell his restlessness; he since has discovered that his openness to others and interpersonal skills make him an effective community social worker with adolescents. He is no longer as restless.

Step 3: Understand that vocational success and fulfillment are also rooted in our character, not just in our minds and technical competence. Many varied strengths contribute to success, including ambition, drive, and hard work as Jane told us; people skills as Billie, Chen, and James Ferguson, chairman of General Foods, told us; an ethical sense as many people in the study told us. Educating primarily for technical knowledge and skills risks not only future vocational obsolescence but also future character gaps more difficult to fill when older.

Step 4: Work to become more mature. Maturity is a common strength shared by vocationally fulfilled men *and* women. Reread Chapter Three. Identify the strengths associated with maturity that we need to acquire. Then like Billie, self-consciously seek to acquire them—even though we are not yet called to a specific vocation. The more mature we become, the better prepared we will be to create our own fulfilling vocation the rest of our lives—regardless of how our own needs may change, as Jane's did, or what the vocations of the future will be.

Step 5: Learn to use maturity's strengths in all areas of our lives, not just in our work. Billie shows us how to take our problem-solving skills and apply them to both work and family issues. Applying them in many different situations strengthens them. For this reason, vocationally fulfilled men (though not women) generally succeed in their other adult roles, such as their marital, parental, and citizenship ones.

Step 6: Whether a man or a woman, if our principal goal is to succeed as an entrepreneur like Jane, then we should value and cultivate strengths more typical of men, such as a willingness to take risks, assertiveness, and self-reliance. However, don't let such masculine strengths overshadow people skills that are more typical of women, especially if we value our colleagues' respect and loyalty. Chen, Billie, and Harry remind us how critical these skills are for success as administrators. Bill Spaulding, the founder and CEO of his marketing firm, also reminds us not to carry our masculine strengths into our familial relationships.

Step 7: Don't be content to let work be or become only a job. Try to find work that is a calling. Why? Chen and the larger group tell us that in the long run, we'll be happier and healthier if called to our work. Our lives will be more of a unified whole, rather than a collection of many individual pieces that rub and grind against each other.

Step 8: If you are a male who wishes to be fulfilled in your vocation, cultivate the more adaptive strengths typical of men. The study's sixty-five men tell us that to be satisfied vocationally, learn to become self-sufficient and ambitious. Vocationally satisfied men are assertive and forceful; they make decisions easily and willingly take on competitive risks. Their maturity enables them to function well under stress. Because of their tough skins, criticism and rebuff do not destroy them. However, such strengths may be less useful in selected vocations, such as the nurturing ones like teaching.

Step 9: We, especially women, may have to just accept that familial and vocational success can be deeply conflictual, as Billie, Marty, and Alice Matthews warn us. Because feelings of being torn between fulfilling our marital, parental, and vocational roles are so widespread in contemporary families, I examine some future paths men and women can take to minimize the negative effects of such conflicts.

What Path in the Future to Both Familial and Vocational Success?

Alice and Jerry Matthews and most others in the study found familial and vocational success to be difficult to achieve at the same time. Many men claimed that their fathers' one-sided focus on achieving damaged their fathers' healthy growth and limited their familial success. The men want to create a healthier way of life. Surveys confirm Roger's belief that more men are beginning to distrust exclusive commitment to vocational success. If true, the change in values may reflect a societal equilibrating principle at work preparing the groundwork for a generational change in values about what maleness means.

If men wish to mellow their number one vocational selves and become better marital partners, parents, and friends, they will have to grow beyond the typical masculine strengths necessary to make a lot of money, achieve leadership positions, and feel fulfilled in their work. Vocational success of almost any variety that is too tied to such strengths will lead to familial, even vocational, failure, as Bill Spaulding risked.

I am troubled that not *one* of the typical masculine traits necessary for a woman to succeed vocationally contributes to how good a wife, lover, and mother she is. Some of the study's unhappiest husbands had wives who had succeeded in their vocations after I had interviewed them in their early thirties. Their wives had become so absorbed, self-sufficient, emotionally distant, and assertive that their husbands, while proud and respectful of their success, felt that their marriages and sex lives had dried up and died. Jane's husband, Vince, was proud of her success until she began to not need him. With the exception of the Leightons, Barnetts, and Lees, and a few others, most men and women had not resolved conflicts between their intimacy and vocational needs. Andy's and Marty's painfully strenuous labor to create a mutually fulfilling resolution offers hope that the conflict between career and intimacy can be resolved *if* deeper conflictual sexual forces don't erupt. They show us that to integrate familial and vocational roles successfully within marriage requires that men and women be much more androgynously mature in the future than has been necessary in the past.

Clearly defined gender roles within a family can have both healthy and unhealthy consequences. Specialization of role and of the underlying character that supports it, like breadwinning men needing masculine strengths and child-raising women needing nurturing ones, makes for efficiency. It creates a mutual dependency that can make the family a more stable unit. It also provides the opportunity to develop high expertise in the role. But such role clarity, when excessively proscriptive, can have unhealthy effects, as feminists have rightly charged and Andy told us, on both women and men. The effects are aggravated when a society segregates and limits the development of what it defines as inappropriate gender potentials.

On the other hand, abandoning role specialization to be expert in both familial and vocational roles can cause severe stress as well. Strain will be most acute in those who have not developed the strengths required to succeed in the other gender's traditional domain. Furthermore, a family of two self-sufficient familial and vocational experts is potentially unstable; either can separate more easily and still survive. The psychic instability latent in two-career families can be moderated by the development of a mutual need for each other whose fulfillment is given priority by each partner, as the Leightons and Chens show us. Achieving this requires considerable maturity since the relationship will have to be recreated continuously.

If we value for ourselves or our children growing up in ways that best prepare us or them for the varied demands of the future, I don't think we have a choice. We should value becoming more mature and androgynous. Society and our schools will have to help us educate children more maturely and provide the cultural climate that values androgyny more than it does masculinity or femininity alone. As a parent or teacher, don't raise boys to be so masculine and girls so feminine that they make fun of or suppress strengths popularly attributed to the opposite sex. They will need such strengths in the future.

Living involves much more than just vocational success and intimacy. Adults rank religious-ethical ideals, health, and happiness higher than wealth or even a good sex life. Maturing means growing beyond ourselves and our immediate self-centered interests. As religions have taught us, the road to fulfillment and happiness leads away from narcissism toward other-centered and transcendent goals and ideals. So the next section of the book examines the character of people who contribute selflessly to their communities and of those devoted to religious beliefs and ethical ideals. It concludes by bringing together what I have learned about healthy and happy men and women.

Part Four

Enhancing Other-Centeredness and Well-Being

Chapter 17

BEING A MODEL CONTRIBUTING CITIZEN

We can succeed not only as good family members, friends, and workers but also as citizens of our community, nation, and planet. As we mature, we begin to extend our self's boundaries, so spontaneously and beautifully expressed by the father I quoted in Chapter Three who said, "I approach selflessness with my child more than I do at any other time. . . . I'm also now more concerned for people other than myself. You become oblivious to yourself . . . your self really drops out of your thinking."

Growing up means, among many other things, becoming more caring and empathically other-centered, developing altruistic values, and emotionally understanding that though each of us is unique, each of us is also like everyone else. It means integrating more self-centering identities, like "I'm a Californian," or "I'm an American," or even "I'm a twentieth-century male or female" with more universal other-centering ones, like "I'm a citizen of this planet," or "I'm a Greek of Plato's time," or "I'm a crew member of 'Star Trek's *Enterprise*." It means feeling part of a historical procession of humans and of an expanding community whose current and future welfare takes precedence over our own selfish interests and whose well-being we assume responsibility for nurturing. More immediately, it means being a contributing and responsible citizen in our larger community. Recall from Chapter One that being a contributing citizen ranked eighth in importance to adults—ahead of sexual fulfillment, same-sex friendships, leadership and power, and wealth.

We strengthen the values and character necessary to contribute to and serve others and our communities when we assume responsibility for giving our talents, time, and energy to others. By high school, for example, students who contribute to extracurricular, athletic, community, church, and other service activities have already begun to develop the character strengths that predict their future effectiveness. *Schools of Hope* summarizes the evidence about the character of students who actively extend and give of themselves to other-centered activities. They not only do better academically and use drugs and alcohol less frequently, but they also act more ethically, feel better about themselves, and are more mature than adolescents who don't participate or contribute. Furthermore, young fathers differ from married men who are childless: they are more other-centered and mature. So isn't it reasonable to expect that middle-aged people who are model contributing citizens also share similar strengths?

To answer this question, the men and women of the study were ordered from 1 to 8 in terms of their increasing contributions to others and their communities. Their increasing assumption of responsible citizenship activities was defined by how consistently they had volunteered to work for nonpaying community and professional groups the past decade; their level of responsible activities assumed; the number of *different* types of community and professional activities served; and local or national recognition for their contributions, including professional but also nonprofessional honors and awards.

When in their mid-forties, 20 percent of the men and 25 percent of the women had not volunteered to serve others or been elected to a leadership position in their communities or professions within the preceding ten years. Billie scored 5 a decade ago for her contributions, among others, to national commissions and service to her city's mayoral commission on the handicapped. Ten years later, her extensive local hospital visitation and homeless services, state board involvement in Alzheimer's activities, and national service and leadership for veterans would place her near the top of the entire group.

Andy scored 4 ten years ago for, among other activities, his political campaign and civil rights activities; now he would score a 7 for his extensive contributions, which are, however, exclusively confined to his professional activities as a member and chairperson of numerous boards and review editor for journals, his receipt of national and international awards, and efforts to establish a national foundation to finance continued research in his field.

Ten years ago, Marty received a 7 for her work with the peace and civil rights movements, National Organization for Women, and other extensive feminist leadership activities. Now she might score 2 because she has turned so deeply inward and confined her activities to generating ongoing menopausal women's support groups.

Both Jane and Chen scored 1 for no or only minimal contributions as citizens a decade ago. Jane would still score 1 today, but Chen might score a 7 for his contributions and leadership, which, like Andy's, are exclusively limited to serving professional groups. (Incidentally, recall his commitment to universal scholarly values and dedication to defend them—a most apt example of the extension of self beyond its parochial and historical roots.)

In his mid-forties, Harry was selected as *Fulfilling Lives'* exemplar for being a model citizen. He scored an 8 for being one of the group's five most involved in their communities and professions. (Another one of the five had received a prestigious foreign national award for extraordinary service; another had been chairman of numerous nonprofit community boards and of a United Fund drive as well as a faithful participant in local school and church activities.) As I have described, Harry has devoted much of his life to helping others and his community but without sacrificing his family or career. The heavy demands of his current administrative work have limited his voluntary involvement to serving his church's program for the homeless once a week, being a member of an educational organization's board (for which he received a coveted award), as well as membership on several national medical boards. He would be scored about a 6 at this time.

The Personality of the Model Contributing Citizen

The computer-drawn portrait of exemplary contributing citizens revealed four themes: They enjoy being parents; they competently fulfill their other adult roles; they are ethically sensitive, optimistic, idealistic, and principled leaders; and they are androgynous, particularly masculine (though the contributing women are also seen as interpersonally skilled, given their loyalty, compassion, and sympathy).

Enjoys Parenting

Doesn't this portrait of the person who contributes to others make sense to you? Wouldn't the seeds of wanting to contribute to our community sprout first in caring for our immediate families? Enjoying being a parent—one of the more demanding and selfless roles an adult assumes—reflects and nurtures an other-centered and giving character. With such a character, it is not that big a step to want to give to our larger family: our community. Erikson calls this the stage of generativity in our lives and claims that it contributes to our adult maturing, which it in fact does.

Competently Fulfills Other Adult Roles

It is also not surprising that those who contribute to their communities have the coping strengths plus extra energy and time to initiate other activities and take on other responsibilities. Harry is a fine example. He not only knows how to manage and get things done, but he radiates energy—lots of it. Remember that energy available for new interests and commitments is a visible sign of a person's maturity—Harry was more mature than 85 percent of the other men ten years ago. He had the personality resources to succeed in his principal adult roles.

Ethical and Idealistic

Those who select persons for responsible positions know intuitively to note how they have extended themselves into their communities. Clarke Williams, CEO of Century Telephone Enterprises, said, in speaking of the people he prefers to hire, that being a good citizen is a "very good sign of character. . . . If you hire someone whose head is in the sand on the outside, you'll probably find that his head is in the sand on the inside." He is reaffirming a principal finding of the study: We carry our competence and success from one role to another, because they manifest our underlying character.

Certainly, giving our time and energy so generously to others must be renewed by *enduring* idealistic commitments and hopes that we can make a difference to others. Harry's colleague gave him top scores for his ethical sense and commitment to ideals and principles. Harry also told us this when he said that he had a "high sense of trying to do right by my fellow man" and "deep concern" for "the morality of a situation."

Androgynous Character

The androgynous and masculine character of male and female community leaders is predictable. You could infer from my description of Harry that he was androgynous, scoring higher than all but 15 percent of the study's men. His androgyny was due more to his feminine interpersonal skills, however, than to his masculine ones, which the judges rated him to have more of than six out of ten of the other men.

Male and Female Personality Differences in Citizenship

We have learned that men and women who succeed in the traditional roles that historically have been their principal responsibility share a defined and coherent character. Women whose partners were maritally happy had many shared strengths; their husbands did not. Men most satisfied with their vocations also shared many strengths among themselves—the women much less so.

Community leadership roles have been the province of males for centuries, so it is not surprising, therefore, that the male community leaders shared almost three times more strengths than the female leaders did. They were happy and fulfilled and had been so since adolescence. (This was not true of the women who contributed a great deal to their communities.) After Chen, Harry was the second most consistently happy and productive man of the group; he had functioned at the same high level of mood and achievement ever since he graduated from college. Men like Harry, who are deeply and responsibly involved in their communities, are mature, particularly in their stability and autonomy. They are energetic, self-confident, decisive, calm, self-controlled, and resilient. They also accurately understand themselves. Indispensable to good leaders is the ability to understand empathically how others see them. The men but not the women community leaders excelled in this strength. Overall, the men who contribute to others are healthier, both mentally and physically, than men whose heads are "in the sand."

As I said earlier, I had not anticipated how pervasively traditional gender roles shape our character and contribute to our success in so many areas of our lives. I might not have been so surprised by this result if I had been a woman. Feminists have told us that people who are in a subordinate or oppressed position, as women have been since Eve, are more sensitive to how their prescribed roles affect their behavior. I don't know if and how the changing roles of women will affect their historic feminine character and their future community leadership opportunities. Will studies of successful middle-aged women thirty years from now fail to replicate some of the differences I have found? Or will women's heritage limit how successfully they will adapt to the changing demands of their adult roles? Young women now think about work and careers and wrestle with what their number one, two, and three selves will be much earlier than their mothers ever did (some perhaps never did). More now begin their adult years as breadwinners rather than as mothers. Will they develop as clear and defined a masculine-type character as men? Or will they come up against some biologically and historically rooted feminine character traits and needs that tell them that their calling is to be a mother? Or as we move into a more and more interdependent vocational and political world, will their interpersonal skills become more necessary and open the door for a new type of vocational person to step through? Community and public leadership positions are now much more available to women, even in rural downeast Maine, where women are tax assessors and town "selectmen."

One of the stronger shared strengths of both men and women who voluntarily serve others is a deep and principled ethical sense. This sense is grounded on a religious commitment for some, though not formally so for Harry and the others I have introduced you to. In the next chapter you will meet Jim Pryor, the study's most religio-ethical—and controversial—person. The chapter then explores what the larger group tells us about the character of religious and ethical persons.

Chapter 18

JIM PRYOR: CREATING HIS OWN RELIGIOUS AND ETHICAL PATH TO WHOLENESS

Religion and its handmaiden—virtue—continue to be sources of conflict in American cultural and political life. Religion has become secularized for many and embroiled in political and social issues for others. It continues to be at the center of others' lives—and has even been profaned by some TV evangelists addicted to sexual affairs. *Virtue* is becoming another one of those old-fashioned words, like *calling* and, increasingly, *sin*, *salvation*, and *grace*, which adolescents tell me they seldom use or have heard of. Does a religious faith still contribute to success, health, and happiness as early Americans believed? Does old-fashioned virtue still pay off in the long run, as religion has promised, in this day of Wall Street greed, political deception and meanness, and on and on?

Religion as a Source of Hope

What is left for religion to give us? Religion's symbols formerly provided hope. I am not sure they still do for many Americans. They did for only a few of the study's men and women. I am sometimes asked, "Is a religious faith necessary to be healthy and happy?" Because the topic had not been thoroughly studied, I used to reply, "I don't know." Now, I have a glimmer that the answer is, "Traditional religious faith is not necessary to be healthy and happy, but it sure helps some."

Years of studies have shown that conventional signs of religiosity, such as attending church, reciting prayers, reading the Bible, signing pledge cards, and reaffirming a statement of faith, tell little about a person's well-being or personality. The practicing devout may be just as serene, healthy, and fulfilled as the nonpracticing believer, agnostic, or atheist—or just as tortured, wracked by doubts, and insane. I remind you of Andy's and Job's suffering trials. Andy calls himself a religious person who believes in a supreme being and attends the Unitarian church. Though he ranked twenty-fourth among the study's sixty-five men on a combined measure of religio-ethical commitment a decade ago, he is an exceptionally good man dedicated to serving others. Job was also a good man, of great rectitude, devoted to God. Remember that with God's consent, Satan inflicted every imaginable suffering, pain, and disaster on him to test the depth of his faith in God. Despite Job's laments about why he was being punished so cruelly, he did not abandon God. Though God eventually "gave Job twice as much as he had before," even a life of 140 years, Job teaches me that we go to church, read the Bible, and pray to know God better, not to receive a jigger of healthiness or a fix of happiness. God can't be bribed by our goodness, though most of us probably don't believe Job's message in our hearts.

Just how religious were the study's men and women? Not very for the majority. Was religion a source of hope to them? Not for most. Only about one of every four spontaneously said religion sustains their hope as Table 18-1 shows.

Table 18.1. Attitudes Toward Religion

	Percent of Men	Percent of Women
Religion is my main source of hope and energy	8	15
Religion provides a reason to live these days	2	10
Religion sustains my hope	22	29
My strongest convictions are religious	5	15

Religion provided sustenance to a few. Betty, who led daily Bible study groups, reminds us how nourishing a religious belief can be to our hope. When asked, "What is your primary source of hope?" she responded simply, "I know that all things that touch my life come from the hand of God, so there is a purpose in everything we face and in all of our relationships with people."

Jim Pryor found religion opened a deeply inward path to hope and wholeness.

Jim Pryor's View of Hope

Jim Pryor, the highest scoring and judged religio-ethical as well as the most religiously articulate by far of the 105 men and women, replied to the questions about hope this way:

What are your main sources of hope? "I know inwardly that feelings of despair are merely self-illusions. . . . It is as if God is constantly going into hiding. 'Can you find me? When you find me you will experience the warmest embrace imaginable because my nature is a loving one.'"

Why live in days of such despair? "The blessing of life is its opportunity for adventure and discovery, and the very involvement in this process of creation and discovery is . . . to feel one is making a contribution to a movement that has unlimited meaning and value."

Do religion or other beliefs sustain hope for you? "To the extent to which one unburdens oneself of all ordinary religious, political, and social hopes and beliefs, one will come into touch with reality that is so fundamental that it cannot be shaken by any opinion or result. This reality is imperishable and immaculate, complete, full, and absolutely hopeful and trustworthy. . . . Ordinary beliefs in fact keep us asleep."

What are your strongest convictions? "There is an intelligence that includes my own and uses my own that far surpasses anything personal. It has absolute power and is absolutely beneficent with respect to my life and the welfare of the entire cosmos. I need only cooperate with this higher force and my welfare and happiness are assured."

Jim's Crime and Trials

Jim's Crime

Who is Jim Pryor? He is the study's most controversial person. I suspect you and most other readers will condemn his beliefs and acts and accuse him of being a modern-day Judas to the Christ in whom he believes. You may even claim that he fully deserved the suffering he has endured the past decade, which has been inflicted by what he caustically calls the government's Imperial Forces—its federal courts. Jim is a convicted felon sentenced by a Reagan-appointed federal judge to five years in prison and stripped of most of his wealth. He was caught carrying undeveloped photographic film over state lines that pictured adolescent males in sexual relationships with each other in an Asian country. The prosecutor argued that the youths appeared to be younger than eighteen. Under federal statues, every person less than eighteen is defined as a child. Making, transporting, or even possessing a depiction of a child in a sexual act is a felony.

To feature Jim Pryor as the study's most religious person—which he was by every measure I had—may upset you. But when religions are concerned about our personal lives, as most are, they inevitably come into conflict with our sexual lives, as Western religions certainly have historically. For Jim, religion became his path to wholeness—some might say salvation—as well as transcendence of his sexual compulsions.

I have known Jim for thirty-five years. I have great respect for his intellect, deep understanding of the Bible and other religious works and traditions, knowledge of cultural, esthetic, and literary works, and personal courage. I have tried to remain empathically open to what his search for God may tell us about healthy growth and what he believes God's message is for us today. When asked what legacy he hopes his life will leave behind, he replied, "Here was a fellow who thought for himself and encouraged others to do the same." He hopes you too will do the same while reading his story.

Jim graduated from college with the dream of amassing "significant worldly wealth and power." In his early thirties, he dreamt of creating an architectural "cosmic cathedral"-like home of great beauty on acres of California's scenic coast, which he had since bought. When I visited him in his mid-forties, he had indeed fulfilled his youthful monetary dream. As a successful commodities trader earning profits on many days of $50,000, he owned two interconnected houses filled with thousands of books, high-powered stereo systems and records, museum-quality crystal, blown glass, paintings, a stable of fine horses, and a home in Asia to which to retreat. He had nine people on his payroll to support this style of life.

Concurrent with his decade of entrepreneurial success, he searched for God by becoming a follower in succession of three living spiritual guides who shaped his religious philosophy (Vernon Howard, J. Krishnamurti, and Robert Gibson) and the teachers Jesus and Buddha. Walt Whitman's *Leaves of Grass* became his own bible. Increasingly discontent with "living. . . [such an] outwardly beautiful [materialistic] life," he found four years after my 1982 visit "that the true treasure is within. The outer treasure may be quickly lost. That was the brilliance of my being arrested. That evening standing out in the cold winter air with my hands handcuffed behind my back, I knew that my lifestyle was gone, right then and there. How liberating it was to see that one can walk away from such luxury and not have to have it."

Jim's Trials

Jim and his attorney (well-known as a defender of First Amendment rights) did not dispute that he had carried undeveloped film picturing adolescent boys making love into the country and across state lines, which a local film developer had reported to the FBI. He was subject to a maximum fine of $300,000 and thirty years in prison, though he had not been aware of the law that had been passed the previous year making such transport a federal crime. The drawn out-legal arguments centered on the law's reference to film *depicting* pornography with minors, since unprocessed film is not a "depiction" of anything but itself. Seven of the Supreme Court's nine justices sided with the prosecutors, but to cover its tracks, the Justice Department asked Congress retroactively to amend the law to include unprocessed as well as developed film.

Jim was sentenced to five years in a college-like prison, where he was a model prisoner. He wrote "I discovered . . . that there is a vast field left open here for contribution to the common good. . . . Most of the inmates are not inclined to do much for the community. . . . So I have elected to contribute what I can which is much easier for me to [do] because while I loathe the mentality that put me in prison, I am not personally vindictive toward those whom I have encountered in what we call our system of 'justice,' though many prisoners are." Jim created gardens around the chapel, became the assistant to the chaplain, was elected by the prisoners to head their social/educational club, and served as toastmaster of the prisoners' variety shows, all of which made him "the 'Most Visible' prisoner on the campus." In spite of this, others, such as a friend who had robbed eleven banks for which he received a three year sentence, were paroled early. Jim served his full time.

Jim's next trial began nine months after he had moved to a conservative rural mountainous area, where he lived in a log cabin by a pond. Though living a celibate life, he was invited to appear on a televised panel talk show to defend sexual relationships between males. The program was seen by a local resident.

His next trial began like, in his words, "a Jericho trumpet in crescendo; the frenzy never abated." Copies of the program's discussion were distributed around the county, meetings were called, young people were warned by posters to avoid Jim, a local mountain man threatened that if he did not leave he would be driven out, his grocery store owner refused to serve him, his electric transformer was shot out, and one night someone strangled the two black swans that he had bought for his pond. After receiving several death threats, Jim decided to leave, which he did on a Christmas Eve.

When I visited Jim ten months later, he was living in a small third floor room with his computer and some of his records, occasionally dabbling in commodity trades, and working for a national organization trying to increase awareness of gay issues, including age of consent laws. As cooperative, open, and honest about the most intimate details of his life as he has always been, I was impressed (as I was with Marty also) by his self-acceptance and composure, almost serenity, as he discussed the details of his trials. He was walking the path to self-transcendence, having finally found his calling to fulfill his "vision of service to humanity . . . [through his organization] as the vehicle."

What does Jim's life teach us about the religious path to fulfillment or, in Jim's words, "enlightenment and personal integration," and the character of religiously devout and ethical persons? I explore three sources of his calling to serve God in his way: his esthetic temperament and needs, religio-ethical view of sexuality, and emotional health and maturity.

Jim's Religious Path to Wholeness

Jim's Esthetic Temperament

Though educators and philosophers say that mature persons develop a coherent philosophy of life, few of the men and women could articulate a well-thought-out *Weltanschauung* that integrated their talents, needs, values, and personalities. Jim Pryor was a singular exception. When I saw him in his mid-forties, he had become dissatisfied with commodities trading. He was struggling to create a new way of life that brought together his strong sensuous, esthetic sensibility and acute mind under the guidance of an embracing religious philosophy. Fragments from my analysis of his tests reveal the measure of his effort to create such a philosophy:

> He is a basically stable, highly imaginative, and very bright person whose mind is inseparable from his esthetic feelings. Objective reality is strongly colored, infused, by feelings that are largely benign and sexual. He may well dramatize life which for him certainly is not dull, flat, without spice and verve. I don't mean he can't be realistic; he can make good judgments. I see no bizarre or disorganized ways of thinking. His mind is open to hunch, intuition, and mythic, primitive, even divine inspiration. His mind is more appreciative than critical, more tender than tough-minded, more dramatic and colorful than disciplined and precisely crafted. Its flexibility enables him to see issues from different perspectives. He has good analytic skills and can be accurately self-critical. He is introspective and able to put intellectual distance between himself and his impulses to which he can accommodate in conventional ways if necessary.
>
> My concern is that given his obvious talents, impressive esthetic sensitivity, and the maturity to be so open to his impulses and feelings without distorting most of his judgments, he may not find a way to integrate his esthetic sensuousness with some fulfilling channels to the world of work.

"Absolutely true," he exclaimed. An evolving religious philosophy became his integrative route and provided him the strength and serenity to endure his subsequent trials. As we will see, his understanding of God grows out of his esthetic sensitivity to beauty, harmony, and inward openness to what he feels is the sanctity of our body's sexuality—in his eyes, a gift from God.

Religion's Integrative Path for Jim's Sexuality

Jim believes that religion is the most important and fulfilling aspect of his life. It is his life; it is not about "mechanical morality, like lists of dos and don'ts . . . but about God, which is the unity of all life. Everything is related to everything else and everything can contribute to everything else. When the commandments say to love God first and then love others and yourself second, I . . . [believe] my career is to serve others, to give value to society. A career is to contribute to the world I live in; that is my career—to benefit humanity."

His five most important goals for his life are to "be enlightened . . . [and] self unified; increase the light of humanity; kinship with nature; embody love as understanding; and experience love as shared space."

Jim's central question is his relationship with God. For him "God is my great friend, the universe, Truth, beauty . . . I am discovering life on God's behalf. I am God's agent to discover Itself. God has infinite possibilities. . . . My true aim or purpose is to give God glory, to express what is God, not to expect that there are any shoulds to living except to love and to grow." He accepts his trials as God giving him work to do from which to learn more about his path to wholeness. Believing in immortality, Jim looks forward to his ultimate trial—dying—with

> unmitigated joy. . . . I am here having an experience on planet earth and am having a growth experience. This life has been given to me to experience various relationships and to gain certain insights. But I don't need to be identified with this earth or hold onto it. I don't need to be attached to it. When I'm finished with this growth experience here, I have no doubt there are far more wonderful, spectacular things to experience in the universe. . . . This life is

a very minor preliminary to astounding joys and fulfillments and gratifications that are on the way and to which death is a liberation.

Jim's calling is to liberate humanity from societal and personal constraints on how we love and grow. He wants to contribute to our living in true freedom by becoming conscious of and living our own truth. "To give God glory is to increase consciousness" of the good which God has fashioned. So the path to wholeness is to become clearly aware of one's own potentials and assume responsibility for their development and use.

To be able to love God and others as ourselves is God's gift to us. Sexual love is also God's gift as well as the potential for expressing it with both males and females. To deny to anyone the possibility of discovering his or her own potential to love, even sexually, is to abuse them. Jim's more focused calling is to create a society in which everyone's awareness of their potentials to love is increased. He believes that "since personal integration is to be preferred to personal disintegration. . . not to express the love that is indicated to me would be a betrayal of God in the most profound way."

When pressed to explain how he would answer those who claim that having sex with his own sex betrays his Christian beliefs, he irritably responded, "That suggestion is utterly unconscious, uncomprehending, unfortunate, born out of ignorance. This is the state of mind of a person who says that sexual relationships in all cases are harmful and wrong. They may be tremendously beneficial . . . they may . . . [open up] persons to a life they could never know otherwise . . . [and introduce them] to the wholeness of life that might have eluded them the rest of their entire lives."

Jim's sexual relationship with Charlie after his release from prison proved to be the path to deepening his understanding of God's second commandment and so transcending sex's imperative. Charlie was a twenty-year-old bisexual whom Jim helped to support in numerous ways. Jim's evolving religious inwardness prepared him to learn the difference between sex and sexuality of which Andy had spoken. Fundamentally, he eventually discovered that he wanted not a fleeting sexual experience but a "deep and lasting and soaring" relationship with another. In Jim's words, Charlie taught me my central task is to create and maintain an open space with another human being. . . . Charlie was the vehicle for showing me that if I opened the space and if it happens to be filled that's fine. It is not my place to inveigle, seduce, charm, and use any manipulative way to do anything in a personal way except to maintain this openness. If it doesn't happen to be filled, I don't have to be neurotic about it. I don't have to feel denied. God is fulfilling me in stupendous and astounding ways. . . . I have more to give another human being by far if I find that mutuality on which to build. If sex is not there, I don't have to have it. I will support human beings at whatever level they happen to be, but not hold them up artificially or substitute my sense of what they should be for what they are in fact.

I don't have to go out hunting. At the present time I am beyond that. Finding someone else, seducing and winning him over is presently nonsense. It is froth signifying very little. So Charlie was the last gasp of that particular way of life. When I moved away, I knew that was finished and that I would never come back to that kind of relationship again and I haven't.

"Why did you stay in the relationship for so many months?"

"Maybe I couldn't terminate it any more quickly out of whatever fear was present at the time. Fear of being without this kind of outlet? Fear of the unknown?"

A favorite Biblical passage of Jim's is, "There is no fear in love; but perfect love casteth out fear: because fear hath torment. He that feareth is not made perfect in love" (1 John, 4:18). He understands the critical word *love* in the passage to mean emotional openness or vulnerability. Love is a divine gift enabling humans to connect with another. The only adult teacher who reached Jim when an adolescent was a coach who asked him, "What are you up to? You are living in isolation; you are obviously not connected." Sex became a way for Jim to connect with another, whether male or female. Materialistic extravagance during his commodities trading days also connected him to the outer world. Once his equilibrating principle and the Imperial Forces took charge to show him he did not need outward treasures, he turned inward to deepen his connection with and seek an eternal friendship with God.

To my question about his primary source of hope, he simply said, "My relationship with God." How would he answer the youth who asked "What is there to live for?" "There is unimaginable richness to live for: joy, truth, beauty, goodness, a sense of absolute overflowingness, radiance, personal power." To "What religious beliefs sustain you?", he replied, "What sustains me I don't regard as a belief. I regard it as a relationship, a living reality, a moment-to-moment discovery."

Jim's Emotional Health and Maturity

When Jim appealed his court sentence, he asked me to write the judge about his character. The law was the law. That I could not dispute. But I could dispute the judge's character diagnosis of Jim as an "immature and sick pervert" based on one specific act. From my years of knowledge of Jim and the hundreds of personality measures that I had secured about him during that time, I felt confident that he was (and is) not an immature or sick pervert. He was (and still is) mentally healthy and of average maturity when compared to other competent adults. The judge's moralistic bias about his act was only that. But she had no basis to jump from one act of breaking the law to her character diagnosis that Jim was a "sick" person and therefore a "menace." Another person who might have broken the law similarly might well have been an immature, sick, and perverted menace.

The word *mature* must refer to a person, not to a specific act. Chapter Three and Saint Paul insisted that we are not bits and pieces of indiscretions and poor judgments. We are adapting whole persons. Any assessment of our maturity must look at all of us, not just parts of us. Jim's current path is leading, in his words, to greater "self-control and freedom," or what the model of maturity would identify as self-transcendence.

Do you still doubt why he adapted so serenely to his years in a federal prison and became the leader of his fellow inmates? So religion, as history has shown us for centuries, can aid individuals to transcend desolation and sorrow and ground them to an absolute and beneficent source of hope—God, Jim's great friend.

Religion Is for God, Not for Success and Happiness

When I turned to the entire group of men and women for insights about religion, success, and happiness, I had to conclude that religion is for devotion to some transcendent purpose or god, not for success and happiness. Are traditionally religious, churchgoing, and devout persons more successful than the nonreligious? No. Healthier and happier? No. Do they share any familial, parental, or personality traits? Practically none.

Nevertheless, the few results provide some tantalizing ideas to ponder. The differences between the more and less religious individuals' personalities affirm religion's potential hope. Religious women and men are seen by their peers to be virtuous, idealistic, and understanding persons of strong convictions. The religious women are judged to be mature, self-confident, optimistic, reflective persons, who, like Betty, stand up for and defend their beliefs without apology. The religious men are more feminine, especially in their interpersonal skills. Like Jim Pryor, the religious man is loved by others who view him as gentle, sensitive to their needs, and eager to soothe others' hurt feelings.

The last tantalizing hint about traditionally religious persons is that for the only time in the study, a positive adult outcome may be rooted in an unfavorable family background. The hints are few but consistent. The religious men's and women's fathers had been either remote and withdrawn or absorbed in themselves; the men, in particular, reported that they had needed their fathers to depend on. Had God become the father they desired but never had when younger? Jim's father did not fit this portrait. While he knew of Jim's sexual preferences and supported him, he was a "free spirit, as if he never belonged to this world." Jim feels he is like his father: serene, detached, affectionate, warm, and idealistic.

The answer to the question about religion's contribution to our health and happiness is: "Traditional religious beliefs and commitments contribute to some individuals' well-being; they are *not* necessary to succeed and be healthy and happy." The answer did not surprise me. Other students of religion's contribution to our well-being had alerted me to its probability. The peccadilloes of the TV evangelists Bakker and Swaggart remind us that professed faith and practice not rooted in and consistently integrated with our character can even destroy us.

I pursued the question further by exploring religion's handmaiden: virtue.

Virtue Pays Off

For many, religion's meaning is found not in what we profess but in how we actually live ethical and therefore virtuous lives committed to transcendent values or ideals. The study's religious women and men, like Marty, Betty, and Jim, were highly ethical, but other ethically committed ones, like Billie, Jane, Harry, and Chen, were not deeply religious. When asked about the strongest convictions that gave them hope and energy, more than a third of the 105 men and women described *only* a humanistic ethical ideal that valued goodness in others and their responsibility to nurture it and to create a better society: "I want to turn out strong, moral, hopeful children." "I believe in the essential goodness of human beings." "I am not here just for myself; I draw my vitality by being helpful and valuable to others." "I conduct a personal continuing inquiry into the meaning of life and the ultimate good of society and how to achieve it." "The world can be improved and everyone must join in to make it a better place." "I have faith in you and me."

I can make four fairly firm assertions about virtue.

First, sensitivity to ethical issues and holding ideals are highly valued by most as essential to living.

Second, virtuous men and women are indeed more successful, happier, and healthier than unethical ones. Unquestionably, old-fashioned virtue does pay off in most of the good things of life.

Third, ethics and ideals are rooted in our character, particularly the strengths typical of other-centered, stable, and autonomous persons.

Fourth, it may be easier for women than men to be virtuous because virtue is rooted in interpersonal strengths more typical of women than of men.

Ethical Qualities Are Highly Valued

Americans highly value being ethical and idealistic despite ceaseless examples of unethical and cynical behavior: the dishonest gaminess of political TV ads, daily revelations of premier companies like Unisys and General Electric allegedly bilking the Defense Department, illustrious senators on "the take," and surveys reporting that the majority of California high school students cheat and don't care if others do. Ethical ideals ranked fifth in importance in my survey of several thousand adults. When I ask teachers to name the five most important strengths their students need to be effective adults in the future, they always include honesty and integrity. The study's men and women spontaneously identified the virtues necessary to succeed in their principal adult roles—values that religions have advocated for centuries: honesty, compassion, integrity, commitment, and courage.

When we study a group of exceptionally good and effective men and women, we discover that their peers rate them to be honest, deeply ethical and principled persons of high integrity. Their colleagues rate their integrity and ethical practices to be their most distinctive of thirty vocational strengths. With the exception of Jim Pryor, Vince Allen, and another man who had been in jail overnight for an alcoholic binge, none had been troubled by the law.

Virtue Brings Success, Health, and Happiness

Are ethically mature and idealistically committed men and women successful, healthy, and happy? Are those who say of their strongest convictions, "I don't have any," "I really don't know," "I like to use power and enjoy while here," "I am motivated by dollars to be successful," and "I believe only in myself" less healthy and happy than those who affirm the worth of others and the desire to help them and create a better world?

The answer is yes. Virtue pays off royally in success, health, and happiness.

Virtuous men and women succeed in all of their principal adult roles. They are good marital partners, competently fulfill all of their various marital responsibilities, and feel fulfilled as parents. They are also good lovers, both by their own and their partner's signs of a good lover. The virtuous men and women are also comfortable openly sharing almost anything with their close friends. Finally, they are mature, physically and emotionally healthy persons. No wonder they are happy and fulfilled and seen by their peers to be living full and satisfying lives. If I take a slightly less rigorous stance about what results I accept as probably true, I can also say that virtuous men and women are rated to be great friends by their friends, are responsibly and extensively involved in serving their communities, and have mature children. Virtuous men are also vocationally fulfilled and viewed as such by their colleagues. But this is not true of virtuous women, probably because the meaning of work differs so much among them.

Regardless of how I measured "virtue," it is clear that it does *not* bring higher incomes—just good health, happiness, and self-fulfillment in the long run.

It is no mystery why being a virtuous person pays off in success and happiness. How do you feel if your lover or children are dishonest, duplicitous, untrustworthy, and selfish? Or if you have a colleague who cheats, lacks integrity, is sociopathic, and stabs you in the back? Or if you have a friend who is too morally insensitive to know when he is transgressing? Unethical people just create a great deal of pain and misery for others and eventually for themselves. They must always be on guard to protect themselves from the discovery of their lies and deceits or suffer the pain and misery that guilt provokes. I do not recommend Reverend Dimmesdale as a model to live by if you rank happiness and health as high priorities for your life.

Virtue Is Rooted in Our Character

Our ideals spring out of our character. So do our ethics. Virtue is not a pleasing garment to put on and take off at will—it is part of us. The men and women recognized this truism when they spontaneously described what kept them going on down days: "There is something internal to my character," "I am not the pessimistic type," "I am an eternal optimist," "I have a tremendous amount of energy I have not yet begun to tap." They sensed what I found.

Perhaps you would like to match yourself against the more outstanding traits that virtuous men and women share in common. If you are virtuous, you are, above all else, psychologically mature. You are also a cheerful optimist, hopeful, decisive, energetic, and reliable. Your peers also see you as sympathetic, tender, open, and loyal. Intriguingly, and perhaps because of your self-confidence, you seek out new experiences and are willing to playfully take risks to continue growing.

Some character strengths are more visible in virtuous men than women and others more visible in women than men. If you are a virtuous man, you are cooperative, gentle, understanding, and sensitive to others' needs. Because you feel in control of yourself, others see you as calm and not easily upset by stress. If you are a virtuous woman, you are an independent individualist, willing to learn new things and stand up for what you believe.

So hope—having ideals, principles, and ethical maturity—is firmly rooted in our personality, especially in feminine interpersonal strengths for both men and women and also some masculine ones for women. Again, just as we saw for successful men and women, virtuous persons have also developed the strengths typical of the opposite sex.

Virtue May Be Easier for Women Than for Men to Acquire

Have you ever wondered why it is males who usually get into trouble from kindergarten on? Why are our jails jam packed with about 85 percent males and only 15 percent females? Who more often bribes, fights, steals, rapes, and whores around? Will the ratio of males to females who get into trouble change as women get an equal opportunity to bribe and sleep around? I am sure there is no one simplistic answer to my question. But I have three clues that suggest it may be easier for the typical woman to be virtuous.

Clue 1 is that virtuous men (and women, too) are clearly understanding, sensitive to others' needs, sympathetic, and have all the other interpersonal strengths that typically describe women. Jim Pryor's friends and colleagues gave him top scores for being an ethical person; he ranked fourth among the sixty-five men in understanding, sensitivity to others' needs, and other similar interpersonal strengths. Since men are seldom raised to have such feminine interpersonal traits, they may have to work harder to be virtuous.

Clue 2 is that the men's peers saw them as a group to be less sympathetic, compassionate, sensitive to another's needs, understanding, and so on than the women's peers rated the women to be. Do virtues like honesty, integrity, and a deep ethical sense grow out of the more "feminine" quality of our relationships with others? If so, then women may be more predisposed with the character to be virtuous.

Clue 3 is that the men thought of themselves (and their colleagues agreed) as less ethical and idealistic than the women rated themselves to be. Might this be because "real" men find "ethics" irrelevant to their principal identities? Somewhat playfully, I created a macho index that combined the judges' ratings of the core attributes of the historical American male, as Tocqueville described him 175 years ago: forceful, self-sufficient, dominant, masculine, aggressive, and competitive. The answer to my question is yes. The macho male may or may not be very ethical; his maleness does not contribute anything to being ethical. (Incidentally, macho males succeed in only two ways: Their peers judge them to be leaders who enjoy using power to make a lot of money. Aren't these the areas that virtue seems to be most egregiously lacking these days?)

So could it be that being virtuous comes easier to women than to men because, for whatever biosocial reasons, they are more attuned to their relationships with others? Do men have to work harder to develop, if not their consciences, the values that will govern their relationships with others? Are males of other cultures, like the Balinese, who are raised to be gentle, kind, and sensitive, as ethical and idealistic as females of those cultures? I don't know.

You may now be asking what some implications are of the result that the wellspring of virtue is a person's character. Three come to mind immediately.

Only if transcendent religious beliefs, like a belief in God, are deeply incarnated in virtuous ways of getting along with others will religion contribute much to our success, health, and happiness. Signing a pledge card just won't do it, unless we have ethical characters already.

Second, if you wish to raise your children or educate students to be virtuous, do not settle on a sermon, morning prayer, or flag salute. Instead, create a home, school, or classroom that enhances the maturation of character, especially the kind of interpersonal strengths that apparently support virtue.

Third, if George Bush had been serious about wanting a "kinder and gentler" nation, then he should have selected women, like his wife Barbara, to be his vice-president, secretary of war, and a majority of other cabinet positions.

We have seen that men and women who succeed in their adult roles and are virtuous are happy and healthy persons. The book's next chapter directly examines the personality of healthy and happy men and women, which are adults' two most highly valued goals.

Chapter 19

A Toast to Good Health and Happiness

Four themes course through the lives of successful and fulfilled men and women: their generalized competence in living, psychological maturity, androgyny (particularly their feminine interpersonal skills), and virtue. A fifth theme is their health and happiness. We are like a multifaceted crystal and though each facet has its own special character, each also reflects the crystal's principal organizing properties. As I begin to examine the state of the crystal itself, you can probably anticipate what the men and women will tell us about their well-being. The chapter summarizes what I have learned about the state of the whole person.

The adults who ranked the twelve values that you also ranked in Chapter One prized happiness and good health most highly. The study's men and women also valued happiness and health highly, even more for their children than for themselves when they were in their mid-forties and their kids were still at home. Of the ten wishes I asked Marty to list she wanted to fulfill before she died, her first was, "to have raised healthy, happy, strong kids." Andy's, after maintaining his "good health until the end" and a "good relationship with Marty," wrote, "to see my children grow into mature adults." Billie's answer was, "My children can do whatever they want to do." Jane's was, "To see my children successful." Harry wrote, "to see my children happy and successful." And Chen wrote, "my children's health." Their wishes remind me of our American right to life and the liberty to pursue happiness.

But what are good health and happiness? How do we tell who is healthy and happy and how to achieve these goals? These are more slippery and subjective questions to ask than "Who is a successful parent, lover, or physician?" At least I can eventually find out how the men's and women's children turn out, count how many lovings they have each month, and ask their colleagues to rate their competence.

Physicians and psychologists—philosophers too—trip over the meaning of good health and happiness. Rather than talking of health, physicians describe symptoms of its absence. Rather than talking about mental health, psychologists talk about the absence of symptoms of mental illness. The National Institute of Mental *Health* should be called National Institute of Mental *Illness*, if its budget priorities are a clue to what it means by "health." Ironically, some speak of "positive mental health," as if "mental health" doesn't mean "mental *health*." Others prefer *well-being,* the term I use, to include both physical and mental (or psychological) health *and* happiness. Have you noticed that I have equated maturing with growing healthily? Because others do not accept my equation, I do not include my test of dimensional maturity in the measure of well-being. Actually, the study showed that for all practical purposes, well-being and psychological maturity are the same.

Although professionals dispute what health means technically, you and I know when we feel good. We know when we're not up to par, even if physicians can't find anything wrong with us. We know if we are better or worse than we were last week or year. I can no longer race up even a few steps without pausing to catch my breath. I could, if I wanted, even plot my changing physical health from my doctor's annual cholesterol count, blood pressure readings, and dismal weight record. But I leave that up to him. We know how to improve our health. We know what smoking does to us. We struggle to eat less fat and more fiber and make our lives less stressful. We know we should assert our willpower, though most of us have trouble finding it.

Happiness is something else altogether. We and others can judge how happy a person we are but *how* to become a happy person is a much more elusive to answer than to stop eating so many hamburgers. The Declaration of Independence guarantees Americans the right to pursue happiness—but how? Some students I know think getting money, partying three nights every weekend, and having frequent sex is the way. A mother wrote me recently she was really going to be happy when her teenager left for college. Another told me that finding Jesus made her happy.

What are the ways to happiness? To anticipate what the research told me, "The pursuit of happiness is not by way of seeking pleasure but by way of developing our character." A golden parachute, a Ferrari, cocaine, or a cellar of vintage wines may give us pleasure but not happiness if we don't have the character that predisposes us to enjoy our pleasures or be happy if we do find Jesus. The Declaration's signers should have guaranteed us "life, liberty, and the opportunity to develop a mature character," not "the pursuit of happiness," too often translated to be "the pursuit of money." My amended guarantee is not a fighting or elegant slogan, but it is much more accurate psychologically.

Identifying Healthy and Happy Persons

So that I did not inflict my biases on the results by prejudging who were the study's healthier and happier persons, I assessed their well-being as comprehensively and objectively as possible by combining their self- and judge-ratings and measures of their physical and mental health and happiness in a way that allowed me to rank the women and men in their overall well-being. Among the women, Billie ranked first, Jane sixth, and Marty seventh of the forty women, probably because she was undergoing the turmoil of therapy when I saw her ten years ago. Among the men, Chen ranked first and Harry ranked fourth in overall well-being. Andy ranked third in mental health and happiness, after I had excluded the measure of his physical health because of the reemergence of his earlier symptoms. Of the study's sixty-five men, Jim ranked twenty-second in well-being.

What Does a Person's Well-Being Predict?

Physically healthy men and women are mentally healthy. Mentally healthy men and women are also physically healthy.

Body and spirit are inseparable, a truism doctors of years past who used to see us in our homes knew in their bones. Specialized physicians who run us through their offices, concentrating *only* on our leaky bladders or wavering hearts don't seem to understand this truism.

Happy persons are physically and mentally healthy. Energy for living is not drained into preoccupations about constipation and ringing ears, or obsessive worries about children and paralyzing hangups about performing sexually in bed. Of course, unhealthy persons can transcend their bodily pains to experience serenity, perhaps even happiness. Andy's maturity enabled him to accept and adapt to his crippled leg and spreading paralyses to his arms and become one of the happier men of the group. Good physical and mental health, however, makes it easier to create a happy life for one's self. Feeling happy may improve our health—both bodily and mentally.

Just as virtue pays off, so does well-being. Healthy and happy men and women *succeed in all of their familial roles*. They and their partners agree about their competence. They are maritally happy, successful and sexually compatible lovers, and fulfilled parents, possibly because they are open and self-disclosing. Their children are also mature for their age. It is not surprising that good health and a happy disposition contribute to how well we succeed, particularly in our familial roles. Imagine playing vigorously in bed with our lover or hiking and camping with our children in between asthma attacks, arthritic pain, and unpredictable attacks of diarrhea. Living with a hypochondriac or ceaselessly suffering person can be wearying and discouraging. Or even worse, living with a morose grouch who sees every rising sun as his last can darken every day. They do provide one solace, however. They force us to find the stuff of which saints are made.

Success also contributes to good health and happiness. It strengthens our feelings of competence, self-confidence, and maturity. We feel good about ourselves and what we have done and can do. That warm glow must just do something good to our blood flow, endorphins, immune system—and spirit.

Men and women who are physically and emotionally healthy and happy have been *happy and productive persons throughout their adult lives*, which again suggests that our happiness is deeply rooted in our character. Adolescents living fully, productively, and happily are more likely to turn out to be happier when they are middle-aged than adolescents unhappily limping along on three instead of four physical and psychic cylinders. The same principle holds true for men and women in their sixties. Those happy with their current lives had been more mature and productive when adolescents.

The relationship between well-being and vocational success is questionable because of male and female differences. Men who succeed vocationally—regardless of how we define their success—are healthier and happier than men who fail. This is *not* true for women who succeed. Just because a woman earns a lot of money, holds a major leadership position, or enjoys her work does not mean that she is either physically healthy or happy. These differences are even sharper when we examine the mental health of vocationally successful men and women. Vocational success or lack of it apparently just does not affect a woman's mental health. That a woman's traditional familial role but *not* her work outside of the home predicts her well-being may trouble you. It does me. It contradicts some surveys that find that working women declare they are healthier and happier than nonworking women claim. Given the ambiguity of the meaning of vocational success for women, I have to say its relation to their well-being has yet to be firmly established.

Nevertheless, the relationship between a woman's well-being and her vocation is too important and timely an issue to ignore the possibility that full-time work may be irrelevant to her well-being. If work outside of the home is not a reliable source of a woman's well-being, what happens to her future health and happiness if her traditional sources of well-being—her familial competence and fulfillment—are diluted or only partially tapped? Will her well-being actually decline as her intimacy relationships become less intense and less fulfilling? A number of the study's working women struggled with just that question. Remember Alice Matthews, the pediatric physician, torn between the demands of her career and her children and her guilt about relying on her husband so much? Others felt that their friends were slipping away and bemoaned the "thinness" of their emotional and social lives. Is success in traditional nurturing fields like teaching and nursing an easier route to well-being for feminine women? As younger women organize their identities increasingly around their careers rather than their intimacy roles, will their route to well-being become more like that of men's? If so, how healthy and happy will they be in their middle and later years? Someone should really examine these important questions in depth.

The Personality of Healthy and Happy Persons

Healthy and happy men and women are mature and androgynous. They are well integrated, stable (though not rigid), and autonomous persons, as well as optimistic, growing persons. Their peers respect them for fulfilling their potentials. Such people so accept themselves that they can freely share their feelings with others. Their self-control engenders a positive emotional attitude about living. They have the strength to control their own talents, make their own decisions, and direct their own growth. Like Billie and Harry, they are in charge, "on top," of themselves.

I have been impressed by how frequently strengths like willingness to risk climbing out of our personal ruts to try new things, optimism, and feeling in control of ourselves contribute to our success and well-being. These strengths also contribute to recovering from debilitating illnesses, as Andy demonstrated in his dogged persistence to adapt to the loss of his leg. If you asked me to prescribe how you can grow up to be healthy and happy, I'd say:

- Don't ever give into the temptation to remain mired where you are
- Believe you can continue growing
- Assert your will to change yourself
- Learn how to make your mind and character work for, not against, you
- Think "Billie, Harry, Andy, Marty, Jane, and Chen" the next time you feel stuck in your ruts

Adults are right to value well-being so highly, for it predicts so many good things in life. By identifying the core strengths of healthy and happy persons, we now know where to begin to improve our well-being and so increase the odds that we will succeed in our adult roles. We also now know that the personality of mentally healthy and happy men and women is generally similar. When growing up, men and women need to keep their eyes on becoming better integrated, stable, and autonomous. In addition, men also must work on becoming more interpersonally mature, women also on developing a stronger sense of themselves.

Parental Roots of Adult Happiness and Mental Health

I could not trace the roots of the women's or men's happiness back to any parental trait. Apparently, there is no cookbook recipe I can give parents about how to raise their children to guarantee that they will become happy middle-aged adults. Happy adults have had such diverse upbringings and parents that they share no common familial home or parental traits. The book's principal actors and actresses have already told us this. Billie had seven "parents." When she was five, Marty became the "mother" to her own inept mother and alcoholic father and their children. Jane was almost destroyed by an authoritarian and smothering mother. Andy felt his mother loved him only conditionally; his father was emotionally unreachable. Harry's parents held him to too severe expectations. Chen's parents left him for three crucial childhood years. Only Jim's mother gave him "unbounded support and love"; his free-spirited father supported his "finding his own way."

As adults, we are the primary agents of our own happiness. We can not blame our parents for our unhappiness. Or as parents, like Harry, concerned about our children's future happiness, we can press no obvious buttons or pull levers that will *directly* contribute to their subsequent happiness. They will just have to work on their own to make their lives happy and fulfilling ones.

Again like me, you may be now saying, "Unbelievable. You mean that parents have no influence whatsoever about how happy their children will be as adults?"

"No. I don't think we can say that." Parents can directly affect their children's personality which in turn affects their well-being. However, their *direct* impact on their middle-aged children can no longer be seen. They *indirectly* contribute to their children's later happiness by enabling them to mature in the ways described earlier; for their children's youthful and adult maturity contributes in a major way to how happy they will be by middle age.

If you pushed me, I would agree that when an adult is still emotionally tied to his parents or, like Marty, fighting to be free of their lingering presence, maybe it is more difficult to make one's own happiness.

But the more mature we are, the more our happiness is in our own hands.

Generally, emotionally healthy adult men more than healthy adult women come from similar parents and homes. (Chapters Twenty and Twenty-Two will grapple with why girls' healthy growth is more complicated than boys' and why their personality is a much poorer predictor than a boy's of their future well-being.) Chapter Thirteen's prescriptions for creating a strong family that produces successful and healthy adult children summarize what parents contribute; *Fulfilling Lives* provides the appropriate qualifications always necessary when prescribing how to raise children.

Though we now have a sturdier understanding of men's and women's mental health and happiness, we do not yet know much about why they differ in their physical health—the topic of the next chapter. The differences, which bothered me for months, opened up insights for me about how our male and female bodies affect our healthy growth.

Chapter 20

MALE AND FEMALE PATHS TO PHYSICAL HEALTH

The meaning of men's and women's well-being is remarkably similar, but the meanings of a man's body apparently differ from a woman's. Men's physical and mental health are almost one-of-a-piece; they are rooted in similar character strengths. Women's are not. Although women's mental health is inextricably meshed with numerous character traits, their physical health is not. Physically healthy men differ from unhealthy men in their personalities; physically healthy women do *not* differ from unhealthy women in their personalities. What do such differences in the meanings of men's and women's bodies tell us about maleness and femaleness?

Men's and Women's Differences in Physical Health

Men and women differed in their physical health in two puzzling ways. First, the women reported many more specific signs of bodily dysfunction than the men did, but, strangely, neither they nor their peers rated them less physically healthy. How could this be? The women worried more about their bodies: They more frequently rated themselves tired, tearful, and constipated; they reported more headaches, nipple pains, heart palpitations, cold hands and feet, as well as reduced concentration. Neither age nor menopausal status accounted for the women's bodily inefficiencies. *But* reporting many more signs that their bodies did not work well did *not* predict their overall physical health or symptoms of mental distress.

Second, men's—but not women's—overall physical health is associated with well-defined personality traits. Physically healthy men succeed more consistently in most of their adult roles than unhealthy men. They are better husbands and lovers, have more sexually compatible and faithful relationships, are fulfilled fathers, satisfied breadwinners, better leaders, and contribute more to their communities as citizens. They may or may not make good friends. Their maturity is seen most clearly in their *stability*; they are calm, not moody or easily hurt by criticism, and so are predictable.

Physically *unhealthy* men are, among other things, indecisive pessimists, not in control of their lives. Not motivated to strike out on different paths, they are rigidly stuck in deep ruts. Their lack of confidence robs them of the courage to risk altering their life styles, even taking decisive steps to deal with their poor health. They don't see themselves (nor do those who know them best see them) to have the motivation or skills necessary to cope with their poor health.

We and doctors responsible for our health should not ignore our character, particularly the traits I just listed. The traits could be keys to improving our long-term physical health. Educating a man how to plan, experiment with, get more control of, and feel more optimistic about what he can do with his way of life may more effectively prevent a stroke than prescribing a daily aspirin.

Since my visit, Jane's husband, Vince, had had a heart attack. She called to complain bitterly, "He's not doing anything to alter the way he lives. He says 'What's the use?' He resists every suggestion I make about changing his diet. He won't even tell me how he feels about his attack. I think he's given up. I think he's suicidal."

Having known Vince for thirty years and concerned about him, I asked, "Can I do anything?"

"Would you try? But I don't think anyone can reach him."

I tried. She was right. Only his physician could possibly help, but my hunch is not for the long haul, if he prescribed only drugs and ignored Vince's character.

On the other hand, women's physical health seems to be irrelevant to anything else about them. Healthy women are good marital partners and have mature children but that is all their health says about them. Furthermore, healthy women share few personality strengths in common, a result other researchers have also found.

Men's and Women's Bodies
Do Make a Difference

I puzzled for months to understand why women report signs of bodily distress but neither they nor their peers rate them to be less healthy than men and why women's physical health is less well integrated with their personalities. Two hypotheses provoke intriguing ideas about the meaning of femaleness and maleness. First, women's shared menstrual cycles shape the meaning of their bodies differently than men's erections do theirs. Second, women's and men's bodies make it easier to grow up in different ways: for women, in other-centeredness; for men, in stability and autonomy.

Menstruation and its panoply of physical symptoms are not signs of "sickness" for which women are responsible. From adolescence to middle age, menstruation reminds them every twenty-eight days that they can create babies. They learn to accept—even celebrate as Marty did—their biological cycles and accompanying distress as inherent to their femaleness. Women may learn how to become sensitive to their bodies' periodic messages of rich and varied feelings that can so affect their relationships. They thus learn the language of their feelings in a way that most men do not. They also learn how to go with and not fight their bodies' temporary inefficiencies and claims upon their attention and energy. Their tears, irritability, and moodiness do not signal personal weakness for which they are responsible; they might for "stiff-upper-lipped" American males.

Moreover, men experience no similar *periodic* reminders of their bodies, varied subtle feelings, and vulnerability. Their bodies hover for months at the periphery of their awareness like fleeting indistinct shadows. Men take the reliability and efficiency of their bodies for granted—until their stamina begins to fail when they can no longer clamber up 4000 Himalayan steps without interminable pauses or swim the fifty laps they did only several years ago. No prods recurrently turn men inward to enrich their inner worlds, the language of feelings, and awareness of how their bodies affect their relations with others. A symptom becomes a personal, not a gender, issue of their responsibility. Their bodies and physical health then become spurs or challenges to cope with. They consequently become intertwined with idiosyncratic coping personality traits.

For example, men who believe they must be real "men," and not simpering cry babies, learn to deny messages of pain. Clamping their teeth together, suppressing pain, plugging ahead regardless, they make the committee meeting or play all four quarters. That's real "character." When last visiting my physician, I overheard him order a desperate wife to get her husband out of his committee meeting and to the nearest emergency room immediately. He had awakened with the left side of his face paralyzed; it had returned almost to normal before he manfully left for the office, ignoring his wife's protests that anything was really wrong. My doctor thought he had had a possible stroke and might have a more massive one any moment.

Women also know their bodies differently in another important way. Because they share hundreds of similar gender-related menstrual experiences from puberty to menopause, they regularly and empathically reexperience their common biological identity with each other. They become more sensitive to, understanding of, and accepting of each other's temporary inefficiencies, moods, and tears. Marty emotionally "knew" her periods biologically bonded her to her sisters.

Men experience no comparable periodic bodily reminders of their biological commonality and vulnerability, though they have shared one biological similarity while growing up: puberty and its most prominent enduring problematic outcome— their heightened erectile responsiveness. Until I read Richard Handy's book, *Male Sexuality*,[1] (the most insightful book about maleness of which I am aware), which describes his impotence and its effects, I had not realized how the richly varied meanings of erections could contribute to a man's identity and influence his relationships. How boys learn to cope with their embarrassingly unpredictable and visible erections apparently can etch even more deeply their competitive, dominating, controlling, and inhibiting interpersonal styles.

Effects of the Body on Maturing

Our bodily changes produce psychic effects—some we may not yet know of— that fashion the different meanings that females and males attribute to their physical health. One particular effect, however, helps me make sense of the differences in the women's and men's results. A girl's predictable menstrual periods may not spur her to develop as individualistic and autonomous a self as a boy's unpredictable erections may. Her individuality is periodically tugged by and partially reabsorbed into a commonly shared menstrual experience which she cannot control and therefore must learn to *adjust* to and accept, or, as Marty learned to do, *adapt* to and celebrate. Gender similarities can override more individualistic meanings of her body. May this not be a reinforcing biological reason for women's alleged "communality" and salient other-centered maturation? May this not also be why so many of the women's bodily signs of "dysfunction" did not predict their individual physical health? Also, in spite of such signs, may this be why neither the women themselves nor their peers rated the women to be less physically healthy than the men and their peers rated the men to be?

Whereas most women learn to yield to and interpret their bodies' given cycles as signs of being nurturing females, men learn to control and *use* their bodies as signs of being achieving males. Handy claims that the essential unpredictability of pubertal boys' visible erections, so responsive to any strong stimulation, makes their drive to control their public appearance and associated emotional arousal or excitement more urgent. He shows how erections acquire, as a result, many diverse and individualizing meanings, including excitement, sexual desire, emotional control, competitiveness, dominance, and aggressiveness. Handy illuminates why so many around the world were fascinated by Lorena Bobbitt's trial for cutting off her husband's penis—a man's "proudest possession," according to one news report. Or why Anita Hill's charge of sexual harassment by Clarence Thomas at his Senate nomination hearing for the Supreme Court was dismissed by the all-male committee. Or why males dominate, abuse, and look upon women as their possessions.

Learning to deal with such meanings draws on individual personality strengths, especially the ability to control one's body as well as the threats to that control, such as women or other sources of excitement. Seeking to master unpredictability rather than to yield to predictability leads to greater individuality and so stability and autonomy. Obviously other reasons than just learning to control their erections contribute to men's use of their bodies to control and achieve. However, the unpredictability of erections provides an "athletic playing field," so to speak, for reinforcing self-command and then testing and stabilizing it in all of the thrill-seeking ways adolescent males do. Their bodily route, more likely than that of girls, leads to greater individuality. Their bodies become more fused and integrated with their personalities. As a result, their physical health becomes a better predictor of their personality than women's physical health does.

I shall provoke you further. You may think that I underestimate how women learn to use their bodies to get what they want. Many societies expect girls to learn how to enhance their physical attractiveness to please males and so confirm their femininity—and desirability. Boys also mold and groom their hair, squeeze their pimples, and build their muscles. Yet, historically have not girls' bodily routes to growing up been more proscribed by their role of adjusting to boys' expectations than boys' bodily routes adjusting to girls' expectations? Male rather than female types of bodily competence lead to a more stable sense of self independent of the opinions of others. That the men's physical health but not the women's predicted many adaptive coping strengths is consistent with the gist of my argument.

Given the changes in the meaning of being a woman, I hesitate to claim that the study's middle-aged women's results, at least as I have interpreted them, may still apply to younger women who have grown up in a different cultural era. As girls participate more actively in team sports, test themselves against boys in Little League, trek Himalayan trails, and survive marine boot camp, their physical health may acquire more masculine meanings in the future.

I have now completed telling you about the personality of men and women who achieve the twelve goals that you ranked in Chapter One. Roger suggested that I give you a summary capsule of what he calls "zingers" about growing beyond ourselves and enhancing our well-being. I then return to examine how similar and dissimilar men's and women's paths to fulfillment are.

Chapter 21

TEN FACTS ABOUT OTHER-CENTEREDNESS AND WELL-BEING

You may think the following "zingers" are only common sense or obvious ideas that you can read in any popular magazine. But I think they are more than just personal opinions whose merit we must take on faith. They are firmly supported now by evidence that makes them *believable* zingers for me. Do any of these prescriptions zing for you?

Zinger #1: To increase your odds of succeeding and becoming a happy adult, begin by selecting a "normal" family. Evidence? Harry Barnett. He had one mother and one father who raised him, enjoyed being parents, and who he was fond of. He did not have to become a premature parent at the age of five or run away from home to preserve his sanity.

Zinger #2: To become a good citizen and community leader, learn to enjoy helping children grow up, develop the skills of being a competent adult, get hold of some ideals and principles, and become androgynous. Evidence? Harry and the computer's portrait of men and women who voluntarily contribute to their communities.

Zinger #3: Hold onto your religious faith for spiritual, not material, reasons. Evidence? Religious persons are no more successful, physically or mentally healthy, or happy than nonreligious ones. But a religious faith may contribute to your health and happiness as it did for Jim; it is just not essential to fulfillment and well-being for everyone.

Zinger #4: Be virtuous; it pays off in corporal rewards in the long run. Evidence? Honest, compassionate, principled men and women who have integrity and a deep ethical commitment have all the good things that religions have always promised us: success, health, and happiness. Religions have wisely not promised that virtuous people will be wealthy. They may or may not be. Blessedness is not necessarily accompanied by money.

Zinger #5: To have good physical health, pay attention to your mental health. To have good mental health, don't neglect your physical health. Evidence? The study clearly shows that they go together, as wise people have known for centuries.

Zinger #6: To succeed in most adult roles and be happy, learn how to create a mentally healthy life. Evidence: By most measures of familial success, mentally healthy men and women are better marital and sexual partners, as well more fulfilled and competent parents, who raise their children to be mature. Mentally healthy men are also involved in their community activities and fulfilled in their vocations. Mentally healthy women have close friendships with other women. Both are psychologically mature.

Zinger #7: To become mentally healthy, learn how to become more stable, autonomous, and androgynous. Evidence: A convincing core group of strengths describes the mentally healthy woman and man. More than intellectual and even interpersonal strengths, mentally healthy persons have strongly grounded and independent selves. They are self-determining, self-reliant, self-confident, and resilient persons. Mentally healthy men are interpersonally feminine. Mentally healthy women are typically masculine, though not excessively so, in their individualism and willingness to defend what they believe.

Zinger #8: To succeed and be happy, keep in good physical shape, particularly if a male. Evidence? Men in good physical health consistently succeed in more areas of living than men in poor health. Though the men and women did not differ in their overall physical health, a healthy body may mean something different to a woman than to a man. Her menstrual periods may sensitize her to her body's changing moods and provide a biologically shared identity with other women that men only experience through shared achievements.

Zinger #9: To be happy, work hard to become more mature. Evidence? Happy men and women share many similar character strengths. They are well integrated, stable, and autonomous persons. Happiness is the payoff for becoming more mature.

Zinger #10: To become virtuous and enhance your well-being, develop a mature and androgynous character. Evidence? The most consistently prominent traits of virtuous men and women, as well as the biggest contributors to their well-being, are their maturity and androgyny.

The prescriptions may sound like variations on the same theme. They generally are. Though altered in emphasis and limited by our traditional gender roles, the prescriptions reflect the underlying structure of the effectively functioning individual. Some prescriptions may not sound new or violate your common sense; this reassures me about the validity of the study's methods and worth of its results. What zings for me is that the ten zingers are now more firmly grounded in scientific research, not just on opinion and bias. They suggest which common sense ideas may more likely be true.

We have discovered that men and women need to develop their neglected or contra-sexual potentials to succeed and be happy. Though their paths to wholeness may criss-cross each other, occasionally run parallel, and at times travel the same route, the results suggest that their paths begin to merge as maturing proceeds. The next chapter compares how men and women mature and why and then examines in some detail women's path which seems to be less clearcut.

PART FIVE

Becoming More Mature in Today's World

Chapter 22

MEN'S AND WOMEN'S PATHS TO FULFILLMENT: SAME OR DIFFERENT?

It is fashionable nowadays to idolize our differences and ignore our similarities. Some feminists argue that women develop differently than men. A female critic of *Fulfilling Lives* claimed its model of maturity did not fit women but offered no argument or evidence to support her bias. An African-American or Hispanic might argue similarly. The argument will not be resolved by opinion but only by as intensive other long-term studies comparing the maturing of different kinds of people.

This chapter provides evidence that men and women are much more similar than dissimilar, that they mature similarly, and that the contributors to their maturing are also similar—though not identical. We have consistently seen that both need the same strengths to succeed in being good marital partners, lovers, and entrepreneurs, as well as to be mentally healthy and happy. Men and women need different strengths to enjoy frequent sex and be vocationally fulfilled. Societal values and expectations of what males and females should be can so block, distort, and channel growth that their underlying similar maturing potentials are obscured.

Proponents of the argument that men and women develop differently risk ignoring how systemic healthy growth is as well as its guardian—the equilibrating principle. They risk confusing what is with what could be. Seeming male and female differences are not necessarily healthy differences. Because women are nurturers and communion-oriented, other-centeredness becomes for some the sine qua non of maturity. Or because men are self-reliant and self-sufficient, autonomy becomes for others their key to maturity. By not locating female and male development within a comprehensive and valid dimensional model of healthy growth, only one dimension, such as other-centeredness or autonomy, is elevated to the keystone position of a woman's or man's maturity. Taking such a tunneled view of healthy growth risks ignoring the equilibrating principle. Billie was an exemplary "nurturer." But counseling revealed her other-centered maturation was too exemplary; it blocked the healthy growth and fulfillment of her other impressive potentials.

The argument that women and men mature differently is flawed for another reason. Because men are viewed as more autonomous and women more other-centered—and my evidence supports this popular notion—doesn't mean that if freed from their culture's procrustean molds of what they should be, men and women would not mature similarly. Again, Billie is a good example. It took her forty-one years to stop trying to please others before she could assert, "I feel that I now have come to terms with what I am and am functioning as a healthy adult for the first time in my life." Or it took Jane thirty-five years before she could say, "I like myself now. I didn't before. I'm more self-confident now. I feel more confident to say no. I'm not afraid to offend others any more." Both developed stable and autonomous ideas of themselves—after years of painful struggle. When we actually study how successful men and women adapt to their different roles, we discover that their maturity predicts the same successes. This can only mean that maturity means the same for both.

Men's and Women's Similar Maturing Paths

Men's growth is simpler to understand than women's during their adult years. The men's growth did not take any right-angled or surprising turns. Think of Andy, Harry, and Chen; only Jim's veered elsewhere. The men's maturing path from the thirties into middle age remarkably resembled the one they had traveled in their twenties and early thirties. Nine of the ten principal changes that occurred then were the same most important ones that took place from their early thirties to their mid-forties. However, only about half of the *causes* of such growth were similar. Do different experiences at different times in our lives have similar maturing effects?

You might reflect back to what you were like when you graduated from school and then what you are like now and try to identify how your mind, relationships, values, and view of yourself have changed. How might you score such changes using the categories of the model of maturing? Then try to figure out what the principal causes of those changes were.

Before describing how the men and women grew from their twenties to their mid-forties, I must comment about the rate or timing of such changes. If you are an unmarried twenty- or thirty-year-old, you may report less growth than the study's men did about those years. Why? They had settled down and committed themselves to their vocations and begun their marriages and families by their mid- and late twenties. Since the challenges of these commitments were the principal determinants of their growth, I'm not sure what will spark your continued growth if you are like Roger and have postponed assuming or don't plan to assume such commitments. Are today's younger generations as mature and healthy as earlier generations were when their age? Or will they turn out in the long run to be happier and healthier when middle-aged? By delaying making commitments, will they make more lasting and healthy ones by middle age?

Societal changes in "timing" are one reason I and others studying adult development over many years do not accept the idea that there are age-fixed stages or crises to growing up in the adult years. Maturing is continuous and similar from the twenties to middle age. However, the specific developmental tasks and level of maturity required to adapt to them fluctuate as a result of changing societal expectations about when it is "time" to marry or have children or settle down to earn a living. Career women, for example, who postpone having children until their mid- or late thirties face a different psychological task than women who have children in their late teens and early twenties. Career women need to be more sure of themselves and their priorities to avoid communicating resentment and rejection to a child whose need for their constant presence interferes with fulfilling their career aspirations.

Men Maturing from Their Twenties to Early Thirties

The principal growths the men experienced from their early twenties to early thirties were increased self-awareness and self-integration, certainty about who they were, and caring for others. The principal causes of such maturing were their partners' personalities and their type of occupation. (No information was available about the women's growth during these years.)

Some typical quotes from the men's interviews when they were in their early thirties illustrate how they had grown the previous decade. To appreciate just how much loved ones can help us grow, I will first tell you what the men said of their premarital selves and then of their marital ones.

The men used similar words to describe what they were like before they settled down with their partners. "I was a hermit." "I found socializing difficult before I met her." "My dealings with others were harsh." "I was very crude as a bachelor." "I was a very closed and uncommunicative kind of person." One man's wife-to-be really shook him up. "I was sitting in that chair over there and she said to me, 'Look, when are you going to stop this formal behavior and this aloofness and admit we have a relationship?' That really blew my mind. Challenged my whole life and my way of relating to people. She dared to say, 'I can see through you.' A little female [a pre-women's movement comment] had dared to challenge my behavior and make me look at myself."

The men spoke differently about themselves after living with their partners for years. One man's comment is typical. "She's leveled me a few times. Said that I'm not all I'm cracked up to be. Accused me of being dull and having a tunneled view of life because I work and do nothing else. Not that interesting a person. That taught me I'm missing out on things, like how flowers grow, how my son is growing."

I like this one. It shows how living with another can tell us what we are like and what we should be.

> She has helped me to learn what I don't have to be. I don't have to be a perfectionist. I don't have to be deadly serious about everything I do. She has helped me to have fun, to laugh at myself. She has challenged me when I've been

pompous or pedantic or petty. She's really made me feel that no matter what happens she will stand with me and by me and that gives me a great sense of security and confidence in what I do.

Do you now understand my comment about the effects of delayed timing? The longer some men postpone assuming the trials and joys of committing themselves to an enduring relationship, the harder time they may have getting over being crude, unsociable, uncommunicative hermits.

Men and Women Maturing from Their Thirties into Their Forties

The men's and women's interviews in middle age about how they had changed since their early thirties were also scored for the categories of the model of maturing. With only two exceptions the men and women reported similar maturing changes, so I combine them now. They both reported as their major changes

- Becoming more aware of themselves
- Thinking more relationally or integratively
- Becoming more other-centered in their relationships
- Stabilizing their self-concepts
- Becoming more aware of their values
- Stabilizing their values
- Developing more autonomous selves

The men also reported feeling more together in their sense of self, primarily because their values had become more stable and certain. As Jane reported, the women also grew to like themselves better and to get a clearer sense of their priorities.

To make these categories more meaningful, I'll translate each into predictions I made to Roger, if he grew into middle age in these ways. Roger will continue to discover more about what is behind his partly closed mine shaft door. If he yields to Beth's wishes and has a child, he will discover how angry he could be when provoked. He will actively make more connections between the heroes of American novels and their historical and social settings. If he stays with Beth, he most likely will become more caring and compassionate; if not and he restlessly continues going from one woman to the next, then I doubt he will grow much in other-centeredness. He probably will settle even more firmly into his number one self by accepting and integrating the assertive maleness of his fighting dogs into his day-to-day relationships. He should become clearer about what he wants out of his life; he might even summon the determination to begin writing the historical novel he has been dilly-dallying about for years. And as he develops a more autonomous sense of self, he won't need to ask me how he can continue to grow up.

Causes of Men's and Women's Maturing Into Middle Age

What kinds of experiences contribute most to how men and women grow into middle age? Do you recall from my second interview with Billie that I gave her fifty cards, each of which had a different possible cause of change—such as her husband, her job's demands on her time, and the women's movement? She then sorted them into categories in terms of their influence on the changes she had mentioned and then explained the effects of the more influential causes.

The principal prods to the men's and women's maturing into middle age were again quite similar so I report them together. Both identified as the most influential contributors,

- Their partner's personality
- Being a partner to their spouse
- Being a parent
- Their children
- Receiving counseling
- Physical and mental health

For the men, their type of occupation and its demands as well as becoming middle age also affected many. For the women, the women's movement decisively affected their maturing.

I illustrate how only one maturing change—increased self-awareness—occurred as a result of the men's experience. Recall that they had grown most in their self-awareness from their early thirties to their mid-forties. The main cause of their *increased self-awareness* continued to be, as it had been in their twenties, their partners' personalities and their relationship with them. Beth would have continued to provoke Roger to edge further through his mine shaft door if he had stayed with her. The next most influential spur to the men's increased self-insight was counseling. Recently, one of the study's men wrote me a postcard. His wife had told him two days before my visit that she wanted to divorce him. He had angrily locked her out of their house several evenings before when she had come home later than he expected. Not expecting her to take that step, he was torn apart and paralyzed for five years before his misery reluctantly drove him into counseling. His card read, "Eight or nine sessions with the counselor were wonderful for me. I learned why I had done what I did. I'm extremely happy, and I hope to be married before the end of the year."

The remaining principal causes that goaded the men to become more aware of themselves had a lot to do with growing older. Approaching middle age and their changing health began to tell them that they could not play as fast a tennis game as they used to. (Logging out my dead spruce trees tells me that if I am going to trek again in the Himalayas, I had better do it soon.) If middle age is still ahead of you, I can alert you about many other changes you may face, such as what your vocation's demands on your time and energy may do to you or what contributes most to developing more firm values and more caring personal relationships. But then growing up may be more interesting if you don't know what is in store for you.

Though the maturing path that middle-aged women took from their early thirties to their forties is similar, it twisted and turned in ways that perplexed me for months.

Women's Different Maturing Path Into Mid-Life

Understanding how females grow up to succeed has been dogged by four seemingly inconsistent and unexpected findings. For me, the book remains incomplete until I make some sense of them. The results that have perplexed me most are:
- Women's vocational satisfaction is consistently not related to or integrated well with their personalities
- Women's physical health predicts little else about them
- Mothers and fathers contribute much more to their daughter's adult success than they do to their son's

- Women's parents and adolescent personality contribute almost nothing to their mental health when adult

Three clues helped me frame a hypothesis to explain these diverse results:

1. The women's objective tests and peers identified three similar women—Billie, Marty, and Jane—to be among the more successful and happy ones of the study.
2. Stability and autonomy are the core strengths of mentally healthy and happy women as well as of men. Their interpersonal skills are not.
3. Androgynous strengths are necessary to succeed and become mentally healthy.

Women's Conflicting Sources of Maturing

My hypothesis is that women's maturing has been more conflictive than men's. Women's biology, parental enmeshment, and overdeveloped feminine interpersonal strengths have blocked their maturing. Their equilibrating principle's potential for encouraging maturing has, one might say, been put on hold.

If you are a woman, I hope that the hypothesis won't inflame you. Harriet doesn't like it. Her reaction was, "At least women are trying to grow. Men aren't." I'm not sure where that leaves me. Anyway, the hypothesis is the only one that makes sense of the women's findings for me. Other women already have proposed similar ideas, for which the study now provides the scientific support. I shall briefly review the evidence and then describe in more detail why the women matured as they did in their adult years.

Biological Influences. As Chapter Twenty suggested, women but not men share similar recurring biological experiences, like menstruation, pregnancy, birth, and nursing. These experiences strengthen and reaffirm a communizing rather than individualizing identity. The consequences of developing such an identity are numerous and pervasive: the development of interpersonal skills that further communal harmony, language that is sensitive to and articulates feelings, and values that conserve social rather than promote individualistic traits and roles. Too developed communizing strengths can block the development of individualizing potentials and so hinder maturing.

The suggestive evidence? The women's peers rated them to be more interpersonally feminine than the men's peers rated them to be. Women's bodily health and adolescent personalities did not predict much about them as adults. This suggests that gender and over socialization into typical feminine roles may have suppressed or obscured their individual talents and needs.

Parental Enmeshment. Women but not men remain emotionally close to and enmeshed in their families of origin far into their adult years. They also look back to their mothers more than men for support. Worldwide, fathers do not expect their daughters to "get out on their own" as early and in the same way that they expect their sons to. They early model and expect their sons to roam, explore, climb trees, get drunk, gamble, race cars, and generally "get into trouble." Fathers also have a biological ally. After all, testosterone is an assertive, intruding, penetrating, risk-taking hormone. So boys are often goaded to learn how to cope, achieve, and master themselves on their own.

For centuries, girls have been raised to stay home. The consequences of such enmeshment are, among other things, valuing security more than risk-taking; reaffirming a prescribed identity rather than fashioning one's own; and, by not testing themselves against a rich variety of challenges, other than interpersonal, not discovering and expanding new interests and developing latent, particularly assertive strengths.

The suggestive evidence? Women satisfied with their vocations or serving their communities as leaders share few character traits because they have not been raised to succeed in those ways. Parents continue to contribute more directly to their adult daughter's than to their son's successes; fathers influence more their adult daughter's than their son's vocational success. Two reasons help explain why women continue to be more affected by their parents than men are.

First, women are more sensitive and responsive to parental cues and expectations than men are. The women's parents occupied more of their daughter's emotional life space than they did of their son's, as the interviews and tests showed. The women valued their parental (even parent-in-law) relationships more than their husbands did. They also did not feel as understood by or act as equals with both parents.

Like Marty and Jane, though not to the same pitch, the women felt divided and distressed by their mothers with whom they still felt like children. More than the men, they felt that their mothers had rejected them when younger. Also, the women disagreed and argued with their mothers much more than the men about almost every topic, most notably about sex and ethical-religious issues. When we are so emotional and unsettled about our relations with another, that person can affect us in singularly enduring ways. In contrast to the men, few of the study's women had "freed" themselves of their mothers by their forties: not Billie who at the age of forty-one still "wanted more" from her dead mother; not Marty who was still arguing internally with her mother in therapy; not even Jane who still simmered and fumed about her mother, who she wouldn't allow to visit her grandchildren. By their fifties, all three had made peace with their mothers—even Jane, though grudgingly.

Second, the women's parents continued to influence their daughters because they were in flux, unsure of their future, and searching for a more comfortable identity. By their mid-forties, the men, with only one exception, had themselves together. But many of the women had not, except for a few like Billie, Marty, Jane, and Sue. If we are unclear about our priorities and who we are and want to be, we may be more vulnerable to continuing parental influences. When we are unsure of or have not tested ourselves in many different ways and found our path, we may reach back to find support from our families. We "call home" more frequently.

Overdeveloped Interpersonal Strengths. I now raise some controversial issues. Do not forget how much typical feminine interpersonal skills like compassion, sensitivity to the feelings of others, and understanding contribute to adult success. Some writers about women believe that their interpersonal skills and values are *the* pinnacle, *the* measuring rod, *the* summum bonum of female moral and personal growth. The study's adult women resoundingly say otherwise. The core of their maturity and well-being is their stability and autonomy, not their other-centeredness.

The equilibrating principle warns us that every outstanding strength can be a potentially fatal weakness if it is not integrated with other strengths. Scholastically talented but interpersonally immature youth are at risk of failing in their familial and vocational roles as adults. Or too self-sufficient autonomy, as occurs in men, not integrated with other-centered interpersonal skills can produce an arrogant and self-centered narcissist who fails in his familial roles.

So also, too developed feminine interpersonal skills, as occurs in some women, like Billie, can block continued growth. When such potential strengths are not integrated with a strong and independent sense of self, they can produce a conforming adjustment but unhealthy adaptation. Women have always faced unhealthy trade-offs for adjusting. Women are more depressed and have lower self-esteem and self-confidence than men. The negative effects of being raised to be a woman who pleases and conforms to others' expectations are several: Interpersonal adjustment bars discovering potentials that might disrupt harmonious relationships; one's self-worth depends on others' approval; and so maturing remains blocked and well-being elusive.

The suggestive evidence? The women's peers judged them to be more compassionate, sensitive and understanding than the men's peers rated them to be. Regardless of how I measured the women's and men's maturity, mental health, and happiness, their stability and autonomy consistently were at their center. Their feminine interpersonal strengths were not; they are necessary but not as critical to maturity and well-being.

Androgynous women and men are mature and healthy persons. Women's and men's mental health is predicted by their masculinity, though not, however, by core qualities like aggressiveness, competitiveness, and forcefulness. It is predicted by strengths characteristic of autonomy and stability, like self-reliance, courage, decisiveness, and self-confidence. A psychology of women that ignores such strengths to overemphasize their interpersonal ones risks entrenching women's past psychic oppression even more; it will undermine women's potential to be healthy and happy individuals. The meaning of a woman's maturity and well-being has to be much more complex and multidimensional to be faithful to how she grows healthily.

As long as women fulfilled their traditional feminine roles, they could adjust successfully to being wives, mothers, and lovers—roles that their mothers had modeled and prepared them for. Those who wished to work could be satisfied in a limited number of nurturing vocations, for example, teaching. They did not have to modify their feminine identity in such jobs, for their interpersonal skills contributed to their vocational success. Until the late sixties, therefore, the values of the women's parents and their upbringing matched those needed to succeed in their traditional roles.

But the world changed in the late sixties in ways the women had not been prepared for. They discovered that they had been raised to play a social role that did not fit many of their talents and needs. They became enigmas to themselves because many had not discovered who their "real" selves were. They did not feel strong inside themselves. They told me, "All I am is an empty eggshell." "I am a wife to my husband, a mother to my children, a daughter-in-law to my mother-in-law. I don't know who I am." Or, in the words of the unexcelled leader of the League of Women's Voters and other community groups, whom I quoted earlier, " All I am is a collection of roles put together by a committee."

None had talked like that in the sixties when they were in their late twenties and early thirties. Twelve years later many women told me that they had no strong sense of themselves. They had identified with their other-centered interpersonal roles at the expense of developing stable and autonomous selves.

I could not trace the roots of the women's mental health back to their parents or their adolescent personalities because neither had prepared them to develop the strong autonomous selves that are the core of a mentally healthy woman. The study's nonresults mirrored the women's transitional steps away from identifying with a prescribed social role to fashioning a more centered and independent self.

The intriguing question now becomes, "How did the women, raised to be collections of roles, develop more mature personalities?" Billie, Marty, and Jane show us how modern women may have to grow to become successful, happy, healthy, and distinctive individuals. Marty struggled for years to grow beyond her biological nurturing disposition—without denying it. All three had to separate emotionally from too intense involvement with their mothers and discover their more androgynous, particularly latent masculine, strengths. Each developed a defined stable and autonomous sense of herself that integrated her feminine other-centeredness into a healthier, more whole self.

The Maturing Effects of the Women's Movement

Though the women grew in ways similar to those that the men did, their leading edges were stability and autonomy, while the men's were awareness, other-centeredness, and integration. The women grew most in altering their ideas of themselves as women; they became stronger, more independent, as Billie, Marty, and Jane have taught us. I hazard the guess that as they developed more stable and autonomous identities, their mental health improved and they became happier.

Their pattern of growth reflects an irrepressible human urge toward wholeness and shows the equilibrating principle diligently at work in the lives of middle-aged women—as well as of men, but not as noisily. The centuries-old view that women should be only accommodating homemakers and mothers had become too maladaptive and suppressive of their urge to wholeness. Though the feminist movement had been preparing us for such a revolutionary change for decades, the integration and consolidation of its values precipitously occurred only within the few years that passed between my two meetings with the women.

Before analyzing the maturing effects of the women's movement, two of their other principal causes of their growth deserve comment. Two-thirds of the women had sought some form of counseling since I had seen them in the late sixties and early seventies. Although many wanted advice about specific family issues, a not inconsiderable number had entered long-term therapy because of depression and self-doubts. Analyses of their tests suggested that some were really grappling with their identities as women rather than with classical neurotic conflicts and symptoms. Their upbringing as females had turned out to be inappropriate for the roles that they and society now expected.

The older women felt most provoked by their teenage children, who were demanding the freedoms and opportunities that the women's movement had brought. As one mother told me, "I feel like my adolescent daughter trying to figure out what I want to do the rest of my life, particularly now as I see her leaving home in a few years. We're dealing with the same issues. It's scary."

I had had no glimmers of the potentially radical effects of the women's movement upon the women's sense of self when I interviewed them in the late sixties. Twelve years later, it ranked seventh out of the 50 reasons that might have contributed to their growth in the meantime. Few women had *not* been affected by their movement. Eighty-five percent had been changed: 25 percent dramatically; 28 percent moderately to considerably so; and 32 percent somewhat. It affected most prominently the maturation of the women's self-concepts and values.

When we self-consciously seek to test and discover what we are and could be, we sometimes engage in what appear to be immature behaviors. So when women began to wrest control of their identities from men—who for centuries had told them how to act and what to become—they had to experiment to learn what identity would be most integrative for them. Very predictably, some, like Marty, plunged into exaggerated excesses, self-centered liaisons, and potentially self-destructive experiments. These transitional calamities can mask, however, great resilience and other undiscovered strengths that slowly begin to emerge in time, as they did for Marty.

Typical signs that reasonably mature people are finding their way out of their "adolescent" identity experiments are liberation of energy, enhanced self-confidence, a more mature assertive autonomy, and heightened creativity. Marty, Jane, and Billie all followed such a path.

I best make sense of how the women matured as a result of their movement by using the model of maturing to provide the signposts of their growth. The first is that the women's movement made all of us more *aware* of the immature effects of women's historic gender role. After speaking on this theme at a woman's conference, an anonymous woman slipped the following poignant note into my coat pocket.

> I am one of those women
> Tossed and turned by various claims
> Vacillating between feelings of confidence,
>   and fears of being discovered a "phony."
> Trying while at a National Conference
>   to "forget" my parental responsibilities
>   but not being fully able to do so.
> Though my husband says he's glad to fill the gaps.

> What's shaped my hesitation,
>   my ambiguities,
>   my goals?
> While those may be strengths,
> I experience them more often as limitations.
> Where is the power I seek
>   to claim my full personhood,
> And what price will be paid
>   if I am able to fully exercise that power?

She tells us what a "collection of roles" feels like. She, like other women, had become aware how much she had lived for others at the expense of developing her own "personhood," her own strong sense of self.

The next signpost along the maturing path was for the women to learn that their doubts and hesitations were not theirs alone. They became more *other-centered* in their concept of themselves by identifying with women throughout history. Marty got right to the nub of this phase, when she said of the women's movement, "It taught me that I have sisters, that there is a sisterhood and that a lot of pain that I was feeling was also shared by other women. Furthermore, that the reason for the pain was outside of myself."

"I'm not sure what you mean. Could you give me an example?" I asked.

Marty answered, "The pain of feeling trapped as a mother and wife. Other women were feeling that same type of trapped feeling. There was something historical about that. Women have felt that for a long time."

The third signpost that marked the maturing effects of the women's movement was the encouragement of women to get in touch with how they really felt and thought, which then became *integrated* into their views of themselves. I had not anticipated the number of women who talked of taking over the political and social views of their partners. They wanted to please and not provoke argument or disharmony; they also did not know what they thought. Joan, the artist and most typically feminine homemaker in the study, said that the women's movement "gave me the courage to say what I am thinking is okay, a kind of validation. It's strange that a woman needs that validation. Just to be . . . just to think what she wants to. Just to think that what I had on my mind was okay to say."

What I heard women like Joan telling me was that they now had permission to no longer be good little girls trying to please their parents. Again, Marty's path seemed typical. Achieving integration involved the struggle to free herself from being fused with her parental, particularly maternal, internal presences. She eventually learned how to meet her mother as an independent but loving equal.

The last two signposts were a growing certainty of a more firm, *stable* sense of self and a feeling of being in control of their own decisions and acts and so more *autonomous*. These two themes ran through one interview after another. It was Jane Allen who forcefully insisted that "My idea of who I am has totally changed. I like myself. I didn't before. I'm able to do anything if I set my mind to it. I'm self-confident, much more aggressive, much more. I have always been aggressive, but I never knew the strength I really have. I feel more confident to say no. I am not afraid to offend others any more."

Cynthia more quietly spoke for the other women who had traveled the same route. "I am more independent and rely on my parents less. I don't need approval from other people now. I accept whatever I choose for myself. Just that I can take responsibility for myself without being a shadow of my parents."

Both had become their own persons.

From a historical viewpoint, some form of the women's movement was inevitable. From a practical viewpoint, exaggerated self-centeredness, broken marriages, and wounded children were, sadly, also inevitable. Any such extraordinarily fundamental shift in the meaning of femaleness demands a heavy price in suffering and hurt. How long such emotional damage will continue is unknown. Much depends on women's determination to continue growing, men's adaptability, and women's and men's success in working together to create healthier definitions of femaleness and maleness for themselves and their children. While many are now being grievously hurt, we must not forget that millions of women and other minorities have also been emotionally maimed for centuries because society had denied them the opportunity to grow healthily.

Reactions of Men to Women's Maturing

Since the personal meanings of femaleness and maleness are so reciprocally intertwined, changing the meaning of femaleness presages changes in the meaning of maleness. Inevitably! Men have been struggling not just to adjust but to adapt to women's and their own needs to grow more healthily. Roger believes that increasing numbers of younger men are becoming more sensitive to women's needs and learning how to adapt to more assertive women. It is older men, more set in their traditional gender role and benefiting from it, who suffer the effects of women's maturing more acutely.

How have middle-aged men reacted? They have adjusted more than they have adapted. Of the men I studied, 83 percent claimed that the women's movement had affected them, mostly their values and relationships with their wives. While a respectable 32 percent said that the women's movement had also altered their concepts of themselves as men, its *actual* impact had been much more modest. The women's movement was the seventh most important cause of the women's maturing but thirty-eighth of the men's. They had adjusted but only reluctantly begun to adapt by actually altering their deepest beliefs and attitudes about their maleness. Just as Billie's and Marty's path prefigured the route other women began to take, so Andy's and Harry's path is the one that more men will begin to follow. They not only adjusted but also adapted.

You may feel that my hypotheses miss the mark. I feel, however, that there is enough truth in them to begin to bring this book to a close. I shall end by telling you the hope for our society that the men and women have given me.

Chapter 23

A Perspective on Hope

Readers of *Fulfilling Lives*' earlier versions urged me to sum up what the study told me about how to grow healthily in today's changing society. Roger wrote, "Soar, and say what you believe it tells us today."

Perhaps it is the teacher in me, or the arrogance of age, but I have accepted their invitation to get on my soapbox to talk about three issues: what impels maturing, why developing healthy identities is more perplexing today, and what our society can do to help today's children grow up to succeed.

What Impels Maturing?

I have learned that we mature for many reasons, but if three are absent then we begin to die psychologically. To mature, we must be in an *alive relationship* with others, whether as workers, partners, parents, friends, even as communicants and believers in God. Erich Fromm, a wise psychologist, taught me that also.

"Not just a 'relationship,' but an 'alive' one," he insisted. As a psychoanalyst, he participated actively in growing with his patients. "When I become bored in therapy, something is wrong. For growth to occur, our relationship must be alive."

"And the effects?" I asked.

"My best self-analysis comes from my work with patients when we are both alive in our relationship."

"I'm not sure I understand what you mean by 'alive'?"

"Waking up more and more to become aware of yourself, others, and the world around you. Becoming more excited."

The men and women have helped me understand Fromm's definition more precisely. Their greatest growth occurred when a trusting and accepting relationship encouraged their vulnerability and openness to the influence of a respected person they loved.

However, just being in an alive relationship is not enough; another impetus to grow must be present, a *basic drive*. Roger mentioned it, almost off-handedly, when he tried to explain why he had changed since he wrote, "It's time for me to grow up, but how?" He wrote, "Something inside but I can't put it into words. Something else pushes me to keep growing . . . not give up." Carl Rogers, the founder of client-centered or nondirective therapy, believed we have an "inherent tendency" to grow wholely. I do too. The equilibrating principle is its guardian and spokesperson. Fromm also believed that each of us has a "basic drive. . . to grow," though, he felt, we vary in its strength. Billie's drive to grow healthily was exceptional as were Andy's and Marty's determination to make their marriage succeed, Jane's doggedness to "make it on her own," Harry's devoted commitment to his family and community, Chen's single-minded calling to be a scholar, and Jim's consuming search for God.

Our drive to grow varies for many reasons, including our genetic histories and biohormonal experiences that contribute to our restless vitality, even from the moment of birth. The drive to grow also goes hand in hand with the need for more alive relationships. Societal agents, such as families and schools, can subdue if not snuff out our drive to grow, as I see in so many of the schools I visit. In a nationally recognized school, 55 percent of the teachers described their students to be apathetic; 85 percent of the students believed that high school was boring; only 20 percent thought that their teachers were intellectually exciting. In another academically superb school, 65 percent of the teachers wished that they were more intellectually exciting people themselves. Fromm tells us no real growth will occur in schools until we create more alive faculty and student relationships. I agree. We need to teach to bring our students and ourselves more and more alive, not to worry about their SAT and achievement test scores.

A third necessary impetus to growth is to have a vision of what we want to become. A hopeful vision of the future inspires us to continue to grow.

Why Developing Healthy Identities Is So Perplexing Today

What is our vision of the future today? A woman in her late twenties reacted to what I had written about the "American, Japanese, and German paradox" in Chapter Fifteen—being so wealthy but so dissatisfied and depressed—by perceptively writing,

> I think this goes deeper than money, though. What about mission? That's what Roger is looking for. Franz Vehrman said, "It is the task of every generation to find a mission, fulfill or betray it." Our generation has not found a mission so we feel we are betraying. What is worse is that we are betraying nothingness, emptiness, thus the existential crisis... We have less personal day-to-day needs to worry about so we can afford to be depressed.

Our times are indeed darker. Or in the words of the author of Proverbs, "Where there is no vision, the people perish." The revised version speaks more directly to the paradox: "Where there is no revelation, the people cast off self-restraint." We live for ourselves. We want things fast. We expect others—our parents, schools, government—to give us what we want. Not just today's students and young adults live for now, but my generation does too. We want our generation's catastrophic medical insurance to be paid for by our children and grandchildren. We want to enjoy now. I have a cocktail napkin that pictures five ice cream cones with the words, "Life is uncertain. Eat dessert first." We have been doing just that, and more of us now ask, "What's been the point of it all?"

Mission? Vision? Calling? Purpose? Number one self? Each points to what we want to be and do with our lives. Our "existential crisis" is that we are freeing ourselves from traditional sources of meaning but don't now know what to do with that freedom.

Where did our meaning come from yesterday? Certainly from our need to survive. As a Depression child, I dug for clams on Long Island's beaches so my family could eat each evening. As a youth of the thirties, I worked for ten cents an hour to get money to buy my two weekly pleasures—one ice cream cone and the Saturday matinee. Survival dictates our view of the world, its possibilities, and so our choices. For most contemporary Americans, sheer day-to-day survival is no longer a determiner of meaning, but finding money for five ice cream cones—those unnecessary extras—is.

Work's meanings have expanded and so provided more freedom. It no longer rigidly commands as much of our lives as it did 100 years ago and still does in most other countries. It no longer consumes so much of our life space unless we decide to let it. American pubertal children worked long hours less than 100 years ago; children still do in Benares, India, weaving silk ten hours a day. The work day and week have shortened since World War II. We work fewer years of our lifetime; we can "retire" earlier. Many of us can choose between many more types of jobs now. We are freer to change our work and create our own work environments. Our ties to our work are gradually coming more under our own control.

Our identity as a Catholic, Jew, or Methodist used to tell us how to act and what to believe. It still often does, but no longer as compellingly for more and more of us. Catholics have sex to enjoy, not just to produce babies. Most Jews no longer follow their dietary laws as strictly. Even some Methodists now drink wine. Beliefs about immortality, heaven, hell, and the devil are myths, not living options, for more and more of us. We are freeing ourselves from religion's traditional meanings.

Our identity as a Daughter of the American Revolution (DAR), a Mississippi black, a Massachusetts' Kennedy, or a Vietnamese refugee used to tell us our status, what we could or should aspire to, what doors of opportunity were open to us. It still does, but again in an increasingly diluted way for more and more of us. Membership in exclusive groups like the DAR no longer has the same clout. Skin color is slowly yielding its deadening grip on hope as competence becomes the way to fulfill the American dream. Our aristocratic dynasties linger on, but less and less prominently. Immigrant status no longer impedes success as firmly for those, like our Asian citizens, whose talent and hard work quickly unlock our educational and economic doors. We are slowly freeing ourselves from family, ethnic, social class, and national status as primary sources of meaning.

We are also modifying the influence of age and gender as sources of meaning. Our developmental age both limits and makes available opportunities for society to program meanings for us. Biological changes, such as the onset of puberty, menopause, and physical decline, powerfully affect our character and how we act. Their relative "fixity" means that aging's changes will continue to be a source of meaning.

Societies vary in how prescriptively they define the meanings of age. We tell our five-year-olds that they must take on the identity of a student—ready or not. Two decades ago we disapproved, even prohibited, the expression of sexuality, affection, and dependency between different age groups more than Italians and Turks did. Take affectionate relationships. Of the ninety-six different possible age and status ones that I surveyed, including an eighteen-year-old boy hugging and kissing a middle-aged woman, Italians approved expressing affection in six times more possible such relationships than Americans did; the Turks approved it in four times more. Americans approved erotic flirtations only when the partners were similar in age. Now, we are less censorious about such relationships. We are securing more freedom to decide if and when we want to have sex, marry, and work. We don't have to marry by our mid-twenties or retire at sixty-five to be considered "normal." Though age still determines many meanings for us, we can override its social constraints more acceptably nowadays.

Like our biological age, our identity as males and females will always be a source of meaning. Handy tells us gender shapes meaning by showing us how rooted maleness, for example, is in the rich meanings of a male's penis and erections. Marty suggests that femaleness may be centered in the meanings of a female's vagina. Within whatever limits biology sets to the meanings of maleness and femaleness, all societies attribute other meanings to them. The study's women and men have shown how determining biosocial meanings of femininity and masculinity are to our health, success, and happiness. The post-sixties' revolutionary changes in gender roles has freed women—more than men—from an oppressive sexism. While gender, and its associated meanings of maleness and femaleness, will always be a source of a person's identity, its commanding influence is diminishing—certainly for women world-wide. Women are becoming more free to create their own meanings of femaleness; eventually men will also be more free to redefine their maleness.

So we are freeing ourselves from traditionally prescribed and commanded sources of meaning. Freedom brings emptiness, nothingness, to those who have depended on prescribed work, religion, status, age, and sexual role for meaning. Remember what the women told us. "I'm only a collection of roles put together by a committee"; "I'm just an empty eggshell"; "I don't know who I am." Emptiness is so painful it drives us to eat five ice cream cones to fill it up, to seek therapy for our existential "crisis," to work compulsively. What do we do with our growing freedom from traditionally prescribed meanings? Only one answer suffices for the future: Create our own meanings.

The inescapable question becomes, "What are the personal strengths needed to create our own mission, vision, calling, purpose, number one self?" Whatever form our meaning takes—to be a Harry as a competent and fulfilled parent, a Chen called to write books, a Marty called to a feminist vision, a Billie transcending her traditional feminine identity to create her number one self as a problem solver, an Andy overcoming his physical handicaps to pursue new discoveries, a Jane gripped by her desire to be a millionaire, and a Jim called to be a friend of God—psychologically mature and androgynous strengths are indispensable to create a healthy, successful, and fulfilling way of life.

Religions have always provided us with visions of healthy growth. We can draw upon their symbols that articulate humans' accumulated wisdom of what it means to grow and become more alive and whole persons. Research is beginning to verify, extend, and project religions' historic insights into modern terms such as "psychological maturity." When men and women have the opportunity to grow healthily, become more mature, or be self-actualized, they grow similarly. They become more aware, other-centered, integrated, stable, and autonomous persons.

The study's men and women call us back to the verities of the past. Billie, Andy, Marty, Jane, Harry, Chen, and Jim show us just how contemporary and empowering out-of-fashion religious words such as "calling," "commitment," and "virtue" are to living a meaningful, healthy, successful, and happy life. They tell us that we do not have to endure nothingness; we do not have to be rudderless; we do not have to start from ground zero to create afresh a vision of healthy growth, authenticity, or self-actualization.

How to Help Today's Children Grow Up to Succeed

We do not grow up alone in a vacuum without help and guidance from others, particularly our families and schools when young. A loving, democratic family that has strong values and expectations contributes greatly to a child's healthy growth and future success. Children not so blessed with such a family need not despair, however. Others—grandparents, partners, counselors—and their own strengths—a strong will, interpersonal skills, and optimism—bring hope.

Today's children do not have as many sources of hope available as yesterday's. Fragile and unstable families, missing parents, inaccessible grandparents, rotating caretakers, chaotic neighborhoods, among other potential sources of hope, explain why teachers see more vulnerable children today. Teachers feel they must be parents more than teachers.

Schools are society's only remaining means to provide all youth with hope. They can empower youth with the maturity to get command of themselves today to be able to create their own meanings tomorrow. They can also witness a vision of what a healthy society and better world could be like. Just as parents can continue to support and guide us after we have left home, so may teachers and schools. Following Haverford men for so many years has taught me that. When in their early thirties, the men selected Haverford College, primarily because of its Quaker religious philosophy, to be one of the nine most important causes of their growth since they had graduated twelve years earlier. Few of them had entered Haverford as Quakers. How could a school continue to influence its graduates so far into their adult lives? Because they had made its values of what a better world could be like their own. Its vision had become part of their character.

The effort to improve our schools is failing because we have not learned how to create schools of hope that educate for maturity—human, not just academic, excellence. A school of hope that consistently educates for maturity witnesses a vision of goodness that the study shows us pays off in future health, success, and happiness. Recall the metavalues that define a mature person: honesty, truth, fairness, compassion, integrity, commitment, courage, and freedom. These values are as intrinsic to the academic enterprise and pursuit of truth, becoming liberally educated, as they are to every great religion's vision of wholeness.

Research tells us that the school that generates hope has

- A distinctive vision of its liberally educating goals that is widely shared by all members of the school and its parents
- Adults that are as committed to the maturation of students' character and selves as to their minds
- A leader whose primary role is to be the steward and articulator of the school's vision
- Teachers who empathically understand the interpersonal world of their students *as their students perceive it*
- Adults and students who have alive interpersonal relationships that are growth-inducing for both (trusting, caring, adventurous, and intellectually exciting)
- Teachers and students for whom teaching and learning are a calling, rather than a job, and whose morale about their work is high
- Teachers and students who emotionally own not only the goals of the school but the means of implementing them within the school *and* the classroom
- Adults and students who value risking together to discover more effective ways to achieve their goals, who are willing to hold themselves accountable for their success and failure, and who reflect about why their school and classroom climates and methods have not been as effective as they had hoped

Schools of Hope: Developing Mind and Character in Today's Youth, building on *Fulfilling Lives*, describes how each attribute can be implemented to transform schools of despair into schools of hope. Now that our work together is completed, I shall end by soaring high to tell you what hope means to me.

Hope is the future alive in the present. Hope prefigures its own fulfillment. Hope disciplines. Without an *alive* hope, we cast off self-restraint and succumb to the seductions of the present: five ice cream cones, drugs, sex now, self-centered aimlessness, violence, even death, as research tells us about so many youths today. "The [suicidal] adolescents we talked to groped for words to describe what they felt was a void in their lives—the lack of anything to stand for, of an altruistic goal."[1]

Without a shared hope, a society drifts, becomes paralyzed by special interests, falls apart into deceit and violence, and eventually perishes. The most serious threat to our future health, success, and happiness is the absence of individual and collective hope, that "void . . . lack of anything to stand for, of an altruistic goal." Nothingness. Emptiness. When I ask students about their symbols of hope, they answer with silence.

The book has been a search for hope—to prod us to learn from our mistakes; to provoke us to think about what we want to work toward and stand for; to identify the character we need, as Andy told us, to be the "large family flying together among the stars" in the future. The result will be not just to "see life on the planet continue," but also to be happy, to have stronger marriages and families, to better the lives of all children, to reclaim work as a calling, and to become more virtuous contributing members of our planet.

NOTES

Preface

1. Heath, D. H. *Fulfilling Lives: Paths to Maturity and Success.* 350 Sansome St., San Francisco, CA 94104: Jossey-Bass, 1991.

Chapter One

1. James, W. *The Principles of Psychology.* New York: Henry Holt, 1890, Vol. 1, 309-310.

Chapter Two

1. Lowenberg, P. Einstein in his youth. *Science*, 1988, *239*, 510-512.

Chapter Seven

1. Vaillant, G. E. & Vaillant, C. O. Natural history of male psychological health, X: Work as a predictor of positive mental health. *American Journal of Psychiatry*, 1981, *138*, 1433-1440; p. 1438.

Chapter Twelve

1. Tocqueville, A. de. *Democracy in America.* New York: Knopf, 1945. (Originally published 1835), p. 105.
2. Tocqueville, [1835] 1945, p. 106.
3. Miller, S. *Men and Friendship.* Two Park St., Boston, MA 02108: Houghton Mifflin, 1983, pp. 197-198.

Chapter Fifteen

1. Mehren, E. After scandal, she adopts her first ambition. *Los Angles Times* Service, 1987, December.

Chapter Twenty-Two

1. Handy, R. *Male Sexuality.* 700 East Amherst St., Buffalo, NY 14215: Prometheus Press, 1988.

Chapter Twenty-Three

1. Giffin, M. E. & Felsenthal C. *A Cry for Help.* 1540 Broadway, Garden City, NY 10036: Doubleday, 1983.

BOOK ORDER INSTRUCTIONS

1. All prices include handling and postal charges for mainland USA. For orders to Canada and other countries, contact Conrow Publishing House, 223 Buck Lane, Haverford, PA 19041-1106 for handling and shipping costs *before* ordering.
2. Only orders *prepaid* in American dollars by personal or institutional check, money order, or certified check can be accepted. Make check out to Conrow Publishing. Credit card charges cannot be accepted.
3. Please clearly print name and mailing address on order if not included on check.
4. Discounts off publisher's list price plus shipping charges are about 35% for individual and 50% for pre-packaged bulk copies of *Fulfilling Lives* and *Schools of Hope*.
6. Pre-packaged discounts given *only* for cartons of 16 copies of *Schools of Hope* and 18 copies of *Fulfilling Lives*. Contact Conrow Publishing for discounted prices for bulk orders of *Lives of Hope*.

	Individual	Pre-Packaged
Fulfilling Lives: Paths to Maturity and Success (Hard cover), 408 pages	$24.00	$325.00 (18 copies)
Schools of Hope: Developing Mind and Character in Today's Youth (Hard cover), 444 pages	$22.00	$275.00 (16 copies)
Lives of Hope: Women's and Men's Paths to Success and Fulfillment (Soft cover), 312 pages	$12.00	Contact Publisher for discount